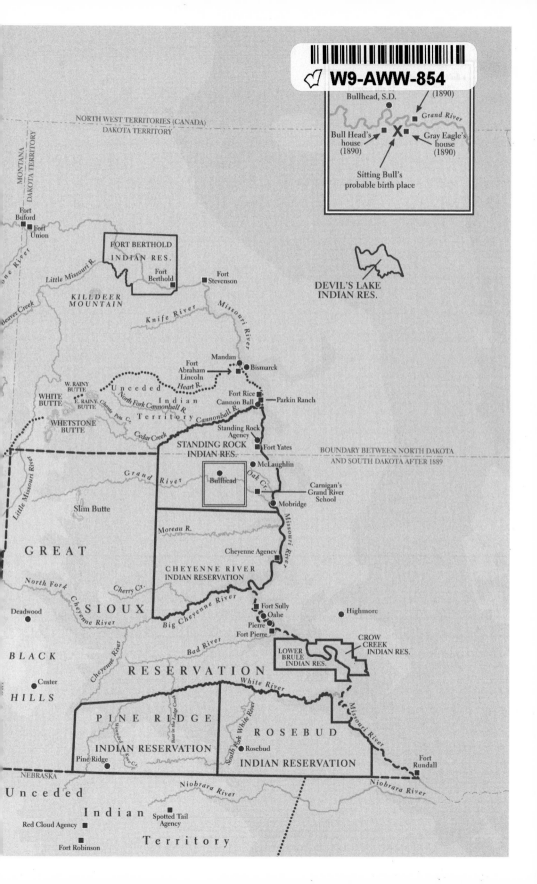

Bullhead, S.D.

(1890)

Grand River

Bull Head's
house
(1890)

X

Gray Eagle's
house
(1890)

Sitting Bull's
probable birth place

NORTH WEST TERRITORIES (CANADA)

DAKOTA TERRITORY

MONTANA

DAKOTA TERRITORY

Fort
Buford

Fort
Union

-one River

FORT BERTHOLD
INDIAN RES.

Fort
Berthold

Fort
Stevenson

Little Missouri R.

KILLDEER
MOUNTAIN

Knife River

Missouri River

DEVIL'S LAKE
INDIAN RES.

Beaver Creek

W. RAINY
BUTTE

WHITE
BUTTE

E. RAINY
BUTTE

WHETSTONE
BUTTE

U n c e d e d

I n d i a n

T e r r i t o r y

North Fork Cannonball R.

Cheyenne Pass Cr.

Cedar Creek

Mandan

Fort
Abraham
Lincoln

Heart R.

Fort Rice

Cannon Ball

Cannonball R.

Bismarck

Parkin Ranch

Standing Rock
Agency

STANDING ROCK
INDIAN RES.

Fort Yates

McLaughlin

BOUNDARY BETWEEN NORTH DAKOTA
AND SOUTH DAKOTA AFTER 1889

Grand   River

Bullhead

Oak Cr.

Carnigan's
Grand River
School

Slim Butte

Mobridge

Little Missouri River

Moreau R.

GREAT

CHEYENNE RIVER
INDIAN RESERVATION

Cheyenne Agency

Missouri River

North Fork

Cherry Cr.

SIOUX

Deadwood

Cheyenne River

Big Cheyenne River

Fort Sully

Oahe

Highmore

Pierre

Fort Pierre

BLACK

Custer

HILLS

RESERVATION

Cheyenne River

Bad River

White River

LOWER
BRULE
INDIAN RES.

CROW
CREEK
INDIAN RES.

Missouri River

PINE RIDGE

INDIAN RESERVATION

Run in the Sage Creek

Wounded Knee Cr.

South Fork White River

Rosebud

ROSEBUD

INDIAN RESERVATION

Pine Ridge

Fort
Rundall

NEBRASKA

U n c e d e d

Niobrara River

Niobrara River

I n d i a n

Spotted Tail
Agency

Red Cloud Agency

T e r r i t o r y

Fort Robinson

Sitting Bull

BILL YENNE

WESTHOLME
Yardley

Frontispiece: One of the most memorable portraits of Sitting Bull, this photograph was taken by David F. Barry in Bismarck, Dakota Territory, probably between 1883 and 1885. (*Montana Historical Society*)

Half title page: Sitting Bull's hieroglyphic autograph. Title page: Sitting Bull's cursive autograph. (*National Anthropological Archives*)

Westholme Publishing, LLC
Eight Harvey Avenue
Yardley, Pennsylvania 19067
Visit our Web site at www.westholmepublishing.com

First Printing: April 2008
10 9 8 7 6 5 4 3 2 1

ISBN: 978-1-59416-060-8
ISBN 10: 1-59416-060-0

Printed in United States of America

The greatest Indian enigma of his time, perhaps of all time.

—*Dictionary of Canadian Biography*

Sitting Bull, leader of the largest Indian nation on the continent, the strongest, boldest, most stubborn opponent of European influence, was the very heart and soul of the Frontier. When the true history of the New World is written, he will receive his chapter. For Sitting Bull was one of the Makers of America.

—Stanley Vestal

I began to see when I was not yet born; when I was not in my mother's arms, but inside of my mother's belly. It was there that I began to study about my people. God gave me the power to see out of the womb. I studied there, in the womb, about many things. The God Almighty must have told me at that time that I would be the man to be the judge of all the other Indians—a big man, to decide for them in all their ways.

—Sitting Bull, 1877

NOTE ON TERMS

SITTING BULL'S name in the language of his people, the Lakota, is Tatanka Iyotanka. Tatanka is the Lakota word for buffalo bull, although it is often used as an umbrella term for the entire species. Iyotanka, meanwhile, implies that the bull is intractable or stubborn. The term "tatanka iyotanka" also is the first stage in an old Lakota allegory of the four stages of life (see page 5).

In this book, where Lakota words are used, my general reference is *Lakota Dictionary: Lakota-English/English-Lakota: Comprehensive Edition*, by Eugene Buechel (editor) and Paul Manhart, published in 2002 by the University of Nebraska Press. In other cases, such as with names, I have tried to use the most widely accepted spellings. I use the term "wasichu" for "white people," rather than the less common term, "wasicun." Wasichu also has the alternate meaning of "the one who steals the bacon," or "fat taker."

PROLOGUE

ONE night, long ago, on the windswept prairies of Western Canada, he stepped into the faint light of a kerosene lantern to speak with a man from the tribe that his people call the wasichu, and that we call Euro-Americans. Jerome Stillson of the *New York Herald* looked into the eyes of this man, who was both the most famous American Indian in the world and a scarcely understood mystery. "Your face is dark," Stillson told this enigma who had come to him in the form of a man. "My people do not see it."

What Stillson said that night many years ago remains true to this day. His name is still the best known of any American Indian leader in history, but despite this, his face remains clouded by mystery, unseen and not truly understood by the wasichu. "He's known around the globe," Mark Holman, the library director at the college that bears his name, told me. "You can go anywhere in the world and mention his name and people know." His fame is assured. He was world famous when he died, and he is at least as well known around the globe today—but why? What is it about him that makes him as relevant and as current in the twenty-first century as he was in the nineteenth century? Who was he and what is his legacy?

He was many things to many people and he remains as such today. He was a warrior, a shaman, a villain, and a hero. He was a showman happily selling autographed pictures of himself, and selling them at a discount to ladies to whom he took a fancy. He was a man of great charisma. Today, his face is not so much dark, as it is like a face illuminated by the lantern, or by the shifting, flickering light of a campfire like that which burned the night he was born or the night he was laid to rest.

Both James Walsh and Adirondack Murray, who knew him and respected him, understood that he projected an indefinable presence and power that made the nineteenth-century term "medicine man" a meaningless understatement. Murray saw him and sensed an oracle of mysteries and saw in him the highest expression of wisdom. Stanley Vestal, who did not know him but probably talked to more people who did than anyone else who has written about him, saw him as the very heart and soul of the frontier, one of the makers of America.

He saw himself as a man, a man who saw things that others did not see. The Lakota have a word for men like him. They call them wikasa wakan, but even that seems a pale way to understand something that can't really be described in words.

What most people know of him today is known through a shifting, flickering amalgam of images, some true, some ambiguous, and a great many that are totally false. His image is like a collection of partially assembled pieces of a puzzle. Like many historical figures with which most of us have only a passing acquaintance, he is known through an often distorted lens. He was a great man, but he was also a human man. Like all great men, he had his weaknesses, his moments of doubt and fear. Like all great men, he was a very complex man who we have reduced to simple terms in order to try to grasp who he was. To do so, we often miss the point.

Though the man is long gone, and his face still remains unclear, his name has never been forgotten. However, exactly who he was remains less clear in that collective memory than what his name has come to represent. The caricature was easy to grasp, but the reality was far more complex than the simplistic image that has been ingrained into popular culture for more than a century.

Who was the man in Stillson's flickering lantern light so long ago? Who was the man behind the face that remained in shadow despite global notoriety? What Stillson hoped to accomplish in his interview on that cold night so long ago was to cast some light into the darkness that obscured that face, and that is what I hope to accomplish in these pages.

This buffalo herd was photographed on the Standing Rock Reservation not far from Sitting Bull's birthplace early in the twenty-first century, but the scene is essentially identical to what one would have encountered two centuries before. (*Bill Yenne*)

1

WANIYETU WOWAPI

H E WAS BORN A VERY LONG TIME AGO into a world very unlike our own, and very unlike the world in which he lived his final years.

He was probably born early in the wasichu year of 1831, though he might have been born a couple of years earlier, or maybe as late as 1837. It is recalled among his people that he was born in the "Winter When Yellow Eyes Danced in the Snow," and this has been calculated to be the equivalent of 1831. His people, the Lakota, reckoned a year from the first snow one year to the first snow the following year; these pictographic *waniyetu wowapi* (winter counts) lead us to 1831. Therefore, that date is the one that most people now use.

A waniyetu wowapi was a document that counted winters. In the language of his people, the word *waniyetu* literally means winter, but it is a synonym for "year." The word *wowapi* literally translates as a document. It might be a single-page document, or a pictograph, or it might be a book in the wasichu sense. The Holy Bible is known in the language of his people as the Wowapi Wakan, literally, the "Holy Document."

In actual practice, a waniyetu wowapi was a series of pictographs paint-ed on a single flat surface, usually a buffalo hide. Later, as they became available from wasichu sources, cloth and paper came into use. There would be a pictograph for each year that was a picture that reminded everyone of a memorable event that occurred during the year, and by which people would recognize and recall the years. Even if someone did not have a firsthand recollection of Yellow Eyes dancing in the snow, they had heard about it through the stories told by older people. Today, there is no one left who remembers Yellow Eyes, and few who remember who he was—but the name is in the winter count.

As George Hyde remembered, and told us a century later, in 1937, Yellow Eyes had many names. He was a wasichu who grew up in a promi-nent St. Louis family with the name Thomas Lestang Sarpy. In Nebraska, there is a county named for this family. As he grew into adulthood, Thomas would share neither his family's prosperity, nor this family's name. It is said that he left home to escape a bad marriage, working for a while for the American Fur Company. In their employ, he traveled upstream on the Missouri River, where he established a trading post in what is now South Dakota. By now, he was known as Thomas Leston, but he came to use the name "Blestan," because to the people with whom he traded, this word sounded like their word for red lake.

In the space of three or four winters, he earned the name Yellow Eyes and took a wife from among the people with whom he traded, and they had a child. Some people say that he had two wives and two children, but that is beside the point. In 1831, a keg of gunpowder blew up next to where he was standing and Yellow Eyes was hurled to his death. To those who saw this, it was unforgettable, and the winter became the Winter When Yellow Eyes Danced in the Snow. Two years later, the Year the Stars Fell, was correlated to 1833 because of the Leonid meteor shower that occurred in November of that year.

But let us return to the winter that Yellow Eyes left the world, which is the winter that the subject of our story came into it.

He was probably born in a cottonwood grove along the south side of what is now known as the Grand River. This place was about 30 miles west and upstream from where the Grand enters the Missouri River, in what is now known as South Dakota. However, in 1881, he told a newspaper reporter that he was born on Willow Creek, just below the mouth of the Cheyenne River. Many years later, he told an interviewer, "I was born on the Missouri River; at least I recollect that somebody told me so—I don't know who told me or where I was told of it." He might have said, and the interpreter did not understand, that he was born in the "Missouri River Country," which would have included the banks of the Grand River.

In the 1920s, old men who had known him when they were young men and he was an old man told interviewers that he was born at a place along the Grand that was called Many Caches. It was known as this because it was here where people routinely camped, and where they excavated caches to store their goods. He may also have been born elsewhere in what is now western South Dakota. If anyone knows for sure, they are probably keeping it a secret.

The conventional wisdom is that he was born in the late winter, during the month called the Moon of Sore Eyes, a time of lengthening days and abating overcast when the sun reflecting off the snow was painfully bright. If he was indeed born in late winter, then it is probable that his family were still in an established winter encampment area such as Many Caches.

Ironically, the place where he later left this world was just a few miles from where he was probably born. Also ironically, the nearest town— Bullhead, South Dakota—is named for one of the men who shot him. Today, this part of the Grand River seems nearly as far from the wasichu world as it was in the fourth decade of the nineteenth century. Those who routinely commute by air between the coasts casually dismiss the Dakotas as part of "flyover country." Indeed, the contrails that criss-cross the dark blue sky on a cold, crisp late winter morning, when snow drifts cover the narrow country roads, are about the only feature one sees out here that allows us to realize that we are not standing here in the early nineteenth century—or the eighteenth, or before. In late winter it can take as long—or longer—to drive to the probable place of his birth from the nearest Interstate highway (I-90) than it does to drive from New York to Washington, D.C.

Today, the confluence of the Missouri and the Grand is submerged beneath the reservoir created by the Oahe Dam, but upstream, near where Many Caches once existed, the Grand River appears more or less as it as it did back in Sitting Bull's time. The sound of the wind rustling through the trees near the place where he was born is still punctuated with the familiar trill of the western meadowlark, a bird that is said to have had a special meaning for him throughout his life, and whose language he is said to have understood. He also had a special relationship with the yellow-shafted flicker. When he was a boy, one of these birds saved his life, awakening him from a nap and warning him to lie perfectly still when a grizzly bear passed so close that the young man could feel the damp warmth of its fetid breath.

When he came into the world during the "Winter When Yellow Eyes Danced in the Snow," the boy who is now universally known as Sitting Bull received the name Jumping Badger. At the time, his father was called Sitting Bull, though he too would be known by other names. Among their people, name changes were common, though not undertaken lightly. As they matured, people were often given new names that better described their character than the names they were given at birth. Indeed, before he took the name Sitting Bull, the elder Sitting Bull had been known as Returns Again, a name that he earned by being a warrior who successfully completed a raid on a rival tribe and came home to tell the tale. Speaking of tales, the way that Returns Again took the name Sitting Bull is also an interesting story.

Returns Again was thought to possess the rare—but not unheard of—ability to communicate with animals in their own language. One day

Cottonwood groves grow in the river bottom land near where Sitting Bull was born. The area has changed only a little since Sitting Bull rode these hills and valleys. (*Bill Yenne*)

while hunting—or in some variations of the tale, one evening while eating dinner around their campfire—Returns Again and three other hunters were approached by the Great Buffalo, who is the earthly manifestation of the deity that provides adequate game to Lakota hunters. The Great Buffalo spoke, but only Returns Again could understand him, so it was known that the message was meant for him rather than his companions.

Speaking to Returns Again, the Great Buffalo named the four stages of life. Everyone has heard the metaphor about the three stages of life in which a person walks on four legs in the morning (a crawling baby), two legs at noon (a walking adult), and three legs in the evening (a person walking with a cane). In the parallel Lakota parable, there are four stages. First is tatanka iyotake, the sitting bull, followed by tatanka psica, the jumping bull, and tatanka winyuha najin, the bull who is standing with a cow. Finally, there is tatanka wanjila, the bull who stands alone.

Returns Again interpreted the message of the Great Buffalo to mean that he should take the name Sitting Bull, which he did. Some years later, when his son became a man and was renamed Sitting Bull, the elder

Sitting Bull (formerly Returns Again) took the name Jumping Bull, the next stage of life in the continuum referenced by the Great Buffalo on that portentous day.

Returns Again had been born around the turn of the nineteenth century, possibly in 1799. Little is known of his ancestors, although his own father is said to have received a King George III peace medal at the time of the War of 1812, when the British were currying favor with the Western Tribes. Returns Again had at least two siblings. Of one brother, Looks for Him in a Tent (Looks for Home), little is known except that he was killed in a battle with Crow warriors in the winter of 1869–1870. Another brother was Four Horns, who later became an illustrious leader of his people. Much younger than Returns Again, Four Horns was born in about 1814 and may have been his half-brother.

The wife of the elder Sitting Bull was called Mixed Day at the time she gave birth to Jumping Badger, although she was later known as Her Holy Door. When Jumping Badger was born, Mixed Day and the elder Sitting Bull had a daughter who was about six years old and whose name was Good Feather. A second daughter, Twin Woman (also known as Brown Shawl Woman) was born much later, although the exact date has not been established. Both the elder Sitting Bull and Mixed Day were ethnically Hunkpapa Lakota, but prior to Mixed Day's becoming his wife, the elder Sitting Bull also had a son named Fool Dog by a woman who was Arikira. Little is known of Fool Dog other than that he remained with the Arikira people. The name Fool Dog pops up from time to time in nineteenth-century lore, including as one of the signatories of the 1868 Fort Laramie Treaty, but it cannot be said for certain that each mention is that of the same person.

JUMPING BADGER was born into the Hunkpapa, a branch, or oyate, of the tribal grouping known to many as the Teton (Titonwan) or Western Sioux, but who refer to themselves as Lakota.

The Sioux did not call themselves "Sioux." That name, which is still used officially by the wasichu after more than 200 years, is a truncation of the word "Nadouessioux." In the language of the Chippewa (aka Ojibwa or Annishinaabe) people, it means "little snakes" or adders. The derogatory term was applied by the Chippewa to all the Plains tribes that shared the Hokan-Siouan language. The Sioux are simply one of the tribes whose language is of this linguistic group, but there are other Hokan-Siouan-speaking people. These include central Plains tribes such as the Iowa, Kansa, Omaha, Osage, Oto, Ponca, Quapaw, and Winnebago, as well as the Hidatsa (Gros Ventre) and Mandan on the Northern Plains. Other tribes who lived in what is known to the wasichu as Virginia, as well as the Biloxi people living near the mouth of the Mississippi River, were linguistically related to the Sioux.

The Sioux refer to themselves by a name that literally means "friend" or "allies," and implies "all Sioux people." The name varies within three distinct Hokan-Siouan dialects. The ethnographers say that from east to west, the three groups refer to all members of the tribe as "Dakota," "Nakota," and "Lakota," respectively. This geographical breakdown is an oversimplification, because the "Sioux" subgroups are all mixed around today, but it is a useful shorthand way to understand the origins of the tribal divisions.

Once living generally in what is now Minnesota, the eastern branch of the tribe, known as the Dakota or Santee, included such subgroups as the Mdewakanton, Sisiton (Sisseton), Wahpekute, and Wahpeton (Wahpetonwan).

The central branch, or the Nakota, living in what are now the Dakotas, included the Yankton and Yanktonai (Little Yankton), subgroups. The Yankton and Yanktonais are also called the Wiceyala or Middle Sioux. When they moved eastward onto the prairie, they had contact with the semi-sedentary farming tribes such as the Mandan, Hidatsa, and Arikara. Eventually the Yanktonai displaced these tribes and forced them upstream to the area of the confluence of the Knife River and the Missouri River, although they continued to trade with these tribes, and eventually some Yanktonai took up farming.

Accounting for about three-quarters of the total Sioux population in Sitting Bull's time, the largest division of the Sioux was—and still is—the branch known as the Lakota or Teton. The Lakota are subdivided into the Oceti Sakowin or Seven Council Fires. These seven subgroups are the Brulé (Burnt Thighs), the Hunkpapa (or Uncpapa, meaning "campers at the horn," or "head of the camp"), the Itazipacola (Sans Arcs or No Bows), the Minneconjou (Miniconjou), the Oglala, the Oohenonpa (Two-Kettle), and the Sihasapa. The latter group, also known as the Blackfoot Sioux, are not to be confused with the Blackfeet (Siksika) tribe, who were culturally similar in the nineteenth century, but who speak an Algonquian language, and who were and are geographically separate.

The people of Jumping Badger's council fire, the Hunkpapa, took their name from their handed-down right to pitch their tipis at the outer edge, or head, of a circular encampment to serve as the defenders of the camp. The Hunkpapa were, in turn, divided into the Canka Ohan, or Sore Backs, and the Icira, meaning the band that separated and then came back together. The family of Sitting Bull belonged to the latter.

At its apogee, the total Sioux homeland spanned the area from the Rocky Mountains to the Mississippi River, including the southern parts of what are now Montana, the Dakotas, and Minnesota, as well as Wyoming, Nebraska, and parts of neighboring states and the Canadian provinces of Saskatchewan and Manitoba. Like the other Plains people, the Sioux were generally a nomadic people without fixed settlements, whose culture and economy revolved around following the great buffalo herds across the Plains. When Jumping Badger was growing up, the lands across which the Lakota people ranged were mainly north of the Platte River, west of the Missouri River, and east of the Bighorn Mountains, an area at least twice the size of New England. The Hunkpapa, like the Sihasapa, ranged in the area between the Cheyenne and Heart rivers to the south and north and between the Missouri River on the east and Tongue River to the west.

Being born Sioux, Jumping Badger had one thing in common with Americans born in our own time. He was born into the political entity that was the unquestioned—if not unchallenged—superpower for as far as anyone could see. At that time, and for many, many generations before that time, the Sioux had dominated the Northern Plains. Smaller tribes, including the other Hokan-Siouan-speakers as well as the Kiowa, the Pawnee, and many others, feared the Sioux and paid them tribute.

The principal rivals of the Lakota included Siouan-speaking Crow, or Absaroka, who lived to the west in what is now Montana, and the Assiniboine—known to the Lakota as Hohe—who lived to the north in the region of what is now the border between the United States and Canada. Farther to the west, along the front range of the Rocky Mountains, mainly in what is now Montana, the Lakota occasionally came into contact with the Shoshone and the Blackfeet as well as with the Salish and Kootenai people whom the wasichu called "Flathead." Linguistically, the Shoshone were related to the Uto-Aztecan-speaking peoples of the Great Basin and farther south into Mexico. Having originated in the area north of the Great Lakes, the Blackfeet spoke an Algonquian dialect; while the Salish and Kootenai people were linguistically related to the tribes of the Pacific Coast.

Another major antagonist for the Lakota had long been the loose alliance among the Hidatsa, Mandan, and Arikara peoples. As noted above, the former two spoke a Siouan dialect, but the Arikara spoke a Caddoan dialect and were linguistically related to the Pawnee people. The wasichu trappers and traders often referred to the Arikara as the "Arikaree" or "Rikaree." Over time, the name became shortened to "Ree." This latter nickname is seen widely in books and other references to the Plains tribes during the nineteenth century.

While the Sioux, and most Siouan-speaking people, were nomadic, the allied Hidatsa, Mandan, and Arikara tribes engaged in agriculture and had fixed settlements. At the time that Lewis and Clark reached their great "city" near the confluence of the Missouri and the Knife rivers north of today's Bismarck, North Dakota, in 1804, it had a population greater than the wasichu city of St. Louis, Missouri. By the 1840s, however, diseases spread by wasichu traders plying the Missouri River had decimated these three tribes. There may have been many more than 30,000 Sioux in the eighteenth century before the wasichu brought germs to which the Sioux had no resistance, but all the numbers prior to the mid-nineteenth century are rough estimates. In the 1830s when Sitting Bull was young, there were probably between 20,000 and 30,000 Sioux, with the Hunkpapa Lakota estimated to have comprised 10 to 15 percent of the total Sioux population. In 1866, while involved in treaty negotiations, Newton Edmunds, former governor of Dakota Territory, counted 20,790 Sioux, of which 10.1 percent were Hunkpapa. The average of the five best estimates done between 1850 and 1869 is 18,298, of which the Hunkpapa proportion is estimated at 12.2 percent.

In 1890, the Indian Bureau listed 19,270 Sioux as living on reservations, of which 10.3 percent were Hunkpapa. Also in 1890, the United States Census reported that the total Indian population of South Dakota, where most of the Sioux lived and where most Indians were Sioux, as 19,845. By comparison, the 2000 United States Census counted 108,272 people who were ethnically Sioux (up from 78,608 in 1980), and 45,088 who were part Sioux. As such, the Sioux are currently the third largest native tribe in the United States after the Cherokee and Navajo.

No discussion of Sitting Bull or the Lakota people is complete without a mention of his totem animal, the great beast that was the centerpiece of the economic and spiritual life of all Plains people. The Lakota called it tatanka, modern biologists call it the North American bison (*Bison bison*), and nearly everyone else calls it the buffalo. Of course, zoologists will tell

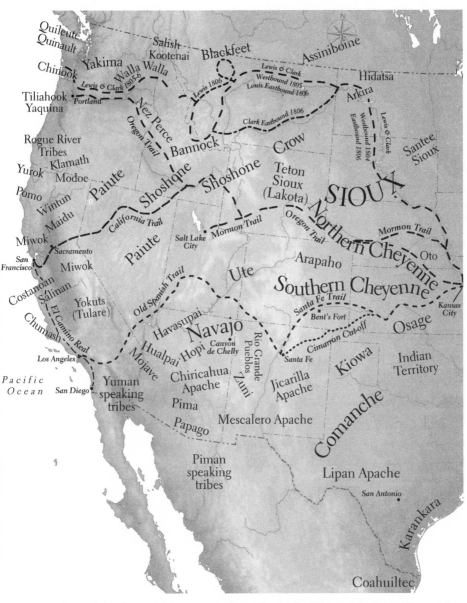

General distribution of American Indian tribes in the West and the key trails used during the first waves of westward migration during the nineteenth century.

you that, strictly speaking, it is not a "true" buffalo. It belongs to the family Bovidae, as do domestic cattle. The North American buffalo is closely related to the European bison, or wisent (*Bison bonasus*), but only distantly related to the true buffalo species of Africa and Asia. However, it is universally referred to as the buffalo, so we use this term. As J. Walker McSpadden wrote in 1917, "Early settlers called it the buffalo, and it has been a buffalo to Americans ever since."

The buffalo is the largest land animal in North America. While a moose stands taller at the shoulders, a buffalo is longer and weighs more. An adult male may weigh one ton. Certainly, the buffalo was the most numerous large mammal ever to exist in North America. When the Europeans began to explore the continent in the sixteenth century, they discovered buffalo as far east as the Atlantic seaboard, and they found immense herds numbering in the millions on the Great Plains from Mexico into Canada.

Because the great herds were nearly gone before any organized scientific population surveys were made, we may never know just how many buffalo once roamed North America. Estimates, based on the number that could have been sustained by the food available in their natural environment, vary widely. Andrew Isenberg, in his *The Destruction of the Bison: An Environmental History, 1750–1920* suggests a conservative number of 30 million, while other calculations range as high as 75 million. In the nineteenth century, some estimates—including one made by General Philip Sheridan—exceeded a billion. This unscientific number is almost certainly a wild exaggeration, although it colorfully illustrates how awe-inspiring the sight of the vast herds would have been. There were so many that early observers resorted to phrases such as "numberless," "the country was one black robe," or "the Plains were black and appeared as if in motion with the herds of buffalo."

Anecdotal reports from trappers and explorers who traveled into and across the Great Plains in the early nineteenth century frequently describe single herds numbering 3,000 or more. The Lewis and Clark expedition, encountering a herd at South Dakota's White River in 1806, observed, "The moving multitude darkened the whole Plains. We are convinced that 20,000 would be no exaggerated number." Similar descriptions of solid masses of buffalo stretching for as far as the eye could see are common. In 1869, William Street, an Army officer in Kansas, observed a herd that filled an area twenty miles by more than sixty miles. It moved continuously at one to two miles per hour through a valley for over twenty-four hours. Allowing twenty-five square feet for each animal, the size of this one herd would have easily exceeded one million buffalo.

The buffalo was a principal resource of the Plains Indians, furnishing them with food, hides for robes, skins for shelter and boats, bones for tools and utensils, and buffalo chips (dung) for fuel. It has been said that Indians used every part of the buffalo for something. While this is true, research has shown that they didn't use all of every animal they killed. However, there was clearly a sustainable yield. The enormous buffalo population would have continued to support the much smaller native population indefinitely, had it not been for the use of firearms and horses—and the arrival of the wasichu.

Various parts of the buffalo were favored as food. The tongue was prized by both Indians and later by whites. The hump was especially favored, and the blood, brains, and heart were also widely preferred. John James Audubon observed that the internal organs were also considered as a delicacy, although certain tribes are recorded to have had special preferences. The Kootenai especially prized the heart, while the Blackfeet refused to eat the liver. Buffalo meat was usually cooked, but not infrequently, especially just after a kill, it would be eaten raw. It was the sushi of the Plains.

Meat that was not eaten within a day or so was preserved by drying it into jerky. It was sliced thin and hung on scaffolds over a fire. Jerky was easier to carry because the drying reduced the meat's weight by 80 percent.

Pemmican, a mixture of dried meat, fat, and wild berries, was also prepared. It has been suggested that the legendary strength and endurance often attributed to the Plains Indians may well be a testament to the extraordinary nutritional value acquired from a diet that depended upon a constant supply of buffalo meat—which is now known to be both high in protein and iron, as well as low in fat and cholesterol.

The Plains people used the buffalo hide for robes, shirts, leggings, dresses, belts, moccasins, caps, and mittens. The leather was also used to make tipis, blankets, medicine cases, trunks, cache-pit covers, tobacco pouches, berry bags (the hide of the unborn calf), cooking vessels and buckets, as well as shields, knife sheaths, horse gear, dog gear, saddle bags, lariats, horse-watering bags, boats, rafts, snowshoes, ball covers, and netting for lacrosse equipment. The hair was used in clothing and ornaments, the sinew was used as twine and bowstrings, while buffalo horns and bones were used to make tools and ornaments.

Before the arrival of the wasichu, native people hunted from the ground with bows and arrows by encircling a smaller group separate from the main herd. It was also common practice to stampede huge herds to their deaths, by driving them over cliffs known as buffalo jumps. After the wasichu arrived in North America, the Indians came into possession of horses, and later, guns. These permitted the killing of larger numbers of buffalo and a higher standard of living for the Indians. By the time that Sitting Bull was growing up, the Lakota hunted buffalo on horseback using bows and arrows. During his first hunts as a youth, some Lakota hunters, though certainly not all, had firearms. During Sitting Bull's lifetime, guns became the prevalent means by which the Lakota hunted buffalo.

The buffalo also figured in the legends of the Plains people, and each tribe had an elaborate mythology surrounding the buffalo. Of particular importance was the extremely rare white buffalo. The white buffalo was generally seen to represent the female power of the Earth, similar to the notion of Gaia, or Mother Earth. According to legend, the White Buffalo Calf Woman taught the people to respect their relationship with the earth. She came as a young woman wearing a white buckskin dress and moccasins, and left as a white buffalo calf. To this day, the birth of a white buffalo calf is an event of great significance to Plains Indian cultures.

WHEN little Jumping Badger was born into the Lakota, their lifestyle had changed little for more than a century, but in the century before that, the world of the Lakota had changed dramatically. Three hundred years before he was born, in the early years of the sixteenth century, a wasichu tribe known as the Spanish had come north out of Mexico to explore the southern edges of the Great Plains. With them, they brought an amazing means of mobility that astonished North America's native people. They brought horses.

The Indians whose paths were crossed by the Spanish, begged, borrowed, stole, or traded for these marvelous animals. As the Indians mastered horsemanship, and as tribe after tribe begged, borrowed, stole, or traded with other tribes, the use of horses spread like an unquenchable prairie fire. Horses literally revolutionized the lives and the economy of the Plains Indians, changing the way that they hunted buffalo, the way that they moved their camps, and the way that they waged war. The Sioux, being the unquestioned superpower on the northern Plains, amassed the largest numbers of horses, and naturally became even more of a superpower because of their huge herds of these prized animals. Indeed, the elder Sitting Bull was considered a wealthy and important man because of his many horses.

A number of years after horses arrived on the Great Plains—nobody knows exactly when—another aspect of wasichu technology reached the indigenous people of the region. As with horses, firearms changed the way that the Plains people hunted buffalo and waged war. Traders, both British and French, had come into the Plains, mainly out of what is now Canada. They traded various things, from colorful beads to iron tools, for buffalo hides and beaver pelts. While it seems obscure and incomprehensible to us today, the importance of beaver pelts to the North American economy—and to the story of wasichu exploration and settlement of the Plains and the Far West—in the eighteenth century cannot be underestimated.

The Indians were eager for the trade goods and the traders were eager for the pelts. It was a commercial relationship not unlike that which the Plains tribes had among themselves and with other tribes for centuries. The relationship was the same, but the trade goods were new and different—the traders also brought guns. Firearms, however, were not as widely distributed among the Plains people as were horses. Everybody could use horses, but guns were not as reliable as other weapons. They required dry powder and an adequate supply of balls, and it took longer to get off a second shot with a musket than with a bow. Indeed, in the hands of a Plains Indian, the bow was a potent and formidable weapon and arguably a weapon far better suited for both hunting and for Plains warfare than a musket. The advent of repeating firearms would open a new chapter, but that turn would not come until well after the boy born as Jumping Badger reached manhood.

It was not long, however, before the boy born as Jumping Badger earned a nickname that would be with him until adolescence. When he was just a toddler, his family noticed that he was more careful and deliberate than most his age. Instead of just grabbing at things, the little boy handled them, examining them carefully. He seemed to do things more slowly, and consequently they started to call him by one of the Lakota words for "slow."

He took his first steps amid tipis and campfires of an impermanent Lakota encampment somewhere on the Plains in the Missouri River Country. The Lakota people were always on the move because the buffalo herds were always on the move. As with all Lakota, the group with whom his parents were associated were always literally pulling up stakes to recon-figure their tipis as travois.

One can easily imagine little Slow "helping" disassemble his parents' equipment for the move, or reassembling the camp at a new location. His early days were filled with scampering about the camp, among the half-wild dogs that the Plains people kept, between the smoldering campfires, playing games with other kids and learning to compete. He would also have spent time as a toddler watching his mother and the other women as they went about the Lakota women's daily chores, which were related to housekeeping and processing the buffalo hides and meat brought home by hunters such as his father. Later, he would begin to ride with the elder Sitting Bull.

Most of the people in Slow's camp were related. His uncle, Four Horns, was there, as were many cousins and extended family. Such group-ings, numbering between fifty and one hundred people, living together and headed by a single patriarch, were the basic building block of Plains Indian society.

Slow's group was one of a myriad of Lakota bands that roamed the Missouri River Country. These bands occasionally crossed paths or inter-acted, but generally remained autonomous. Once each summer, howev-er, many smaller bands would consolidate for the Sun Dance, an annual ceremonial festival that was held for more than a week around the time of the summer solstice. The annual Sun Dance involved singing, dancing, drumming, and fasting. It also included the ceremonial piercing of the flesh of the warriors.

The Sun Dance was the most important cultural and spiritual event of the Lakota calendar, and was presided over by what the wasichu called "medicine men," and what modern anthropologists call "shamans." The Lakota called them "wikasa (or wichasha) wakan," meaning men with exceptional and mysterious powers that were often interpreted as supernat-ural. The role of these individuals in society was an amalgam of spiritual leadership and the practical healing ability of a knowledgeable herbalist. During the Sun Dance, the wikasa wakan would typically receive visions that would be important to his respective band or tribe.

Political leadership, meanwhile, usually went to men within the group who were most skilled at exercising such power. Unlike Europe, tribal leadership on the Plains was less about hereditary titles than about proving one's ability to lead. The itancan, the leaders whom the wasichu traditionally called "chiefs," could enforce strict discipline and demand uncompromising allegiance—but only so long as they had the strength of character to command respect. Only the best of the best could be an itancan and remain in such a leadership role.

Leaders within the Hunkpapa Lakota community—as within the Brulé, the Itazipacola, the Minneconjou, the Oglala, the Oohenonpa, and the Sihasapa—usually led autonomous bands. A council of elders from the various bands met occasionally, usually at the ceremonial Sun Dance festival, but aside from this, the Lakota bands rarely camped together or rode together in battle. Had the warriors from these various groups and bands within the Lakota ever unified under a single military command, the history—and possibly the outcome—of the Plains Indian Wars of the latter nineteenth century would have been much different.

Not long after he learned to scamper, Slow, like other Lakota boys, learned to ride and to hunt. His father probably had him on a horse before he could walk, and it was not long before he graduated from rudimentary toys to his first bow, an instrument with which all Lakota boys became intimate as they grew to manhood. The stories told to late nineteenth- and early twentieth-century ethnographers by those who knew him, all say that he was an excellent hunter. He was very skilled with a bow and arrow. Indeed, to become a good horseman and a good hunter defined the transition from Lakota boyhood to Lakota manhood. Killing your first buffalo calf before you reached the age that modern boys attend junior high school was a routine rite of passage.

Horsemanship and hunting skills also prepared the young Lakota men for another constant of life on the Plains—war. For more than a century, romantics have yearned to portray the indigenous people of North America as living in strict harmony with nature *and* with one another before the wasichu arrived to be the catalyst for armed conflict. This was not the case. For example, the age-old and ongoing antagonism between the Lakota and the Crow was as deeply entrenched in the culture, and at least as violent, as that between the English and the French. Scalps of women and children, as well as those of defeated warriors, were considered legitimate trophies long before the wasichu set foot on the Plains. Most men of Slow's generation had fought many lethal struggles with the Crow, the Assiniboine, or other tribes long before they ever faced a wasichu in battle.

As was the case across the globe in Europe, warfare was not all savagery. Just as the honorable European knight fought by the code of chivalry, so too did the warriors of the Plains have a code of conduct. The practice of "counting coup"—simply hitting, rather than killing a foe—was seen as the ultimate standard of courage. A warrior would do this using a coup stick, usually a long stick with a feather attached to the end. Occasionally racing with his friends, he would ride toward his opponent at top speed, often with the element of surprise, strike him, and then ride away to the acclaim of his companions.

It was not for the faint at heart. It was a disgrace to be counted coup upon, and it was considered sporting to use deadly force against someone who was trying to count against you. Many warriors died trying, so success in counting coup was seen as great bravery. Stanley Vestal describes counting coup as having "all the dash and speed of polo, the informality of a fox hunt, the sporting chance of sudden wealth afforded by the modern horse race, and danger enough to satisfy the most reckless."

ACCORDING to the legends, Slow first counted coup at age 14, four years after having killed his first buffalo. According to the best calculations, this pivotal event in the young man's life occurred in the wasichu year 1845 while he was riding with his father and a hunting party in the rolling hills of the Powder River Country of what is now southeastern Montana. As the story goes, Slow and several companions crested a ridge and spotted a group of Crow in the coulee below. Like testosterone-crazed teenage boys often do, they swept down toward their rivals, shouting and taunting.

The scene must have been dramatic. According to One Bull's later recollection of family legend, Slow was naked except for moccasins and breechcloth, but he had painted himself yellow from head to toe. As the Crow men reacted to the attack, Slow picked one, and rode toward him at top speed on his fast gray horse. The Crow had notched an arrow and was ready to shoot when the boy struck his arm, counting coup and knocking the weapon away.

He did not have long to suffer the disgrace of being counted against by the fourteen-year-old. One of Slow's comrades attacked and killed him. Before the swirling fracas ended, most of the Crow were dead.

That night, amid dramatic, age-old rituals around the blazing campfire, the elder Sitting Bull celebrated his son, bestowing the ultimate honor that he could confer—his own name. Jumping Badger, nicknamed "Slow," officially became Tatanka Iyotanka—Sitting Bull. The elder Sitting Bull symbolically moved one step further in the cycle of Lakota life, renaming himself as Jumping Bull. His father also placed a single white eagle feather in the hair of young Sitting Bull. Many years later, when he finally crossed paths with photographers, Sitting Bull would be recorded many times with such a feather prominently displayed.

The story of what happened that day would become one of the most enduring legends in Lakota oral history. Indeed, Sitting Bull himself would recount it many times, just as White Bull carried it into the twentieth century. The legend grew in 1846, when Sitting Bull added a red feather to his insignia. Analogous to the Purple Heart in the modern U.S. Army, the red feather signified a warrior who had been wounded in action.

This incident, and many others that followed, were recorded by Sitting Bull in a series of more than two dozen allegorical drawings. In the same way that the keeper of the winter counts executed allegorical drawings to keep track of important milestones in the life of the tribe, individual people did the same. Sitting Bull began to create drawings that would highlight important events of his life as a warrior over the next twenty-four years. Most of them depict his successful fights with Crow or Assiniboine warriors. None depict his wives or children. Sitting Bull's biographer, Stanley Vestal, refers to these as Sitting Bull's "Hieroglyphic Autobiography."

While Sitting Bull would record the events that marked his coming of age as a warrior, he would omit his spiritual coming of age. It was too personal. The vision quest is a form of solitary meditation and fasting in a remote location, one feature that many North American Indian cultures share with world religions from Buddhism to Christianity. In the Lakota practice, a vision quest is first undertaken when someone in his or her teens, but it often recurs because not everyone obtains a vision on their first quest. Under the guidance of a wikasa wakan, the subject will go off by himself to meditate and seek guidance from Wakantanka, a sacred and mysterious entity that can be generally described as the "Great Spirit" or "sacred spirit" roughly analogous to the Judeo-Christian understanding of an omnipotent God. As we have noted previously, another important deity that the Lakota had in common with many world cultures was a powerful female "earth mother" figure, known as the White Buffalo Calf Woman.

During the vision quest, the subject remains for several days in one place, within a circle having the approximate radius of his own height. During this time, the subject aspires to have a vision that contains a message about his life to come, which usually is delivered by an animal, who will be their spiritual guide. Persons whose visions involved the same animal—elk, deer, wolf, bear, etc.—often joined together into a society dedicated to that animal. Though he didn't talk about it, Sitting Bull is said to have belonged to both the Buffalo Society and the Heyoka, or Thunderbird, Society. Members of the Heyoka, considered to be one of the most prestigious of societies, paint their faces with lightning bolts, because lightning is a manifestation of the thunderbird.

Before he had reached the age when boys today are graduating from high school, Sitting Bull may have been on his first vision quest, and he was certainly beginning to earn a reputation as a powerful warrior. Over the next few years, as his prestige grew and his victories in battles mounted, he was invited to join the fraternity of exceptional warriors known as the Strong Heart Society. Strong Hearts swore an oath never to retreat in battle, and often ceremonially staked themselves to the ground during a fight to emphasize the point. As such, he was authorized to wear a headdress with two buffalo horns, and the Strong Heart sash, a strip of red cloth decorated with feathers. In fact, Sitting Bull was typically more understated with his headgear.

Sitting Bull's uncle Four Horns, meanwhile, had become a "Shirt Wearer," one of four members of a sort of administrative committee that oversaw the execution of edicts handed down by the council of Lakota elders. This represented the highest rung within the hierarchy of Lakota leadership that was available for a man in his late thirties or early forties. As such, he was to be very important as a mentor for Sitting Bull as he reached manhood.

In the autumn of the wasichu year 1856, remembered in the Lakota winter count as the Winter When the War Bonnet Was Torn, Sitting Bull was riding with a hundred-man Hunkpapa hunting—and horse-stealing—party near the confluence of the Powder River and the Yellowstone River. Scouts had detected a large Crow encampment with many head of horses on Porcupine Creek, and the decision was made to attack under cover of darkness.

The raid against the Crow camp was successful, and the Hunkpapa made off with a huge herd of valuable stock without much resistance. At daybreak, however, the angry Crow caught up with the thieves and prepared to strike back. The two sides lined up facing one another and three Crow dashed forward to count coup. The first man did so successfully, but Loud Bear of the Hunkpapa gave chase and jerked his war bonnet off his head. This scene was so dramatic that it became the namesake event in the Winter When the War Bonnet Was Torn.

Sitting Bull engaged another of the three Crow warriors who had ridden forward to count coup. With his horned headdress and other accoutrements, Sitting Bull was obviously a member of the Strong Heart Society—but his opposite number wore the red shirt of a Crow war chief. Coincidentally, both men were armed with rifles, which was uncommon. Only a relatively small number of Plains warriors in a typical 1856 encounter carried guns. Sitting Bull's was smooth-bore muzzle-loader that he had recently acquired from a wasichu trader. The Crow chief had an old flintlock. Both were single-shot guns, so each man knew that he had to make his one shot count.

The two warriors ran toward each other, and the Crow fired first. Passing through Sitting Bull's shield, the round was deflected downward, hitting him in the left foot. With the Crow having shot first, Sitting Bull had the luxury of taking more careful aim than his opponent, and the shot was good. Sitting Bull finished him off with his knife as the Hunkpapa warriors rode to attack—and rout—the Crow.

His wound was to be for Sitting Bull a permanent reminder of the incident. The ball had traveled the length of the sole of his foot, entering at the base of his toes and exiting at his heel. The damage would not heal properly, and Sitting Bull would walk with a limp for the rest of his life. Though he was physically unable to participate in the victory dance that night, his triumph in a man-on-man fight, witnessed by a hundred Hunkpapa, earned Sitting Bull hero status.

As a leading member of the Strong Heart Society and as a Hunkpapa war chief, Sitting Bull was an increasingly important member of the Lakota hierarchy. He was a big man. He stood about five feet, ten inches, notably tall for his people and taller than many wasichu men of the period. He was muscular, with a powerful chest, a large head, and piercing eyes. In his late twenties, he still possessed the deliberate attention to detail that had earned him the nickname "Slow" when he was a toddler.

It was in about 1851 that Sitting Bull married his first of five wives, a woman named Light Hair. There are a few interview references to her name having been Pretty Door, but these may be places where the translator got her mixed up with references to Sitting Bull's mother, Mixed Day, who was later called Pretty Door or Her Holy Door.

As newlyweds, Sitting Bull and Light Hair once in a while went on hunting trips together, and on such a venture, while they were camped near where the Powder River flows into the Yellowstone, a Crow warrior sneaked into their camp. As the somewhat colorful story goes, Light Hair saw his reflection in a spoonful of fat that she was skimming from boiling buffalo bones. Without looking up, she alerted Sitting Bull, who promptly shot the intruder. He got away, but the trail of blood indicated that Sitting Bull's arrow had found its mark.

A few years later, in about 1856, another intruder arrived on the scene, much to the displeasure of Light Hair. Sitting Bull's second wife, Snow on Her, did not feel that she should take a secondary role to Light Hair just because the first wife had Sitting Bull to herself for several years. A feud ensued that is recalled as having been especially troublesome for their husband. The two women bickered constantly, and according to the stories, Sitting Bull slept on his back with a woman clinging tightly to each of his arms, each refusing to permit him to face the other.

Polygamy was common among the Lakota at the time, but the usual practice was for the second wife to be the younger sister of the first wife so that there would be no doubt as to who was above whom in the pecking

Four Horns's copy of a Sitting Bull drawing of himself with a shield in a battle with the Crow. This image records Sitting Bull's near-fatal gunshot wound in 1856. (*Manuscript 1929A. Four Horns copy of Sitting Bull and Jumping Bull pictographic autobiographies, 1870. National Anthropological Archives*)

order. Snow on Her should have accepted that she was the secondary wife, but she did not. Sitting Bull had made a serious miscalculation.

The quarrel between the wives reached its tipping point when Snow on Her unjustly accused Light Hair of having slept with a man other than Sitting Bull. The women of the village convened a council, demanding that Snow on Her name names. She could not. One of the older women demanded that any man other than Sitting Bull who had known Light Hair should admit it, and that if any man lied, she would kill him herself. Caught in a lie, Snow on Her went away in shame and moved back to her parents' tipi.

The exile of Snow on Her was temporary, however. Light Hair died in childbirth in 1857, and Snow on Her returned to Sitting Bull's tipi. The son of Sitting Bull and Light Hair survived his mother's death, but died at about the age of four. Sitting Bull and Snow on Her had at least two children, Many Horses was born in 1863, and Walks Looking in 1868.

By this time, Sitting Bull had married his third wife, Red Woman. With her, he had at least one child, who was also born in 1868, and who died at the age of nine.

In the meantime, Sitting Bull's sister, Good Feather, had married Makes Room, a Minneconjou Lakota itancan, and had given birth to two sons, White Bull, born in 1849, and Lone Bull (later One Bull), born about a three years later. Both of them died in their late nineties, a month apart, in 1947. They would be among the principal sources of information about their uncle's early days.

In 1857, the same year that his wife died and that he became a war chief, Sitting Bull adopted the four-year-old One Bull as his son. White Bull would technically remain with the Minneconjou, but as a young man he often rode with Sitting Bull and One Bull on raids and hunting trips.

Also in 1857, Sitting Bull adopted a brother, an Assiniboine (Hohe) boy whom he named Stays Back. The story of how they met is one of the most colorful of Sitting Bull's early career as a warrior. Winter had come to what is now northeastern Montana, and Sitting Bull was invited to join in a raid against the Hohe that had been proposed by Stands at the Mouth of the River. At this time, the Missouri River formed the general and de facto border between the Lakota-dominated country to the south and Assiniboine territory to the north. Raiding the Assiniboine involved crossing the Missouri, which was facilitated by the fact that its surface had frozen.

The raiding party made their crossing, one by one, with Sitting Bull in the rear, at a point downstream from where the Poplar River flows into the Missouri. The first raiders across located and attacked a lone tipi, killing a Hohe man as he tried to defend his family. According to the story as it was related second-hand to Stanley Vestal in the 1920s, the Lakota warriors then proceeded to kill the man's wife, her infant, and one older child. A second older child, a boy about twelve, attempted to escape and was surrounded when Sitting Bull finally rode up.

The boy was facing the Lakota defiantly as Swift Cloud was notching an arrow to kill him. When the young Assiniboine saw Sitting Bull ride up, he appealed to him, calling the big Lakota warrior in Strong Heart regalia "brother." This struck a chord with Sitting Bull, who had no full brothers. He intervened, insisting that the bold lad was too brave to die. The others argued with Sitting Bull, but at last they put down their weapons and agreed to let the Hohe live. Sitting Bull then surprised the others by announcing his intention to adopt the boy who called him "brother," as his brother.

When they returned to the Hunkpapa camp, the Assiniboine captive was not exactly welcomed with open arms, but Sitting Bull persisted, overcame objections to his impulsive adoption, and gave a big feast in his new brother's honor. Later, when the Assiniboine learned that the boy had survived the death of his family and was living with the Hunkpapa, they made entreaties toward getting him back. The boy apparently liked his new home so much that he refused repatriation. For this, he was given the name Stays Back, because he remained with the Lakota. Some sources also refer to him as Little Assiniboine, and he would have other names before long. Over the coming two decades, as the boy became a man, he would often ride into battle with his older adopted brother. He would prove so fierce in combat that he earned one of his other names, Kills Often. And in Lakota lore, the winter count for 1857 would carry the name Winter When Kills Often Was Brought Home.

Meanwhile, an important and probably unintended consequence of the adoption was that an informal truce between the Assiniboine and Sitting Bull's Lakota band came into effect.

In the spring of 1859, Sitting Bull's Hunkpapa band was following the buffalo in the headwaters of the Cannonball River in what is now southwestern North Dakota. They were in the process of moving their camp toward a piece of high ground that the Lakota called the Rainy Butte when they were suddenly attacked by an especially large raiding party of about fifty Crow warriors who were bent on stealing some of their horses.

Successfully achieving the element of surprise, the Crow slashed through the Hunkpapa, scattering both the people and their livestock. Amid the chaos and confusion, the Hunkpapa warriors quickly organized to counterattack. The Crow may have achieved a surprise attack, but tactically, they made a mistake. It is far easier to steal horses from a sleeping camp than to attack in broad daylight when the enemy warriors are awake and on horseback.

The melee brought one of the Crow warriors face to face with Jumping Bull, Sitting Bull's sixty-year-old father. They confronted one another on foot. Some versions of the story say that the Crow dismounted to fight the old man, while others say that he dismounted when his horse went lame.

In any case, Jumping Bull shouted that he was going to take on the Crow himself and raised his bow. The enemy raised his single-shot gun, blasted the bow out of Jumping Bull's hands, and rushed the old man with his knife. Sitting Bull's father reached for his own knife, but the sheath had slipped around behind his back and he was unable to reach it before the Crow was upon him. The Crow hacked at the old man with his knife, inflicting a series of wounds to his neck and abdomen. In a grisly coup de grace, he drove his knife into the top of Jumping Bull's head with such force that the blade broke.

By this time, other Hunkpapa were running toward the fight so the Crow jumped on his horse to escape. Alerted to the situation, Sitting Bull arrived as his father's assailant dashed away and he gave chase. He caught the Crow, lanced him off his mount, and dismounted himself. In a rage, he worked the Crow over with his knife, leaving his father's assailant in a mass of bloody bits.

Meanwhile, the Hunkpapa counterattack was in full swing. They reportedly chased the Crow for thirty miles, killing many of them. As they retreated, the Crow left behind three of their women and a baby, who were rounded up by the Hunkpapa. There were many who favored killing the Crow captives in retribution for the loss of Jumping Bull. However, it was Sitting Bull who intervened, asking that their lives be spared. He felt, philosophically, that it had been Jumping Bull's time to die, and that disposing of his killer was enough. The women and child remained with the Hunkpapa through the summer and were allowed to return to the Crow as the leaves began to turn in the fall.

Two moments in the fight near Rainy Butte figure in Sitting Bull's Hieroglyphic Autobiography. Once pictograph shows Sitting Bull lancing and killing the Crow warrior who killed his father. The other image, according to what White Bull told Stanley Vestal, commemorates the capture of three Crow women. It pictures Sitting Bull wearing a war bonnet with horns and a long trail of eagle feathers, while carrying a lance made for him by his parents.

Jumping Bull was buried south of Cedar Creek, near the current border between the two Dakotas, and Sitting Bull assumed the leadership of his family group. He renamed his adopted brother, Stays Back, as Jumping Bull. According to the way it was described in the oral tradition, Sitting Bull's father no longer needed the name.

A contemporary sketch of the Smith, Jackson, and Sublette wagon train departing along the Oregon Trail in May 1830. (*National Archives*)

2

WASICHU ENCROACHING

DURING THE YEARS WHILE SITTING BULL WAS GROWING up, most of the Hunkpapa Lakota living in what are now North and South Dakota had very limited contact with the wasichu. In the eighteenth century, a few French, British, and American traders had been in the country, but mainly on the Missouri River south of present-day Bismarck. A small number of trappers, primarily French-Canadian, had worked the tributaries of the Missouri in the Dakotas, but they had tended to blend in. Many of them lived among the Indians and even had Indian wives, and by the time Sitting Bull was born, a fair number of the trappers with French surnames who were working in the area had Indian mothers.

At the beginning of the nineteenth century, for most wasichu, the interior of the American West remained as a mysterious and forbidding *terra incognita*, a vast void on the maps. Gradually that would change. The expedition of Meriwether Lewis and William Clark passed through on the Missouri in 1804–1806, but they kept to the river. Aside from one potentially deadly disagreement with Black Buffalo's band near present-day

Pierre, South Dakota, in September 1804, they had virtually no contact with the Lakota. They did, however, spend the winter of 1804–1805 camped across the river from the huge Arikara-Hidatsa-Mandan city at the mouth of the Knife River north of present-day Bismarck.

Other wasichu followed Lewis and Clark into the upper Missouri, but they continued to be mainly trappers and traders. The settlements they established were mostly trading posts, and they were mostly on the Missouri because river boats were the principal means of transportation for the trade goods going north, and for beaver pelts and buffalo hides gong south. John Jacob Astor's American Fur Company operated a post at Fort Pierre—near the present site of Pierre, South Dakota—as well as Fort Union (originally Fort Henry), which was built in 1828 farther upriver near the confluence of the Missouri and the Yellowstone. In between, Fort Berthold was situated near the mouth of the Knife, not far from where Lewis and Clark had wintered. Here, the wasichu could conduct commercial activity with the Mandan, Hidatsa, and Arikara.

It was probably at one of these posts—possibly Fort Pierre—that Sitting Bull had his earliest ongoing contact with the wasichu. However, beyond the broad valley of the Missouri River, the Hunkpapa saw little or nothing of the wasichu during the years that he was becoming a man. Most of their fights were still with the Crow.

While the upper Missouri country remained remote for the wasichu, farther south it was a different story. During the second quarter of the nineteenth century, the number of wasichu on the central and southern Plains mushroomed. They weren't coming to stay, they were just passing through, but their numbers were growing. A few decades after Lewis and Clark became the first wasichu to travel all the way from the Mississippi to the Pacific, the flow of wasichu across this expanse became nearly continuous—except, of course, in the winter.

In 1821, William Becknell, a trader from Kansas City, took a mule train load of manufactured goods overland to Santa Fe, the northern outpost of recently independent Mexico. Within a year, wagons were following what would come to be known as the Santa Fe Trail. Gradually, settlements grew up at strategic points along the Santa Fe Trail. Perhaps the most famous was Bent's Fort or Fort William, established in 1833 by Ceran St. Vrain, along with William and Charles Bent. It was located on the upper Arkansas River near what is now La Junta, Colorado. This fort, like those on the upper Missouri, was part of a growing number of such privately financed fortified trading posts that would appear in the West, especially across the central and southern areas west of the Mississippi.

Soon the traffic on the Santa Fe Trail would be dwarfed by that on the routes leading to the valleys of California and Oregon, rich with agricultural potential. William Sublette, who had experience with the Santa Fe Trail, imagined an offshoot of that road that would travel all the way from Independence, Missouri, to Oregon by way of South Pass in Wyoming. As early as 1827, he had surveyed the route, and by 1830, the first wagons were making use of what would be known as the Oregon Trail. While the Santa Fe Trail was primarily a trade route, the Oregon Trail was an emigrant trail. Those who traveled it were settlers bound for the lush Willamette Valley south of what is now Portland, Oregon.

The Oregon Trail also carried the California traffic through South Pass, at which point, a separate California Trail branched off to cross the arid wasteland which is now Nevada, and the almost impenetrable Sierra Nevada. Crossing the Sierra, California immigrants then found themselves in the immense and fertile Central Valley of California. Beginning in 1848, a new incentive brought wasichu to California. The discovery of gold in the Sierra foothills initiated the California Gold Rush of 1849 that was one of the largest voluntary mass migrations yet seen in human history. Beginning in the 1850s, the California Trail would be used by an almost continuous two-way flow of people, as many of the prospectors returned eastward on the California Trail after they achieved whatever fortune—or misfortune—the gold fields provided them.

The travelers on the overland trails during the mid-nineteenth century were just passing through the Plains, and not planning to settle. Nevertheless, their continuous flow, and the forts and settlements that popped up along the trails, had an impact on the life of the indigenous peoples in the West in a way that the earlier traders and trappers never had.

All of this, however, was taking place south of the Platte River, and well south of the vast Hunkpapa Lakota hunting grounds between the Missouri and the mountains of central Montana. Other Lakota people, such as the Brulé, Minneconjou, and Oglala, had more contact with the wasichu than the Hunkpapa, and other tribes living farther south had more contact with the wasichu than any of the Lakota.

By the 1850s, there had been serious conflicts between indigenous people and wasichu along the routes of the trails across the southern and central Plains, but the Lakota supremacy on the northern Plains remained essentially unchallenged. Indeed, that supremacy was guaranteed by wasichu law though the Treaty of Fort Laramie. In September 1851, Lakota itancans, along with representatives of the Arapaho, Arikara, Assiniboine, Cheyenne, Crow, Hidatsa, Mandan, and Shoshone people met with the wasichu at Fort Laramie on the North Platte River in what is now Wyoming to sign this treaty. Most of the Sioux who signed the treaty and its amendments were Brulé or Oglala. None were Hunkpapa. The wasichu naively believed that the Sioux who had signed the treaty did so on behalf of all Sioux. The Hunkpapa, who were not a party to the Fort Laramie conference, would obviously differ with this audacious assumption.

Essentially, the United States treaty commissioners, led by Superintendent of Indian Affairs David Mitchell, promised control of the Great Plains to the Indians in exchange for guarantees of safe passage for settlers on the Oregon Trail and its tributary trails. In compensation, the Indians were promised a grant in supplies and trade goods, valued at about $1.2 million annually in today's dollars, through 1901. A similar treaty signed at Fort Atkinson, Kansas, in 1853, added the Comanche and Kiowa as signatories to the same basic agreement.

These early treaties with the Plains Indians merely formalized the status quo on the Plains south of the Platte. The Indians were clearly dominant, but the wasichu were not going away. As long as the wasichu kept moving through, and did not stay—except at a few designated forts—they were generally not perceived by the Indians as a serious threat to their way of life. The indigenous peoples of the Plains accommodated the wasichu for their value as a source of guns and other supplies, either by way of trade or the generous grants being made through the Indian Bureau.

Though the grants to the Indians were seen as charitable generosity by both the U.S. government and the Indians themselves, the practice set in motion a pattern of misguided wasichu paternalism that would ultimately prove to be as detrimental to the indigenous cultures of North America as bullets. It is now understood that the more that the Indians came to depend on the largesse of the government, the more blurred was their connection with their own heritage. Indians whose parents may have seen no more than a dozen wasichu in a lifetime would soon be camping for at least part of the year within sight of wasichu forts in order to avail themselves of free food and other supplies guaranteed by the treaties.

Two cultures so alien could not long coexist. Soon, they would collide. The first serious crack in the detente of coexistence in the Platte River country of the Northern Plains came in August 1854 with the first major battle between the U.S. Army and the Lakota. As with many battles that took place in the West during the nineteenth century, the Grattan Fight— or Grattan Massacre, as the wasichu often called it—was touched off by a miscommunication that got out of hand. In the history of the Indian Wars, this event was just one of a countless number of miscommunications that unintentionally provoked bloodshed.

It happened just east of Fort Laramie at a time when the Brulé Lakota were camped there waiting for their government annuities. High Forehead, a Minneconjou man camping with the Brulé, shot a lame cow belonging to a group of immigrants passing through on the Oregon Trail. A complaint was filed with Lieutenant Hugh Fleming, the post commander at Fort Laramie. He was inclined to let the matter slide in order to maintain peaceful relations with the Indians. However, a capricious young recent West Point graduate, Lieutenant John Grattan, insisted that he lead a detachment to arrest the man who had shot the cow. Fleming agreed, apparently with reluctance.

On August 18, Grattan took thirty men from Company G of the 6th Infantry Regiment to the camp of Brulé itancan Conquering Bear at nearby Ash Hollow. Grattan proceeded to parley with Conquering Bear through an interpreter who is variously described as drunk, malicious, or both. The Brulé offered to exchange horses for the sick cow—a deal that Grattan should have accepted—but Conquering Bear would not surrender High Forehead. The discussion turned to an argument and a shot was fired, possibly by accident. Conquering Bear was shot down even as he tried to stop the ensuing firefight. Greatly outnumbered, Grattan attempted to retreat to Fort Laramie, but his command was surrounded and decimated. One survivor made it to safety, but he soon died of his wounds.

The U.S. Army officially ruled that Grattan had exceeded his authority, failing to defuse a potentially volatile situation. However, the seeds of distrust had been sewn. Rather than letting the incident go, the U.S. Secretary of War—and future Confederate President—Jefferson Davis decided that the U.S. Army should make a show of force along the Oregon Trail the following summer. In August 1855, Seminole War veteran Colonel William Selby Harney led 600 troops out of Fort Leavenworth, Kansas, headed for Fort Laramie. His command included five companies of the 6th Infantry Regiment, two companies of the 2nd Dragoons, and a company each of the 4th Artillery and 10th Infantry Regiment.

This was bound to irritate the Lakota and other people who were camping in the vicinity of Fort Laramie. Indian Agent Thomas Twiss cautioned the Indians to give wide berth to Harney's task force. Most heeded the warning and decamped, but a group of Brulé led by Little Thunder, the successor to the late Conquering Bear, did not. They remained camped at Bluewater Creek, not far from Ash Hollow, where they crossed paths with the troop on September 3. To impress the Brulé with his power and authority, Harney—whom the Lakota called White Beard—told Little Thunder to surrender those involved in the Grattan Massacre.

Naturally, he refused, and as might have been expected, the wasichu officer attacked immediately. The Bluewater Creek fight, often misnamed as the Battle of Ash Hollow, was a resounding defeat for the Brulé. Though Little Thunder himself escaped, most of his people were killed or captured. There were eighty-six Brulé warriors killed in action, along with a number of women and children. In addition, about seventy Brulé women and children were taken captive. Harney lost just seven troopers.

White Beard—who was now also known under the more descriptive Lakota name Mad Bear—would continue his show of force through the winter. It seemed to him as though he had taught the Indians a lesson, for his troopers were unchallenged. In fact, the Lakota merely avoided him. The West was still a vast place largely untraveled by the wasichu, and there were plenty of places where the Lakota could ride and be unmolested by Harney and his blue-jacketed soldiers.

Sitting Bull probably had his first look at a conference between his people and the U.S. Army during the first week of March 1856. General Harney led his task force north to Fort Pierre, where he demanded to meet with Hunkpapa leaders. Among other things, he instructed them that, in light of the events surrounding the Grattan incident, the Lakota would be required to turn tribal members accused of crimes against the wasichu over to the U.S. Army.

In the course of the Fort Pierre conference, Harney couldn't figure out who was the senior chief of the Lakota—because in Hunkpapa society there was no person whose role in the tribe corresponded to the wasichu concept of a "head chief." Undaunted, Harney simply picked someone, a man named Bear Ribs (aka Bear's Rib or Bear's Side), and negotiated with him as though he was the Lakota head chief. He even gave him a certificate confirming that the U.S. government recognized him as the Hunkpapa head chief. Sitting Bull probably witnessed at least part of the surreal transaction, and we can imagine that he found it almost incomprehensibly absurd.

Sitting Bull's uncle, Four Horns, was one of several men officially named by Harney as a Hunkpapa "subchief." In the government's eyes, he became a sort of senior vice president of the imagined Hunkpapa kingdom. Sitting Bull's brother-in-law, Makes Room, was also named as a subchief. He was Minneconjou, but he was married to Good Feather, who was Hunkpapa.

This lack of understanding of the Lakota demonstrated by Mad Bear Harney was emblematic of the way many wasichu leaders would approach relations with the Lakota over the remainder of the nineteenth century. Far from farcical, this fictional command structure dictated how the U.S. government would deal with the tribes in the West, and with whom they would negotiate, often with serious negative results.

For Bear Ribs, the fiction turned deadly. Obviously, there was resentment within the Lakota community that outsiders had come in and picked certain people to serve as "head chiefs." In June 1862, six years after Mad Bear's visit, Bear Ribs was challenged by some assertive young Sans Arc Lakota men at Fort Pierre. Naturally, Bear Ribs stood his ground when a Sans Arc named Mouse confronted him. Mouse proceeded to shoot Bear Ribs, fatally wounding him. Before he succumbed, the Hunkpapa "head chief" returned fire, killing Mouse.

This duel clearly illustrated the growing rift within Lakota society between those who were willing to accept the wasichu influence as the price to be paid for the benefits of their largesse, and those who felt it a matter of pride to have nothing whatsoever to do with the wasichu. Sitting Bull would be counted among the latter.

UNTIL the early 1860s, relations between the Lakota and wasichu were a minor issue for both because there was still relatively little interaction between the two. The number of wasichu north of the Platte River and west of the Missouri River remained small, so avoiding them outside a short radius from the forts was still fairly easy. For the wasichu themselves, the Lakota were not very high on the radar. Indeed, the early 1860s marked the biggest intertribal conflict in the history of the wasichu in North America—the Civil War. For most Americans east of the Mississippi—and for the U.S. Army—the Civil War was the all-encompassing reality of the era. For the U.S. Army, the difficult task of wrestling with the Confederate Army obviously was a much higher priority than scrapping with the Lakota on the northern Plains.

Given the fact that the Lakota were so geographically remote from wasichu centers of population, the probability of a major war between the Lakota and the wasichu seemed equally remote. Meanwhile, the probability that the eastern Sioux people, the Santee, would be involved in a major conflict was also considered unlikely. Aside from minor skirmishes, Santee had lived in relative peace near the wasichu for many years.

Against this backdrop, it came as a profound shock to the wasichu when they found themselves suddenly at war with the Santee in Minnesota, a place where the conflicts with the area's indigenous people were widely believed to be a thing of the past. The Santee lived at agencies and were thought to have been, as the wasichu put it, "pacified." Mainly, this was true, but it is axiomatic that a single violent incident can often unravel the fabric of what seems on the surface to be a peaceful status quo.

On August 17, 1862, some young Santee men murdered five settlers near Acton, Minnesota, and the following day the violence escalated with the beginning of a series of attacks against wasichu throughout Renville County and beyond. Attempts to defuse the situation only led to more killing, including attacks on soldiers. On August 19, the Santee struck the town of New Ulm, and over the next several days, Fort Ridgely—where many wasichu civilians sought refuge—was assaulted several times. After a second attack against New Ulm, Minnesota's state government appointed former governor Henry Hastings Sibley—not to be confused with Henry Hopkins Sibley, the Confederate officer—to lead a state militia counterattack. Sibley assembled a force of about 1,500 that defeated the Santee in a series of skirmishes that culminated in the Battle of Wood Lake on September 23.

There is a corollary to chaos theory called "the butterfly effect." It concerns nonlinear dynamics and postulates that the flap of a butterfly's wings in Brazil can set off a tornado in Texas. In 1862, it took a local uprising by the Santee in Minnesota to set in motion a major series of wars between the wasichu and Lakota in Dakota Territory and Montana that would consume a generation.

With the U.S. Army otherwise occupied by the Civil War, it should have seemed an unlikely moment to begin a new military offensive on the Plains. The summer and fall of 1862 had been a bad time for the U.S. Army. Stonewall Jackson's Confederate armies were storming through the Shenandoah Valley even as Robert E. Lee, newly appointed to command the Confederate Army of Northern Virginia, was blunting the Union drive on Richmond. Union General George McClellan was withdrawing after a failed Peninsular Campaign. It was not time for the U.S. Army to consider opening a new front against a new enemy, but the use of state militias would make it possible.

To demonstrate its commitment to this new front, the U.S. Army had created a new military Department of the Northwest, headed by General John Pope—who had recently been relieved of his command of the Army of Virginia. While Sibley was defeating the Santee in Minnesota, Pope's army was losing miserably to Stonewall Jackson and James Longstreet in the Second Battle of Bull Run. It was time for him to be reassigned.

Within the department would be two military districts. The District of Minnesota contingent was commanded by Henry Sibley, now a brigadier general, who had not disbanded his brigade after the 1862 campaign. Indeed, by the summer of 1863, he had doubled the size of his Minnesota Brigade to more than 3,300 men. Meanwhile, a District of Iowa brigade under Brigadier General Alfred Sully would consist of regiments drawn from both Iowa and Nebraska. The battle plan called for Sibley's force to move into Dakota Territory from the east, Sully's from the south.

Though some of the largest engagements yet to be fought west of the Mississippi would occur in Dakota Territory during the summer of 1863, they received little media attention given that they were completely overshadowed by the heavily documented and very costly Union victories at Vicksburg and Gettysburg.

Sibley's brigade marched west, establishing a base near Devil's Lake in northeastern Dakota Territory, while Sully's men marched north into Dakota Territory along the Missouri River. Sibley made contact with the Santee in the area and arranged for a conference with Santee itancans Standing Buffalo and Sweet Corn on July 24 at Big Mound, south of Devil's Lake.

Thunderstorms threatened during the day while an aura of tension and suspicion hung over the meeting, so when a nervous Santee shot and killed a militiaman he thought was threatening him, violence erupted. Given that there were 2,000 troopers and 1,500 Santee at Big Mound that day, the casualty figures were small. The Santee, who were outgunned by the troops with their artillery, lost forty, but Sibley lost just four. These included the man shot in the beginning, two killed in the battle and a fourth who was killed by, of all things, a lightning strike!

After Big Mound, the Santee scattered, some of them making contact with a large Lakota hunting camp near Dead Buffalo Lake in present-day

Kidder County, North Dakota—about one hundred miles southwest of Devil's Lake. On July 26, as Sibley approached this encampment, the Lakota and Santee drew him into a brief but hard-fought battle by out-flanking his advance guard. Two days later, the Sioux attacked Sibley's camp near Stony Lake. As had been the case at Big Mound, these two battles were brief and casualties light.

It is possible, though not certain, that Sitting Bull was present at Big Buffalo Lake, Stony Lake, or both. In Sitting Bull's Hieroglyphic Autobiography, a picture of an incident that is dated to the summer of 1863 shows Sitting Bull counting coup on a U.S. Army muleskinner and stealing a mule while under fire. Stanley Vestal interpreted it as an attack on Sibley's wagon train on Apple Creek, about a month before the Big Buffalo Lake fight. The subsequent pictograph, also dated to 1863, shows Sitting Bull killing a wasichu in a buckskin jacket. Vestal pinpoints the site as being near Devil's Lake.

These are the first images in the pictograph of Sitting Bull—now in his early thirties—fighting the wasichu. All of the previous scenes, which are calculated as covering the years from 1846 to 1862, show him fighting or counting coup against people from other tribes, mainly the Crow. It may be that his first face-to-face fights with the wasichu occurred in 1863 during the Sibley incursion into Dakota Territory.

The final major engagement in the 1863 Dakota Campaign involved Sully rather than Sibley, and took place about one hundred miles southeast of Dead Buffalo Lake and one hundred miles east of the Missouri River. On September 3, a cavalry patrol under Major A. E. House came across a large Sioux encampment at Whitestone Hill. Recognizing that they had a four-to-one numeric advantage over House, the Sioux prepared to attack. Fortunately for House, Sully arrived with his main force just as the battle was joined. The battle lasted until the Sioux made a tactical withdrawal at dusk.

While Sibley's earlier battles were marked by light casualties, the Battle of Whitestone Hill was just the opposite. Sully had twenty troopers killed in action, and thirty-eight wounded, but the Sioux may have lost between one hundred and three hundred. The Sioux also abandoned three hundred tipis, as well as food and other supplies, which the troopers burned. It is considered unlikely that Sitting Bull was present at Whitestone Hill, although he certainly was aware of the battle.

WHETHER or not Sitting Bull took part in any of the major fights in 1863, he was definitely a participant in the biggest battle on the northern Plains during the summer of 1864. The Sioux losses at Whitestone Hill, especially in terms of irreplaceable supplies, had encouraged the U.S. Army to schedule a similar campaign for the summer of 1864. In preparation for this, General Alfred Sully established a base of operations—called Fort Sully—on the Missouri River a short distance north of Fort Pierre. In 1863, the U.S. Army had patrolled the area east of the Missouri; in 1864, Sully would go west, into the land of the Lakota—riding against people, mainly Hunkpapa, who had nothing to do with the Minnesota uprising of 1862.

It was late summer when General Sully reached the area north of present-day Bismarck with 2,200 men organized into two brigades. He would have come sooner, but there was not enough runoff in the Missouri River until July to float the steamboats laden with his supplies and heavy equipment.

The wasichu soldiers made contact with the Sioux on July 28 in the season of the annual Sun Dance ceremony at a place in northwestern Dakota Territory, in what is now Dunne County, that was known to the Lakota as Tahkahokuty, or the Hunting Ground Where They Killed the Deer. The name has long since been shortened to Killdeer Mountain. The number of Santee, Lakota, and Yanktonai in this enormous encampment is estimated to have been as many as 8,000, but probably there were only about 5,500. At least a third of the number would have been warriors.

Even with the lesser estimate, the size of the camp was on par with the one that George Armstrong Custer would run across on the Little Bighorn a dozen years later. One thing that both of these camps had in common was that Sitting Bull was definitely present.

As with the later engagement, the Sioux knew that the wasichu were coming. It was hard not to detect a force as large as Sully's, especially with supply wagons and towed artillery pieces kicking up a lot of dust, and a hunting party had provided at least twenty-four hours' warning. Sitting Bull and the other Lakota warriors—including his uncle Four Horns and his teenage nephew, White Bull—were prepared when the troops arrived. White Bull's recollections to Stanley Vestal in the early twentieth century are a key source for the Lakota perspective on the battle.

According to White Bull, it all began when a man named Long Dog charged the troops alone. He believed that he was "with a ghost," and therefore impervious to wasichu bullets. He raced out to meet the advancing cavalry, turned, and rode parallel to their forward line at top speed. Whether it was his "charm" or poor U.S. Army marksmanship, Long Dog was not hit as the troops opened fire. When he repeated his foolhardy display, tempting fate a second time, he again returned unscathed. This greatly buoyed the spirits of the Sioux and they opened fire.

Another warrior recalled by White Bull was Man Who Never Walked, who was literally a man who had been born with deformed and useless legs. He insisted that he be allowed to participate in the fight and that he be placed in a travois behind a horse so that he could ride against the troops. Those around him were reluctant to facilitate sure suicide, but Sitting Bull ordered them to assist him. The horse pulling him was shot down, and Man Who Never Walked faced the U.S. Army, sitting in a basket and singing his death song. When his bullet-riddled body was discovered by the wasichu, they were no doubt astonished to see the extent of the man's disability.

Initially, the mounted Sioux warriors held the upper hand against the cavalry at Killdeer Mountain, but they had no defense against Sully's artillery. Despite this, the Sioux were able to withdraw their women and children from the camp, while under fire, suffering minimal casualties. The Sioux lost at least thirty-one warriors, most of them when Sully's cavalry overwhelmed a cluster of Santee snipers hiding in a ravine. U.S. Army estimates of Sioux killed in action ran as high as 150, with the loss of fewer than ten troopers. Four Horns was among those seriously wounded, but he lived to fight another day.

Sully succeeded, however, in his principal objective, that being to capture and destroy food and other supplies. As at Whitestone Hill the year before, this would impose a long-lasting hardship on the Sioux with winter approaching. The general hoped to follow his success at Killdeer Mountain by pursuing the Indians toward the Yellowstone River through the Badlands of what is now western North Dakota. For the most part, the Lakota managed to elude his slow-moving task force, but his superior firepower and active patrols also hampered an attempt by the Lakota to launch a successful counterattack during the second week of August. In the Badlands, both sides—and their livestock—were suffering from lack of water and exhaustion and the Badlands campaign fizzled as they withdrew in opposite directions.

During the campaigns of the summer of 1864, Sitting Bull had an opportunity to size up the wasichu soldiers—known variously as bluecoats (because of their uniforms) or long knives (because of their swords)—as adversaries in battle. According to White Bull in an interview with Stanley Vestal, his uncle had strong opinions of U.S. Army tactics.

"The white soldiers do not know how to fight," said Sitting Bull after one of his early battles with the troopers. "They are not lively enough. They stand still and run straight; it is easy to shoot them. They do not try to save themselves. Also, they seem to have no hearts. When an Indian gets killed, the other Indians feel sorry and cry, and sometimes stop fighting. But when a white soldier gets killed, nobody cries, nobody cares; they go right on shooting and let him lie there. Sometimes they even go off and leave their wounded behind them."

Conversely, many U.S. Army officers were in awe of the Lakota as fighters. For his book, *Soldiers of the Plains*, published in 1926, P. E. Byrne interviewed a number of soldiers who had fought the Lakota. One of General George Crook's staff officers called them "the finest light cavalry in the world." General Charles King said they were "a foe far more to be dreaded than any European cavalry." General Anson Mills, a captain when he fought Sitting Bull and Crazy Horse with Crook in 1876 said they "were then the best cavalry in the world; their like will never be seen again." The Badlands fighting is the subject of another image in Sitting Bull's Hieroglyphic Autobiography, which shows him relieving the U.S. Army of two horses, a chestnut and a buckskin. The preceding image, dated to the winter of 1863–1864, pictures Sitting Bull taking nine horses from the Crow. According to White Bull, he gave a horse from each incident to his sister, Good Feather.

A few weeks later, Sitting Bull recorded the next event in his Hieroglyphic Autobiography, a further encounter with the wasichu which came close to being his last. Toward the end of August 1864, Sitting Bull's Hunkpapa band was hunting in the headwaters of the Grand River when they observed a civilian wagon train under the leadership of Captain James Fisk that was escorted by a small number of U.S. Army troops.

On September 2, near White Butte, on the Little Missouri River, when the train came to a halt because of an overturned wagon, Sitting Bull personally led an attack. In the melee, White Buffalo Chief attacked a soldier, knocking him off his horse and proceeding to attempt to subdue him. However, the man got the best of this Hunkpapa attacker. When Fool Buffalo intervened to assist his colleague, the wasichu soldier responded by ripping the gun from the hands of the second Hunkpapa and breaking his collar bone. With two Hunkpapa unable to overcome the man, Sitting Bull rode up to intervene, but the unnamed soldier pulled his pistol and fired. The bullet entered Sitting Bull's hip, exiting from the small of his back. Obviously, a variance in the trajectory by even an inch could have hit a vital organ and caused fatal internal injuries.

Aided by White Bull, and riding his big sorrel horse, Sitting Bull retreated to the safety of the Hunkpapa camp. His adopted Assiniboine brother Jumping Bull intervened to apply first aid and stop the bleeding, and probably saved his life.

Meanwhile, the wasichu circled their wagons, forming a hastily constructed defensive position which they named Fort Dilts, after Jefferson Dilts, one of their number who was killed by the Hunkpapa. They successfully kept the Hunkpapa at bay until troopers from one of Sully's brigades arrived to relieve the siege.

During his convalescence, Sitting Bull is said to have played a role in the release of a wasichu woman who had been a Lakota prisoner since July 12. Mrs. Fanny Kelly had been captured from a wagon train by the Oglala Lakota and she was later traded to Brings Plenty, who was part of Sitting Bull's Hunkpapa band. Brings Plenty had renamed her Real Woman and had made her his wife. She was apparently quite popular, as he resisted numerous offers from other men who wanted to buy her as a wife. He also resisted when he got word that her wasichu husband was offering to buy her back. The people in the besieged Fisk wagon train had even made an offer to trade supplies for her, but these negotiations fell apart.

Observing that she was homesick, Sitting Bull eventually intervened, using his moral authority as an itancan of the Strong Hearts. He removed Real Woman from Brings Plenty's tipi and arranged for her to be returned to her people by a Sihasapa Lakota delegation on December 9, 1864. Mrs. Kelly later wrote that while she was in Sitting Bull's tipi, just prior to her release, she was treated as a guest, not a prisoner. Sitting Bull's generosity also made an impression on the Hunkpapa, for in the tribal winter count, that winter came to be known as the Winter When the White Woman Was Rescued.

THE end of the Civil War in April 1865 brought many changes. Not the least of these was that the wasichu were starting to travel across the Plains in much larger numbers than before the war. The U.S. government, meanwhile, was of two minds about its policy toward the indigenous people who lived on the Plains. Official government policy would be a confusing contradiction that was the result of the inevitable conflict between the benevolent paternalism of the Interior Department's Indian Bureau and the hard-line approach of the War Department.

The Indian Bureau's gentle—albeit naive—approach was to simply pay the Indians off. The U.S. Army, meanwhile, saw its duty to use a firm hand to control the situation. Unfortunately, official policy would vacillate erratically between the two poles for the next generation. The U.S. Army planned for a continued military presence in the northern Dakota Territory, moving Alfred Sully and his base of operations from Fort Sully to Fort Rice, located where the Cannonball River flows into the Missouri. As Stanley Vestal wrote, paraphrasing the commonly held opinion of most neutral observers of the day, "So long as the Bureau kept on making friendlies out of hostiles, and the Army persisted in making hostiles out of friendlies, neither department could possibly lack employment." As Sitting Bull himself succinctly summarized it, "The white men have too many chiefs."

Two minds also prevailed on the Indian side of the equation, where those "Agency Indians" who were willing to sacrifice a certain degree of autonomy for annuities contrasted with those who were willing to take nothing and sacrifice nothing. Sitting Bull was one of many Lakota who saw the Indian Bureau's largesse as degrading and who simply refused the handouts. They saw the government that offered the handouts as the same government whose Army had offered the carnage they had experienced at Killdeer Mountain. Sitting Bull figured that the Lakota had lived without the U.S. government for centuries, and they could continue to do so. Furthermore, they possessed both the means and the will to resist the government.

Nor was Sitting Bull shy about staking his prestige on an exaggerated demonstration of what the Lakota might expect at the hands of the wasichu should they consider the Indian Bureau's offer of beneficence. Visiting an encampment of "Agency Indians" at Fort Berthold, he told them that the United States was sucking them into dependence in order to annihilate them. To underscore his assertion, he dramatically cut himself with a knife, explaining that this fate awaited them at Sully's hands if they succumbed to the sweet Pied Piper song of the Indian Bureau.

Even as the wasichu were thinking positively that peace was at hand, and that the Lakota could be pacified, Sitting Bull was arranging his counterstrike.Backing up his words with action, he assembled a war party of several hundred warriors to attack Fort Rice, which the more militant Lakota saw as a provocation by its very presence so far north on the Missouri. They struck on July 28, 1865, with Sitting Bull himself in the vanguard. However, the troops not only managed to beat off the attack, but they managed to keep the Lakota out of rifle range with their artillery. This battle was not Sitting Bull's finest hour. When he took no part in the battle after the opening charge, his reputation dimmed within Hunkpapa circles. Ironically, it was in the aftermath of the Fort Rice debacle that Sitting Bull's name first appeared in a wasichu document, listed by Sully himself as one of the Lakota leaders who had resisted surrendering to the magnanimous largesse of the Indian Bureau.

In an August 8 memo to the Assistant Adjutant General for the Department of the Northwest, Sully referenced Sitting Bull's earlier appearance at Fort Berthold, writing: "At one time the feeling was very strong to come in and surrender. . . . [However] a chief called Sitting Bull, hearing this on his return to camp, went through the different villages cutting himself with a knife and crying out that he was just from Fort Rice; that all those that had come in and given themselves up I had killed, and calling on the nation to avenge the murder."

SITTING BULL'S assault on Fort Rice might have dramatically presaged a new chapter in the war between the Lakota and the U.S. Army, but the center of gravity was shifting away from the Dakota Prairies and the Department of the Northwest to the Department of the Platte and a thoroughfare called the Bozeman Trail. The U.S. Army's chief Lakota antagonist in this next chapter would not be Sitting Bull's Hunkpapa, but the Oglala Lakota and the charismatic Oglala itancan named Red Cloud (Makhpyia-luta). A decade older than Sitting Bull, Red Cloud was probably the most important Lakota war chief of the 1860s. The concessions that he was able to win from the U.S. government were unprecedented in the history of the Indian Wars. Sitting Bull would have a role in the conflict involving the controversial Bozeman Trail, but it would be a minor one.

The focal point of what is remembered as the Red Cloud War was the Bozeman Trail, a spur road that split off from the Platte Road, that section of the old Oregon Trail that followed the Platte River. It departed from the Platte just north of Fort Laramie and traveled northwest into Montana Territory through the Powder River drainage, intersecting the Yellowstone River east of the Montana Territory town of Bozeman.

This area of southwestern Montana and northwestern Wyoming is punctuated by a series of rivers flowing generally south to north into the Yellowstone, which flows generally west to east across Montana. From west to east, these rivers are the Bighorn River, the latter's Little Bighorn tributary, Rosebud Creek, the Tongue River, and the Powder River. Though the Powder is one of several rivers, the entire area, about the size of the state of Indiana, is often referred to as the Powder River Country. Parallel to the Powder River on the east is the Little Missouri, which flows into the Missouri just downstream from its confluence with the Yellowstone.

Before the Civil War, the Indians had acquiesced—under terms of the 1851 Fort Laramie Treaty—to wasichu emigrants traveling *across* the

Plains. Now, increasing numbers of wasichu were settling in the lands between the Mississippi and the Pacific, drawn by both tales of gold discoveries and the terms of the Homestead Act that Abraham Lincoln had signed in 1862, which gave parcels of those trackless lands to any farmer who could make a go of it.

The Bozeman Trail was a major departure—both literally and figuratively—from the prewar status quo on the Plains. If the wasichu saw it as progress, the Lakota and Northern Cheyenne saw it as a serious exercise in trespassing in the Powder River Country—and the adjacent Black Hills in Dakota Territory—which was, according to the treaties, Indian land and off-limits to the wasichu.

Red Cloud (*Library of Congress*)

Despite the treaties, the U.S. Army decided on a show of force in the Powder River Country. In August 1865, even as Sitting Bull was licking his wounds in the aftermath of his Fort Rice misfortune, Brigadier General Patrick Conner headed out from Fort Laramie as part of a major operation designed to show the flag in the Powder. Operating farther east, two other cavalry columns were led by Colonel Samuel Walker from Fort Laramie and by Colonel Nelson Cole from Omaha.

After a few small skirmishes, Conner attacked an Indian encampment on the Tongue River in the early morning of August 29. A glamorous cavalry charge quickly devolved into vicious hand-to-hand combat, from which many of the Indians managed to escape. A week later, a large combined force of Lakota and Cheyenne launched a major direct attack on the troops, and a heavy, early winter snow on the night of September 8–9 killed several hundred horses. Though Conner managed to destroy a large stockpile of Indian supplies on the Tongue River, the campaign was essentially a draw.

Sitting Bull's small part in the Powder River Campaign came as Walker and Cole patrolled north of the Black Hills, before cutting back into the Powder River County during the first week of September. In the course of their campaign, they were involved in fights with both the Oglala and Hunkpapa, as well as Little Wolf's Cheyenne band.

White Bull, who was riding with his uncle on this campaign, recalled that Sitting Bull hung back and did not play a very big role in the battles. In fact, his presence there would hardly be worth mentioning had Sitting Bull himself not included four scenes from the campaign in his Hieroglyphic Autobiography. Each of the four pictures shows him taking horses or mules from the troops, and not engaging in the main fighting. The two images in the Autobiography from 1866 also show Sitting Bull taking horses, one from the wasichu, and three from the Crow. Ironically, one of the Hunkpapa itancan who did have an important part in the September 1865 battles was Bull Head, Sitting Bull's long-time rival.

The 1865 campaign demonstrated that showing the flag was a costly and ineffective way to assert wasichu authority in the Powder River Country. With this in mind, the U.S. government decided on a strategy of fixed fortifications to protect the Bozeman Trail. Just as the U.S. Army would use the fixed fire-base concept a century later in Vietnam, in 1866 they began to build a series of forts about seventy to ninety miles apart to guard the Bozeman Trail. Beginning at Fort Laramie, these included Fort Reno, Fort Phil Kearny, and Fort C. F. Smith.

To legitimize the new reality that it had unilaterally imposed on the Powder, the U.S. government did what it seemed to do best when it came to its dealings with Indians in the mid-nineteenth century—it drafted a new treaty. In June 1866, Indian Agent E. B. Taylor and Colonel Henry Carrington met with the Lakota leaders, including Red Cloud, at Fort Laramie to promise substantial annuity payments would be made in exchange for freedom of passage on the Bozeman Trail. The itancan whose people lived in the vicinity of the trail naturally refused the offer, but the chiefs whose bands were unaffected agreed.

In another in a long series of misunderstandings of the Lakota, Taylor wired the Indian Bureau that a deal had been struck. In July, it was the Lakota who struck. Red Cloud ordered attacks on every wagon train, military or civilian, that used the Bozeman Trail. Four civilians were killed in an attack on July 17, and two soldiers died three days later. These were the opening salvos in the campaign that would consume the next two years—Red Cloud's War.

General Henry B. Carrington. (*National Archives*)

The battles that punctuated Red Cloud's War not only got the attention of the national media back east over the coming two years, but are some of the signature battles of the Indian Wars. First came the Fetterman Fight—often still referred to as the Fetterman Massacre. As autumn faded into winter in 1866, Colonel Henry Carrington's contingent at Fort Phil Kearny was working to finish construction. On December 6, and again on December 21, groups of Lakota attacked wood-cutting crews on Lodge Trail Ridge north of the fort. Each time, Carrington sent Lieutenant William Fetterman and a detachment of mounted troops to chase them off. During the second incident, Fetterman disobeyed orders by chasing the raiders across Lodge Trail Ridge. Here, the overextended troops were ambushed.

The tactical engineer of this ambush was a young Oglala warrior named Crazy Horse (Tasunke Witko). Then only in his mid-twenties, Crazy Horse would go on to distinguish himself as both a courageous warrior and a brilliant tactician in a decade of victories against the U.S. Army. Indeed, his name is still synonymous with the ideal of the heroic Lakota warrior.

Crazy Horse and the Oglala wiped out Fetterman's entire command—eighty-one soldiers and civilians—in about thirty minutes. The wasichu called it the worst defeat yet suffered by the U.S. Army in the West. The Lakota called it the Hundred Soldiers Killed Fight. In the wake of this ignoble rout, Carrington was relieved of his command, while the reckless—but martyred—Fetterman became the namesake of a new fort that was located on the Bozeman Trail. However, the U.S. Army remained undeterred in its program of fort construction along the Bozeman Trail.

Also undeterred was Red Cloud, whose warriors would keep up the pressure against the U.S. Army through 1867. This involved a series of minor skirmishes and two major battles, known descriptively as Hayfield and Wagon Box. The former occurred on August 1, when about eight hundred warriors attacked hay-cutters near Fort C. F. Smith, killing an officer and an enlisted man. At dawn the following day, Red Cloud personally led a major assault on another wood-cutting crew near Fort Phil Kearny. As in the Fetterman Fight, Crazy Horse was present, and so too was the notable Oglala warrior American Horse.

The previous winter, Fetterman's detachment was caught in the open, but this time, the soldiers took cover behind a group of wagon boxes located at the wood-cutting camp, and returned fire. They managed to turn back eight separate assaults over a period of more than six hours until a relief column arrived. The siege was lifted and Red Cloud withdrew, having been unable to execute a repeat of the Fetterman Fight. Relatively light casualties were experienced on both sides.

An incident from about the same time as the Red Cloud War found Sitting Bull in combat with the Salish and Kootenai—the people who the wasichu called Flathead. They lived west of the Rocky Mountains, but came to the Great Plains to hunt buffalo. When the Lakota caught them intruding thus—as they did every year—the Lakota reacted harshly. In this particular incident, Sitting Bull and Flying By were leading a war party against the trespassers along the Musselshell River in eastern Montana.

According to Lakota lore, Sitting Bull had a vision, or premonition, of this battle, which he had announced to his band two days earlier. From this, Sitting Bull began to develop a reputation as a wikasa wakan, or shaman.

Having located the enemy camp as he said they would, Sitting Bull engineered an ambush by making the Flathead think that a small number of Lakota—including White Bull, who later told this story—had stolen some horses. When the Flathead gave chase, they were sucked into a trap. In almost cinematic fashion, Sitting Bull sprung the trap just as White Bull counted coup—his first of two that day—with his lance against a Flathead armed with a gun.

A number of Lakota died in the encounter, and among those initially reported dead was Sitting Bull, who had been seriously wounded in the forearm by a Flathead arrow. Though he passed out from shock or loss of blood, he later regained consciousness, found his horse, and rejoined his companions.

By this time, the pendulum of perspective on the official government response to the Bozeman Trail issue had swung all the way from aggressive armed response to one of a negotiated settlement. While some favored the stick, Nathaniel Taylor, who became Commissioner of Indian Affairs in March 1867, favored the carrot. Congress authorized generous annuities if the Plains tribes would adopt a peaceful posture, and a delegation went west in September 1867 to begin negotiating new treaties.

The Peace Commission met first with the southern Plains Tribes at Medicine Lodge Creek in Kansas, and with the northern tribes at Fort Laramie. At the Medicine Lodge meeting, a treaty was easily negotiated and signed. At Fort Laramie, it was another matter. Red Cloud said he'd be happy to negotiate—but only after the U.S. Army abandoned all the Bozeman Trail forts.

The government, preoccupied by the impeachment of President Andrew Johnson, sent the commissioners back to Fort Laramie in April 1868 with instructions to give in to Red Cloud's demands. In an extraordinary compromise with the Oglala, the government agreed not only to destroy the forts, but to grant the Lakota sovereignty over a vast swath of territory across eastern Montana Territory and Dakota Territory that centered on the Powder River Country and included the Black Hills. In the quarter of the Dakota Territory west of the Missouri River that is now western South Dakota, the treaty created a "Great Sioux Reservation." The Powder River Country was marked on the maps as "unceded territory." Farther west lay the Crow Reservation, a fact that likely displeased many of their staunch enemies among the Lakota.

Most of the signatures were affixed to the treaty in April and May, but Red Cloud signed the 1868 Fort Laramie Treaty in November, only after the Bozeman Trail forts were actually set ablaze. He had wrung an unprecedented concession from the wasichu. At no other time or place in the history of the Indian Wars, before or after, would the U.S. Army voluntarily destroy a major defensive line in order to appease an enemy. For his part, Red Cloud remained true to his word. Even after the West erupted in violence in the 1870s, he remained at peace.

As Red Cloud's Oglala were harassing the Bozeman Trail forts in their high-profile series of attacks, Sitting Bull was waging a parallel campaign of his own against the forts along the Missouri River in Dakota Territory. For a man who may not have seen major combat with the wasichu before 1863, Sitting Bull was now engaged in a continuous campaign of harassment against the U.S. Army.

In December 1866, just two days after the Fetterman Fight, Sitting Bull captured the Fort Buford sawmill and traded shots within the troopers at the fort itself as the Hunkpapa burned the stockpiled firewood. While the Oglala were harassing construction of the Bozeman Trail forts, Sitting Bull harassed the crews building Fort Stevenson, downstream from Fort Berthold. In May 1868, a year after Red Cloud's Hayfield battle,

Four Horns's copy of a panel from Sitting Bull's Hieroglyphic Autobiography in which Sitting Bull counts coup on a wasichu soldier during an 1868 skirmish. (*Manuscript 1929A. Four Horns copy of Sitting Bull and Jumping Bull pictographic autobiographies, 1870. National Anthropological Archives*)

Sitting Bull attacked the crews in Fort Buford's hayfield. Sitting Bull's band even ranged as far east as Fort Totten, near Devil's Lake.

Seven of the final installments in Sitting Bull's Hieroglyphic Autobiography depict events that are believed to have occurred in 1867 and 1868. These seven images of Sitting Bull all depict engagements with the wasichu or the taking of their horses. The final two images, believed to be from the following year, show Sitting Bull back where he started, counting coup among the Crow. It is worth pointing out that even as late as 1869, many Lakota still regarded their traditional rivals, the Crow—not the wasichu—as their principal antagonists.

One of these final images commemorates an encounter in the headwaters of Big Dry Creek in the Yellowstone drainage of eastern Montana during the winter of 1869. Two Lakota boys hunting buffalo were attacked by thirty Crow warriors, and one of the boys was killed. The survivor returned to camp to alert Sitting Bull, who immediately organized a counterstrike.

When Sitting Bull and his party arrived, the Crow, who were on foot, took cover in some rocks. In the ensuing fight, all of the Crow were killed, although the Lakota lost fourteen—including Looks for Him in a Tent (Looks for Home), Sitting Bull's uncle and the brother of Four Horns. In the battle, Sitting Bull is recalled to have counted coup three times and to have taken a number of scalps.

When one looks at the volumes of commentary on Sitting Bull, it is easy to see why most people still believe that his principal antagonists on the battlefield were the wasichu. However, the fact is that nearly all of the foes that he met in combat as a young warrior, indeed until he was in his thirties, were members of other tribes, especially the Crow. Even today, one finds a pervasive recognition among both Crow and Lakota of the fact that the two peoples were once mortal enemies.*

Certainly the Crow figure prominently in Sitting Bull's Hieroglyphic Autobiography. If he had continued past 1870 with his drawings, the wasichu might have emerged as the dominant subject of his battlefield pictographs, but we'll never know. Shortly after the incident in which the thirty Crow were killed, Sitting Bull lost possession of his pictographs. They were either misplaced or stolen, but somehow came into the possession of Dr. James Kimball, the Army doctor at Fort Buford, in 1870. Sitting Bull apparently never resumed work on new images for his Hieroglyphic

---

*To get a perspective on relations today between the Lakota and the Crow, I spoke with Bill Yellowtail, the former regional director of the Environmental Protection Agency, who now occupies the Katz Endowed Chair in Native American Studies at Montana State University. Yellowtail, who is Crow himself, told me that this is an aspect of intertribal relations that is largely unaddressed in the literature, but he agrees that it is something that deserves attention. He said that the relationship is currently quite friendly and that there is a great deal of interaction between the two tribes. He explained that since the beginning of the twentieth century, there has been a great deal of information exchanged between the tribes. "There is still an undercurrent of competitive spirit between the two tribes, though," he said. "It takes the form of good-natured joking. We still make jokes with one another and about one another. In one sense it's in good fun, but on the other hand, there's still an edge." Interview with author, May 2007.

Autobiography, although in 1882 he would make copies from memory of the pre-1870 images.

HAVING finalized the arrangements in the Powder River Country, the wasichu decided in June 1868 that it was time to convince the Lakota on the upper Missouri River to sign on to the Fort Laramie Treaty, and thereby to bring peace to that region as well. As an emissary to these Lakota, the U.S. government called upon the services of Father Pierre-Jean De Smet, a sixty-seven-year-old Belgian Jesuit missionary who had first began ministering to North America's indigenous peoples in the 1820s. He is best remembered for his travels throughout the Rocky Mountains in what are now Idaho, Montana, and Alberta in the 1840s. He was both familiar with the West and its native peoples, and widely respected by them. This made him the ideal candidate for the task of convincing Sitting Bull and his followers to sign the treaty. They called him "Black Robe," which was also a generic Indian term for Catholic priests.

Traveling from Fort Rice with an escort of Lakota warriors, Black Robe arrived at the big Hunkpapa village at the mouth of the Powder River where Sitting Bull was camped on June 19. Sitting Bull, who respected De Smet as an important religious leader—despite being a wasichu—invited Black Robe into his own tipi. Sitting Bull saw Black Robe's religion as having much in common with his own. Black Robe had his Virgin Mary just as the Lakota spoke reverently of White Buffalo Calf Woman. However, Sitting Bull told the Jesuit that he had wasichu blood on his hands, just as the wasichu had Indian blood on theirs.

Father De Smet explained many of the features of the treaty, such as the government's promises to feed and cloth the Indians who signed on. To this, according to what White Bull told Stanley Vestal, Sitting Bull very eloquently and succinctly laid out his own perspective on his people and how they wished to live. He told the priest to tell the "Grandfather" (the

Indian term for President Ulysses S. Grant): "I do not want anyone to bother my people. I want them to live in peace. I myself have plans for my people, and if they follow my plans, they will never want. They will never hunger. I wish for traders only, and no soldiers on my reservation. God gave us this land, and we are at home here. I will not have my people robbed. We can live if we can keep our Black Hills. We do not want to eat from the hand of the Grandfather. We can feed ourselves."

During their meetings, Sitting Bull, as well as Four Horns and the others, told De Smet that they would be willing to leave a door open to detente with the wasichu, but that they didn't want peaceful coexistence, they wanted to be left alone.

Having thought that they had made their point, the Hunkpapa leaders returned with De Smet to Fort Rice to sign the treaty on July 2, even though it contained provisions calling for the abandonment of the Bozeman Trail forts, and not the forts on the upper Missouri.

The enactment of the Fort Laramie Treaty, and the end of the decade—according to the wasichu calendar—marked a moment of important change for the Lakota because the treaty formally legitimized the wasichu presence in much of the upper Great Plains. For centuries, it had been easy for the Lakota to avoid contact with the wasichu. Even in Sitting Bull's youth, a Lakota wasn't likely to see a wasichu unless he went to the Missouri River and looked for one. By the end of the 1860s, those days were gone forever. The Lakota could go into the Powder River Country and not see the wasichu, but they knew wasichu were out there— and that they were coming. Things had changed gradually, then quickly. The Bozeman Trail controversy and the expanding wasichu presence on the upper Missouri were symptomatic of a paradigm shift.

Just as the wasichu wondered what to do next in this monumental clash of cultures, so too did the Lakota. Red Cloud had stated his position, backed it up with action, and had gotten what he wanted. Now, he was ready to sign a treaty and accept the wasichu annuities. Both Red Cloud

U.S. Government Indian Peace Commissioners during their conference with Plains Indian leaders at Fort Laramie in 1868. (*National Anthropological Archives*)

and Spotted Tail (Sinte Gleska), the respected itancan of the Brulé Lakota, were given their own agencies. Many of the Lakota leaders who had played an important role in Red Cloud's War became staunch advocates of coexistence. Among the Oglala, these included Red Cloud, American Horse, and Young Man Afraid of His Horses (aka They Even Fear His Horses)—but certainly *not* Crazy Horse.

Although there were many who were willing to follow the lead of Red Cloud and Spotted Tail, there were others—especially among the Hunkpapa—who had long ago decided that they would never accept the wasichu annuities. The two poles represented by agency bands and the hunting bands drifted farther and farther apart.

Between these two poles were less idealistic Lakota who imagined that they might take the best of both. It was reasonable to assume that a person might live at an agency or on the Great Sioux Reservation in the winter, accepting annuities, while occasionally "roaming" into the "unceded lands" of the Powder River Country to hunt the buffalo in the summer. These people came to be known to the wasichu as the "summer roamers," in contrast with the "winter roamers," who rejected the reservation concept

entirely and roamed the unceded lands in the winter as well as the summer — as people had done on the Northern Plains for centuries before the
wasichu came. Many of the disaffected Oglala, including Crazy Horse,
left Red Cloud to join with the Hunkpapa as winter roamers. Even if they
roamed as they had before the wasichu came, there was no doubt that the
wasichu were here now. Among all the roamers there was a growing sense
that they were surrounded by wasichu.

In the wake of the Treaty of Fort Laramie, the Hunkpapa decided to
make unprecedented changes in the order of their society to meet the
wasichu challenge. Those who had laughed when Mad Bear Harney had
come and made Bear Ribs the Hunkpapa "head chief" now rethought the
idea of such a position. In his early twentieth-century interviews with
numerous Lakota who had been adults at the time, Stanley Vestal learned
that "Four Horns and the Hunkpapa warrior societies [including the
Strong Hearts, of which Sitting Bull was a member] proposed to create a
high command, a single head chief."

The Shirt Wearers, the four-man Hunkpapa executive council, called
a conference, probably in 1869, that involved not just the Hunkpapa, but
other Lakota itancan as well. The object of the conference was to break
with all established precedent and select a single "itancan-in-chief" of
more or less all the Lakota north of the Platte. As occasionally happens to
modern politicians, three of the Hunkpapa Shirt Wearers — Loud Voiced
Hawk, Red Horn, and Running Antelope — were at the end of long scandal-plagued terms in office. The fourth man, Sitting Bull's uncle Four
Horns, still had the respect of the Hunkpapa, but he knew that he was getting old and that it was time for the new blood.

Among the other Hunkpapa itancan who attended the conference
were Black Moon, Crow King, Iron Dog, and Long Horn, as well as
Sitting Bull's long-time friend, Gall. The Sans Arc itancan included Black
Eagle, Bluecoat, Brown Thunder, His High Horse, Two Eagle, and
Spotted Eagle. The Minneconjou delegation included Black Shield,

Flying By, Lame Deer, White Hollow Horn, and Makes Room, who was married to Sitting Bull's sister and who was the father of White Bull and One Bull. Also present was Crazy Horse, himself a Shirt Wearer among the Oglala.

To fill this position of "itancan-in-chief," as a man to occupy a post that never before existed in Lakota society, Four Horns nominated his nephew—and Sitting Bull was, in fact, chosen.

Sitting Bull now represented the Lakota who had chosen to avoid the agencies and refuse the annuities, just as Red Cloud now represented the Lakota who had decided to live by the treaty.

Sitting Bull was probably chosen for a variety of reasons. It may have been because of his bravery, and his leadership in battle. Although his recent hit-and-run raids on the Missouri forts were not especially noteworthy, his cumulative record as a warrior—especially in combat against other tribes—was impressive. By the events recorded in his Hieroglyphic Autobiography alone, he had counted coup sixty-three times through 1869. Ultimately, though, his selection as itancan among itancan probably came down to his charisma and his character. Nearly everything that has been said about Sitting Bull by those who knew him tells of his powerful presence and his magnetic personality. From what we know about Lakota concepts of leadership, their itancan led not by demanding blind obedience to decree, but through inspiration and example. This certainly seems to have been Sitting Bull's way.

As with any good leader, Sitting Bull had clearly stated his position on the Lakota and their destiny in the face of the wasichu encroachment. To De Smet, he repeated what he had explained to previous emissaries who came with promises of annuities. He recalled that "I told them I did not want their annuities, nor could I sell my country. My father lived and died here; so would I. And if our white brothers would do right, we would never have had war. I always liked to have goods to trade for, but I cannot bear the idea of having the country filled up with white men. Some are good, but many are bad, and they often treat us badly. Our people are often shot down by travelers over the plains while they are seeking food for their families."

Great leaders derive their power from forcefully articulating what their followers want. As Sitting Bull so eloquently stated—time and again—the Lakota wanted to be left alone.

A lot of people had signed the Fort Laramie Treaty believing—or at least hoping—that it represented an ebbing of the tide of wasichu encroachment into the northern Plains. For a generation, the wasichu had come, pushing deeper into land where the Indians had ridden and hunted many, many generations before. Now, the wasichu had agreed to withdraw entirely from part of where they had encroached. Was the tide of wasichu really running the other way? Time would tell.

Red Horse's drawing of Indians fighting Custer's troops at the Battle of Little Bighorn. In his Sun Dance vision a few days before the battle, Sitting Bull saw soldiers "falling upside down" into the Indian camp. Red Horse was a Minneconjou Lakota leader who was present at the Battle of the Little Bighorn. His pictographic eyewitness account was recorded at the Cheyenne River Reservation in 1881 and preserved for posterity by the Bureau of American Ethnology. (*Manuscript 2367A 1881 National Anthropological Archives*)

3

COLLISION

AFTER THE FORT LARAMIE TREATY OF 1868, THE LAKOTA were a nation divided. Red Cloud, the Oglala leader whose strong stand had wrung unprecedented concessions from the wasichu, was the figurehead of the faction that had promised to peacefully coexist—and who would keep that promise. Sitting Bull now represented the faction that was willing to be peaceful—but who did not want to coexist. Among those who followed Sitting Bull were many Hunkpapa, as well as members of other Lakota bands, including Crazy Horse and many other Oglala. And it was not only the Lakota who subscribed to Sitting Bull's brand of defiance. Their Northern Cheyenne allies also saw no reason to accept wasichu hegemony.

For a few years, these Lakota and their like-minded allies did not have to coexist. The wasichu had been excluded from the Powder River Country, and all of southwestern Dakota Territory, including the Paha Sapa, the Black Hills, which were important to the Lakota and clearly designated as part of the Great Sioux Reservation. For a few years, the Lakota rode these lands and the wasichu stayed away.

However, the wasichu were hovering in larger numbers around the edges of this land that was off-limits to them. Before the Civil War, the wasichu had crossed the Plains in wagon trains. Now, their technology had given them a new and more efficient means to cross the continent—the railroad. Ever since commercial railroads had begun operating in the eastern United States in the 1830s, people had been speculating about a rail line across the continent. In 1862, after decades of surveying, President Abraham Lincoln had signed the Pacific Railroad Act authorizing federal support for such a project. After several difficult years of construction, the Union Pacific Railroad and Central Pacific Railroad had joined their rails at Promontory, Utah, in May 1869 to give the United States a transcontinental rail link. The route generally followed that of the California Trail from Omaha, across the Sierra Nevada to Sacramento. It would be just the first of many.

With this line in place across the center of the country, the wasichu began surveying for a second transcontinental line farther north. The Northern Pacific was to be constructed westward from Minneapolis and St. Paul, and eastward from the Pacific by way of the Columbia River Gorge. The link between the two outer segments would be through Montana Territory—and Lakota land—by way of the Yellowstone River valley. Technically, the Yellowstone corridor was just north of the Powder River Country and arguably not really within the "unceded lands," but when the survey parties, escorted by the U.S. Army, came through in 1872, Lakota eyebrows were raised. Soon, so too were more than a few rifles.

Sitting Bull himself, leading about four hundred warriors, came to blows with Major Eugene Baker's 7th Cavalry troops near Pryor's Fork of the Yellowstone on August 14, 1872. White Bull was also there, and so too was Crazy Horse. White Bull recalled later that the impetuous younger warriors charged the cavalry lines at Pryor's Fork, trading shots with the troopers, daring them to try to hit the Lakota lads on their fast horses. To demonstrate his own bravery in a different way, Sitting Bull strolled to the middle of the battlefield, within full view of the troopers, sat down, and nonchalantly smoked his pipe. This was seen by all as a profound display of bravery and it underscored his growing reputation as a wikasa wakan.

Shortly after this skirmish, the wasichu surveyors left the Yellowstone valley, but it was due to distant factors about which the Lakota did not know—nor did they care. The Northern Pacific Railroad would go bankrupt in the Panic of 1873, and the westward march of the rail construction halted at Bismarck. It would be eight more years before Henry Villard took over the railroad and work resumed on the line across Montana Territory. In the meantime, other things would draw the wasichu into Lakota lands.

The Treaty of Fort Laramie was ambiguous on some points, but quite clear on others. One of the latter was the guarantee of Lakota sovereignty over the Paha Sapa—the Black Hills—that six thousand square miles of picturesque mountain country in southwestern Dakota Territory. Sitting Bull had promised peace if he was left alone, which obviously implied war if he was *not* left alone. It should also have been clear to the wasichu that one of the worst things to do in terms of getting Sitting Bull angry would have been to violate the sovereignty of the Black Hills.

Nevertheless, General Philip Sheridan, commander of the U.S. Army's Division of the Missouri, counterintuitively decided that peace would be advanced by having a military presence within the Black Hills. Sheridan managed to convince President Grant that the U.S. Army ought to at least survey the territory.

Sheridan's understanding of the people who lived in and around the Black Hills was limited, and he felt little need or inclination to change that. So too was his understanding of Sitting Bull. In the early 1870s, Sitting Bull was just a name to the generals in the East. They had heard of him, and they had heard that he represented something big. However, so little was really known by about this Lakota leader as a man that Sheridan questioned whether the individual referred to as "Sitting Bull" was a real person, or merely an allegory for Lakota resistance to the wasichu. He would soon know the truth.

Meanwhile, Ulysses S. Grant, whose aggressive military strategy as General-in-Chief of the Union armies had won the Civil War, had proven himself to be far more conciliatory in his policy toward the American Indians since becoming president in 1869. Because of this, he should have known better than to needlessly provoke the Lakota with a mission of little or no tangible military value.

What neither Grant, nor Sheridan, nor Sitting Bull could know was that the expedition would ignite something that would make Sheridan's violation of the Black Hills a thousand times worse than it might have been—a gold rush.

To execute the pernicious reconnaissance into the Black Hills, Phil Sheridan picked the U.S. Army's 7th Cavalry Regiment, based at Fort Abraham Lincoln, near Bismarck in Dakota Territory. Leading the regiment into the Black Hills would be Sheridan's old protegé, the dashing Lieutenant Colonel George Armstrong Custer.

By the time that the flamboyant Custer led the regiment into the Black Hills in July 1874, a half dozen years in the West, a colorful persona, and the attention of the Eastern tabloid press had made him into a star. He was the ideal model of the intrepid "Indian fighter." His fringed buckskin jacket and his golden hair, which he always wore long, made him into the colorful bad boy who attracted notice and sold papers. Even the Indians called him "Yellow Hair," or "Long Hair."

Despite his apparent foppishness, he had actually been a true hero in the Civil War. Though he had graduated last in the West Point Class of 1862—which was graduated in 1861, nearly a year early because of the wartime requirement for officers—his star outshone those of many who should have been more qualified for command. He fought at Bull Run,

The 7th Cavalry with its support column and wagons during the Black Hills Expedition of 1874. Lieutenant Colonel George Armstrong Custer heads the column, wearing light-colored buckskins and riding a dark horse. (*National Archives*)

heroically commanded the Michigan Brigade at Gettysburg, and developed a reputation for bravery to the point of recklessness. Promoted to Brevet Major General as a division commander, the twenty-six-year-old "boy general" went on to receive Robert E. Lee's truce flag at Appomattox.

After the war, he reverted to his permanent rank of Lieutenant Colonel and went west to fight Indians. He led the recently formed 7th Cavalry Regiment in the Department of the Missouri as it took to the field in April 1867 against the Cheyenne on the Kansas prairies. Almost immediately, the wartime hero started to be known for impetuous behavior that earned him as many detractors as advocates. Having ordered three deserters to be shot, he went AWOL himself a month later when he left his command to dash off to visit his wife at Fort Riley. As a result, he was taken into custody, court-martialed, and relieved of rank and duties for a year. Custer would have to wait until the end of 1868 for the major combat that would define his reputation as an Indian fighter.

The latter would be a massacre—some would call it a battle—along the Washita River in what is now Oklahoma. Custer led the 7th Cavalry as part of Phil Sheridan's 1868 winter offensive. Though a heavy snow obscured the trail, Custer located a sizable Cheyenne encampment on the Washita and prepared for a dawn attack on November 27. The camp was that of Black Kettle, the same Cheyenne Chief whose village on Sand Creek in eastern Colorado had been the target of Colonel John Chivington's brutal—and almost universally denounced—slaughter on November 29, 1864.

Custer attacked using a multipronged assault from opposite directions and achieving total surprise. Black Kettle himself was killed, along with up to one hundred other Cheyenne, including many women and children. The 7th Cavalry lost twenty-one men killed in action, most of them part of an eighteen-man contingent under Major Joel Elliot, whom Custer had sent to chase some escaping Cheyenne.

Despite the heavy civilian casualties, the Washita "battle" assured Custer's media star status as an Indian fighter. Even though he demonstrated a careless disregard for military protocol, his friendship with Sheridan kept him in the field where he could embellish his reputation. And, despite a lack of major action in the half dozen years after Washita, the media saw to it that Long Hair remained the popular archetype of the Indian fighter.

Custer's next major combat actions came in August 1873, when he and Captain Myles Moylan led the 7th Cavalry up the Yellowstone River. Their patrol more or less followed the same route as Baker had the year before when the 7th Cavalry tangled with Sitting Bull at near Pryor's Fork. When a small group of Lakota swept into Custer's camp at the mouth of the Tongue River—planning to steal horses, decoy troops into an ambush, or both—it was Custer who personally gave chase, only to be surrounded by an estimated three hundred warriors. He dashed back to camp, where he and Moylan formed a defensive perimeter. After several hours and a failed attempt to start a grass fire to smoke out the troopers, the Indians broke off the attack. The regimental veterinarian and two other solders were killed.

While camped at the mouth of the Bighorn River a week later, Custer and Moylan were attacked again. As before, they managed to keep the Lakota at bay, but the troops were pinned down for most of the day. It may have been the same band that had attacked them on the Tongue, but Custer estimated that they had held off a hostile force greater than three times that size. The more Indians that America's Indian fighter was fighting, the better.

As we make the comment that Custer should have been taking notes about the fighting prowess and tenacity of the Lakota, we are reminded that he was, in fact, taking notes. Beginning in May 1872, his articles about his own exploits had been appearing in *The Galaxy* magazine. This, and a compendium of the articles that was published in 1874 under the title *My Life on the Plains*, were all part of his creation of his own heroic myth. What we should say is that Custer might have been better off to have made more practical use of those notes.

A year later, when Sheridan had convinced Grant to authorize a survey of the Black Hills, Custer again rode into land that had been guaranteed to the Lakota under the Fort Laramie Treaty. As Custer led the 7th Cavalry into the Black Hills, it was against the backdrop of rumors that there were gold deposits there. The rumors were, of course, true. Long Hair had discovered yellow flecks of the metal that drives men—and women—mad. With his flair for the dramatic, Custer was not shy about allowing the confirmation of Black Hills gold to become public knowledge. The scout Charley Reynolds, who was riding with Custer, carried dispatches to Fort Laramie that reached the East Coast even before Custer got back to Fort Abraham Lincoln. This news, received against the backdrop of the depression caused by the Panic of 1873, touched off the Black Hills Gold Rush of 1874–1875.

Sheridan had sent Custer into what should have remained terra incognita for the wasichu, akin to opening Pandora's Box. Once open, the gates of the Black Hills could not be closed. The U.S. Army was legally obligated to prevent prospectors from streaming into the Lakota heartland, but it was a practical impossibility. Given this situation, the federal government did what it thought to be the best alternative, offering to buy the Black Hills from the Lakota for the equivalent of $100 million in twenty-first-century dollars. To the faction within the Lakota represented by Sitting Bull, such an offer was an insult. No amount of the wasichu's funny paper could equal the value of the Paha Sapa.

In 1875 you could still ride through the Powder River Country and see no sign of the wasichu, but this was no longer true in the Black Hills. In 1869, it had still been possible for Sitting Bull to realistically defy both the wasichu and the "agency" faction of the Lakota leadership. A half dozen years later, that was not the case.

At the same time, for the wasichu in the East, it was easy to stroll city streets or country lanes and see no sign that Indians had ever existed. It was easy to think of Indians as a relic from a distant, ancient past. As the wasichu prepared to celebrate their civilization at the Centennial Exposition in Philadelphia in 1876, it was hard to imagine the clash of cultures—the *bloody* clash of cultures—that would grab the headlines during that summer. For those who thought that the Indian Wars were over, and that the "red man" would simply fade away, a rude shock awaited them. Sitting Bull's dream of more or less peacefully not coexisting with the wasichu appeared as if it would remain a dream.

President Grant, who as General Grant led a decisive end to the Civil War, now sought a decisive end to the Indian Wars on the Plains. The previous policy of gently coaxing Indians to become "agency" Indians had run its course. Sitting Bull's faction had no interest in being gently coaxed.

After years of extending the metaphorical olive branch, Grant was ready for the literal sword. The Grandfather in Washington had run out of patience.

The U.S. Army Chief of Staff, meanwhile, was another Civil War general, William Tecumseh Sherman. He had, even more than Grant, been willing to bar no holds when dealing aggressively with the Confederates. His notorious "March to the Sea" in 1864 had cut the Confederacy in half, left Atlanta in ruins and had graphically demonstrated the concept of "total war."

General George Crook photographed at Fort Boise. (*National Anthropological Archives*)

Grant and Sherman agreed. If the tide of history would not sweep all of the Indians onto the designated agencies or the Sioux Reservation, then the U.S. Army would have to do it and do it now. To accomplish this, the soldiers would begin by sweeping up the winter roamers, which in turn would convey a stern message to anyone who might be inclined to roam off the reservation at any time of year. In order to begin the task, the U.S. Army would have to do what it had not often done. It would have to go into the field in the winter.

It all began with an ultimatum. The U.S. government issued an order that all of the winter-roaming Lakota and Cheyenne bands should be out of the Powder River Country and onto the Great Sioux Reservation by the end of January 1876.

The battle plan of Grant and Sherman was not carrot-and-stick coercion. It was the stick or else. Wielding the stick would be General Sheridan, commanding the Division of the Missouri, and his subordinate, General George Crook, who now commanded the Department of the Platte with headquarters in Omaha. Crook's reputation preceded him. He was a proven tactical master, the hero of the Apache Wars, and of the Paiute Wars before that. As this writer has pointed out, if Custer is the most recognized by the general public among the U.S. Army officers of the Indian Wars, it is George Crook who has become synonymous with the most successful U.S. Army operational doctrine of the Indian Wars.

Crook graduated from West Point in 1852, a decade before Custer's class, and served in the Indian Wars on the California-Oregon border before the Civil War. In the latter conflict, Brevet Major General Crook had distinguished himself leading the Ohio Brigade at Antietam, and was a division commander at Chickamauga and in the Shenandoah Valley campaign. After the war, he reverted to his prewar regular rank of lieutenant colonel, but would work his way back to major general in permanent rank. Most important were his trademark tactics, developed in the Great Basin and Southwest and based on those of frontiersmen and the Indians, who lived of the land. His successful tactical element was a small, highly mobile, and well-armed unit, composed of skilled marksmen, rather than a large, slow-moving column. Crook himself studied the environment in which he would operate, and he studied his opponents so that he came to understand them as well as they understood one another.

Having applied this policy successfully against the Apache, Crook now threw it out the window for the 1876 campaign. He and Sheridan planned a classic multipronged offensive designed to sweep through the Powder River Country and all of southeastern Montana Territory with large contingents of cavalry.

The main offensive would not take place until summer, but a January 31 deadline obviously wouldn't be taken seriously if it was not enforced sooner than summer, so a limited-scale winter offensive was a must. If the winter roamers were to be caught roaming in the winter, Crook reasoned that he'd best take to the field in February.

Heavy snow delayed the beginning of the winter offensive until March, but finally the cavalry headed out from Fort Fetterman on the Platte River,

about seventy miles upstream from Fort
Laramie. Crook led the thousand-man task
force himself, seconded by Colonel Joseph
Reynolds of the 3rd Cavalry. They suffered
through a severe blizzard during the second
week of March as they searched the valleys
of the Powder River Country for sign of
their elusive quarry.

Ironically, of all the scouts in Crook's
command, the only one who seemed capa-
ble of following the trail of the elusive
Indians was a shadowy figure named Frank
Grouard. It was at about the time of the
Powder River fighting, or shortly thereafter,

Frank   Grouard.   (*Missouri
Historical Society*)

probably early in 1869, that Sitting Bull first crossed paths with Grouard.
Originally named Ephraim Grouard, he was one of four children born to
Mormon missionary Benjamin Grouard and a woman he met or married
in Hawaii in about 1846. The family arrived in California in 1852, but
decided to return to the islands a year later. Young Ephraim for some reason stayed behind, was adopted by a Mormon family named Pratt, and
taken to Utah. For unexplained reasons, Ephraim took his brother Frank's
name, abandoned the Mormon life as a teenager, and found employment
as a mail carrier or freight hauler in the Montana.

As the story goes, a pair of Lakota men ambushed Grouard on the
Montana Plains in the midst of a snowstorm, and were brawling with him
with an eye to robbing and killing him when Sitting Bull intervened.
Sitting Bull was so impressed with the fight that Grouard was putting up
that he did as he did when he was impressed with Stays Back in 1857—
he adopted him as a brother and gave him a new name. In recognition of
Grouard's fighting technique, he became known as Grabber. Others,
however, took a long time to warm up the big Hawaiian. Gradually, the

suspicion wore off, and for a while, Grabber was a part of Sitting Bull's trusted inner circle. By 1873, however, he was gone, having abandoned the Hunkpapa for other pursuits. Like a bad penny, though, he would turn up into the lives of the Hunkpapa at inopportune times.

The man whom Sitting Bull had adopted as his brother about seven years earlier had gone through a number of incarnations since leaving the Hunkpapa in 1873, including time spent with the Oglala. By 1876, he had switched sides entirely. Now he way working against the Lakota, with skills learned from Sitting Bull and his family.

On March 16, as they were working their way along the Tongue River, Crook's column caught sight of a pair of Indians. Crook ordered Reynolds to chase them with six companies, assuming they would lead the troopers to the camp of the winter roamers. Reaching the Powder River itself after an overnight pursuit, Reynolds located the expected encampment and attacked an estimated seven hundred Cheyenne and Oglala Lakota. His cavalry were outflanked, outfought, and forced to withdraw. On March 18, the Indians counterattacked Reynolds's camp, stealing back some horses that he had taken from the Indians the day before.

The humiliated Reynolds ran to the waiting arms of the disgusted Crook, who ordered him court-martialed for his bungling of the opening battle of the campaign. It was an inauspicious beginning to a very dark year for the wasichu in the West.

More has been written about the summer of 1876 than any other season in the half century of open warfare between the U.S. Army and the indigenous people of the American West. Those who have written those words will tell you that it requires more words because of its complexity.

Sitting Bull is often cast as the summer's foremost protagonist—or antagonist—with the equally charismatic Custer in the opposing role. As hero and anti-hero they were perfectly cast. No two opposing leaders could have been more unlike. To their devotees, both were heroic in the extreme. To their detractors, each was the embodiment of villainy. The countless winter counts that have come and gone since that climactic summer have seen no diminution of these extreme and divergent perspectives. Indeed, both men have achieved immortality, largely because of one afternoon in the summer of 1876.

Many, if not most, recountings of the story begin with the U.S. Army's complex strategy for taking President Grant's ultimatum to the winter roamers as they roamed the summer months. For the Lakota and Cheyenne, their strategy was simple. Sitting Bull had already articulated it many times: Leave us alone, and let us live as we have for countless winters—or we'll fight you.

For the wasichu, the complex strategy was the three-pronged penetration of the "unceded" Powder River Country. In a replay of his fumbled winter offensive, George Crook himself would lead the southern—and largest—prong out of Fort Fetterman. General John Gibbon of the 7th Infantry Regiment, a veteran commander of forces at Antietam and the Wilderness during the Civil War, would lead the western column out of Fort Ellis, near present-day Bozeman, Montana.

It was widely anticipated among the wasichu that General Alfred Terry, the long-time commander of the Department of Dakota, would place the eastern column out of Fort Abraham Lincoln under Custer's command. Who better to lead one prong of Grant's grand strategy that the tabloid-anointed great American Indian fighter?

It would have happened this way without question had not the tabloid-anointed great American Indian fighter infuriated Grant himself. As the Lakota would have described it, the Grandfather had big trouble within his own lodge. As those who watch Washington, D.C., know, mischief and malfeasance are often not far from the surface, and it is the wasichu newspapers who scratch away the surface. One hundred years later, it would be Watergate. Tomorrow it will be something else. In 1876, it was Secretary

of War William Belknap, involved in graft and corruption in the management of the trading posts at the Indian agencies in the West. The
Grandfather's own brother, Orvil Grant, was caught amid the Indian
agency scandal, using his influence to secure licenses for those who paid
him a bribe.

Custer was called to Washington to testify because he was a regimental commander at Fort Abraham Lincoln, one of the posts that was
involved in the alleged graft in the Belknap scandal. Custer testified, but
so did others—including Orvil Grant himself, who admitted his transgres-
sions. However, how could the furious Grandfather award a plumb assign-
ment to Long Hair, in light of his testimony against Orvil? President Grant
ordered Custer relieved of duty in the summer campaign, but Custer's
mentor Sheridan intervened with a solution. Terry would command the
eastern prong, with Custer merely as a subordinate. Grant reluctantly
signed off on this plan.

The die was cast. By the end of May 1876, all three prongs of
Sheridan's great campaign were in the field.

As Grant ordered Sheridan to implement the summer offensive,
Sitting Bull had no idea what was going on in Washington, D.C.—nor at
Fort Fetterman, Fort Ellis, or Fort Lincoln. He and Crazy Horse had heard
about the Powder River fight in March, and they were sure that they would
cross paths with the wasichu during the summer. But they had crossed
paths with the wasichu before, and they would fight them if they were
attacked. They didn't know that this would be a turning point of history.
Neither did the wasichu generals.

Had many things been done differently, and had the snow not been so
deep, and had the brief 1876 winter offensive brought the decisive contact
with the winter roamers that Crook desired, the summer campaign might
have been different. For one thing, there were fewer Lakota and Cheyenne
in the Powder River Country that winter than there would be during the
summer, and the wasichu seemed not have calculated this. As spring

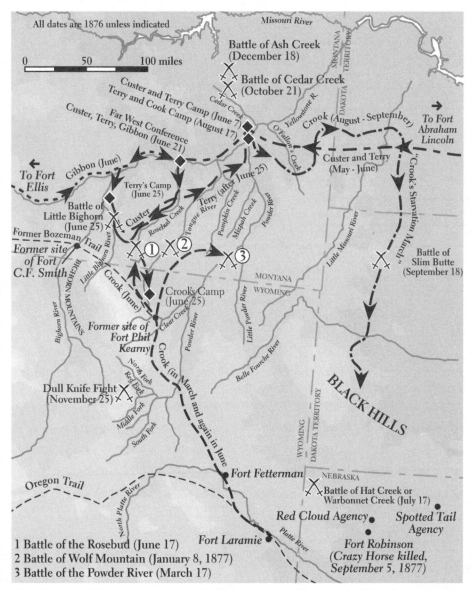

The U.S. Army 1876 campaign against the Plains Indians. (All dates are 1876 unless indicated.)

melted the snows and brought forth the grasses and the sunny days, scores of people who had wintered on the reservation headed west to hunt in the Powder River Country.

When Crook started out in March, he estimated that his task force would face between five hundred and eight hundred warriors, which may have been more or less correct. However, by June, as the three prongs of the offensive moved toward their convergence, there may have been as many as 10,000 Lakota and Cheyenne present, although estimates still vary widely. Among them, were at least 1,500 warriors, and possibly as many as 4,000.

As various autonomous bands came together to celebrate the Sun Dance near the present town of Lame Deer, Montana, they formed the biggest concentration of Indian warriors to be seen in the West since the Civil War. In addition to the Lakota and Cheyenne, there would be some Santee Sioux, including many who had fought in the Minnesota uprising of the 1862.

The huge concentration moved as one group, leisurely traveling through the Powder River County hunting the buffalo, which were still abundant in these rolling hills and valleys. The Indian would camp for several days, then pick up and travel to a new location as hunters ranged far and wide. The Indian multitude is said to have included the Hunkpapa bands of Four Horns and Black Moon as well as Sitting Bull; the Oglala who followed Crazy Horse and Low Dog; the Minneconjou of the Fast Bull, Lame Deer, and Makes Room; the Sans Arc of Spotted Eagle; the Sihasapa of Kill Eagle; and Cheyenne bands led by Lame White Man, Old Bear, and Two Moon.

Though some accounts say that Sitting Bull and Crazy Horse were prepared for a defensive war if attacked, White Bull would later indicate that a battle was considered inevitable. He said that a call had gone out for the warriors from the agencies to come and join the conclave and be ready for a big fight. Even Red Cloud's son is said to have ridden north to join the growing assembly as it camped on Rosebud Creek in mid-June for the annual Sun Dance.

Sitting Bull, in his role as both itancan and wikasa wakan, played a key role in the Sun Dance that summer, ceremonially shedding his blood. White Bull later recalled watching as his uncle danced for hours, staring at the sun as blood ran down his outstretched arms. When it was over, Sitting Bull reported the vision that he had experienced during the dance. Those, like White Bull, who were present when the wikasa wakan recounted what he had seen, would remember that day for the rest of their lives. Sitting Bull told them that in his vision, he had seen many soldiers falling into the camp like grasshoppers. Because they were upside down in the vision, he knew that the soldiers would die. His vision also warned that the people should not mutilate and steal from the upside-down soldiers.

Now, Sitting Bull knew. Time was running out—for the wasichu.

WHILE Sitting Bull was now widely acknowledged as the greatest Lakota itancan—and he was coming to be known as a great wikasa wakan—Crazy Horse would soon earn recognition as perhaps the greatest of all Lakota warriors.

On the day that Sitting Bull reported his premonition, on or about June 14, the great encampment pulled up stakes and moved upstream on Rosebud Creek toward a new campsite. General Crook was not far away. On June 6, his troops had passed the scene of the Fetterman Fight fought nearly ten years before, and moved north toward Goose Creek. On June 16, his slow-moving contingent—which included more than a thousand troopers as well as Crow and Shoshone scouts—crossed into the headwaters of Rosebud Creek. The man who had achieved his greatest success by not using large, cumbersome columns was heading into the biggest battle of his Indian fighting career at the head of one.

By this time, Crook and Sitting Bull knew that they were closing in on one another. Scouts from both sides had seen one another but they were still uncertain as to the location and size of the opposing force. On the morning of June 17, as Crook ordered his column to take a rest, he heard the sounds of his Crow scouts engaging a Lakota war party. The Battle of the Rosebud had begun.

Crazy Horse himself led the attack. Sitting Bull remained on the sidelines, still nursing the injuries from the ceremonial piercings during the Sun Dance a few days earlier.

The battle clearly demonstrated the tactical brilliance of Crazy Horse. He attacked headlong, using a larger and more concentrated force that most Indian leaders ever used in battle, hitting Crook hard and fast. Next, when Crook tried to counterattack, Crazy Horse and the force of about 750 warriors deftly parried each move in what was the biggest cavalry fight in North America since the Civil War. Captain Anson Mills of the 3rd Cavalry later recalled that the Cheyenne and Lakota were "charging boldly and rapidly through the soldiers, knocking them from their horses with lances and knives, dismounting and killing them." It was Mills who called Crazy Horse and his men "the best cavalry in the world."

As Crazy Horse was having a finest hour, the usually competent Crook made a desperate miscalculation. Somehow getting the impression that the Indian camp was nearby, he ordered Captain Mills to take a several companies downstream to attack them. Seeing these troopers ride away from the battle simply energized the attackers, and they renewed their efforts to overwhelm Crook. This, in turn, caused Crook to send word to Mills telling him to come back.

Things were not going well for Crook, now locked in the largest battle of his career in the West, and indeed the biggest battle that most present would ever see outside the Civil War. William Royall's contingent was badly beaten and nearly surrounded as the roughly 750 warriors persisted with one relentless assault after another. Crook may have lost as many as twenty-eight men killed in action, although some sources say it was just nine. Crazy Horse later admitted to have lost three dozen warriors killed.

When it was all over, and Crazy Horse had withdrawn, Crook decided that he had won. Why? Because military doctrine stated that whoever held the originally contested ground was the winner. However, Crook's force had been so badly mauled that it was forced to withdraw from both the battlefield and the campaign. Crazy Horse had just knocked the largest leg of Sheridan's strategy out of the game for more than a month. To make matters worse, Terry, Gibbon, and Custer were unaware that the Battle of the Rosebud had taken place, and that Crook had essentially retreated from the Powder River Country.

For his part, Crazy Horse rode back to camp a hero. The Rosebud fight was celebrated even as the Cheyenne and Lakota picked up to move the vast encampment northward, away from Crook, but toward Custer.

In the week before Crook's June 17 calamity on the Rosebud, the other prongs of the summer campaign had been moving slowly through the valley of the Yellowstone River. General Terry had sent Major Marcus Reno of Custer's 7th Cavalry southward to conduct a reconnaissance mission into the Powder River drainage, and he was actually about sixty miles downstream from Crook on the Rosebud at the time of the battle—without knowing it.

When Reno rendezvoused with Terry and Custer at the mouth of the Tongue River, he reported having seen evidence of a very large number of Indians having camped in the area. Based on this information, Terry correctly deduced that the Lakota and Cheyenne had been in the Powder and Tongue River valleys, and that they had moved west. Therefore, his plan would be to look for them in the valleys of the Rosebud and in the valleys father west. These included those of the Bighorn River, as well as in the area of the Little Bighorn, a tributary of the Bighorn that flowed between the Rosebud and the Bighorn.

On June 21, Terry met with Custer and Gibbon to discuss his tactical plan. Custer was to lead a force upstream on Rosebud Creek, and Gibbon would follow a parallel course up the Bighorn. Custer would then cross westward over the ridge to the valley of the Little Bighorn—referred to by Terry as the "Little Horn"—and march downstream to rendezvous with Gibbon on June 26. Terry imagined that when the Indian camp was located, it would be attacked by Custer and Gibbon's combined force of about a thousand troops. They still did not know that Crook was no longer in the field, or that the Battle of the Rosebud had occurred a few days earlier.

When Custer went into the field the next day, his 7th Cavalry Regiment command consisted of thirty-one officers, 566 enlisted men, thirty-five scouts and interpreters, as well as about a dozen civilians. Custer also brought his regimental band so that they could go into battle to the tune of their theme song, "Garryowen." Amazingly, two of Custer's three brothers, as well as the husband of his only sister, were part of the detachment. So too was his eighteen-year-old nephew, Harry Armstrong "Autie" Reed. The older of Long Hair's two younger brothers, Captain Thomas Ward Custer, commanded the 7th Cavalry's Company C. Tom had the distinction of having earned, not one but two Medals of Honor during the Civil War. Their brother, Boston Custer, had been rejected by the U.S. Army for health reasons, but he was on the books as a civilian contractor. Their sister Margaret's husband, Lieutenant James Calhoun, commanded Company L.

In addition to Boston, the civilians in the group included Mark Kellogg of the *Bismarck Tribune*, who was riding along as an embedded reporter. He was also a stringer for the *New York Herald*, one of the newspapers that had helped to establish and promote the image of Long Hair as the "Great American Indian Fighter." One can imaging Kellogg forming the hyperbole that he hoped to pen as the column plodded over the grassy Montana hills. One line that he knew he could not write would be something about Long Hair's long, flowing locks. For the summer of 1876, Custer had uncharacteristically cut his hair short.

On their second day out, Custer's troopers occasioned upon the site of the big encampment where Sitting Bull's Sun Dance had occurred a little more than a week earlier. It was ironic that soldiers would pass this exact location where Sitting Bull had his vision of wasichu destruction, and that Long Hair would be among them. Despite the troopers marching to the sprightly tune of "Garryowen," Custer had to know that seeing evidence of the Sun Dance amid such a large campsite meant that there were a lot of Lakota and Cheyenne people, and that their warriors were invigorated, as they always were following this ritual. Whether or not he interpreted it as a bad sign will never be known. Maybe he was just glad that he had picked up their trail.

By the night of June 24, the 7th Cavalry had followed the trail into the ridge that separates the valley of Rosebud Creek from the valley of the Little Bighorn. At about 9:00 p.m. that night, Custer's Crow scouts reported back that the Lakota and Cheyenne camp was close. Based on the freshness of the detritus, they confirmed that Custer's enemy was only about a day's ride ahead. Custer was excited by the prospect of attacking the huge concentration as soon as possible. He promptly ordered his men to saddle up for an all-night march, promising them that they could rest tomorrow night in preparation for a dawn attack on June 26.

As the troops moved out, the Crow scouts took Custer to an outcropping of high ground, known as the Crow's Nest, from which he could look down and see the Little Bighorn valley where the huge Indian encampment was. Custer himself reached the Crow's Nest at about 9 a.m. on the morning of June 25 and studied his objective. Because of the smoke from the campfires, it was impossible for anyone in the Crow's Nest to get an accurate estimate of the size of the camp.

As Custer gazed down into the valley, straining his eyes to see something useful, he wasn't thinking cautiously about the size of the force that he would soon face. Nor was he thinking about the exhaustion of his troops after marching all day and all night. Foremost on Custer's mind was the fear that the Cheyenne and Lakota would break camp on June 25 and that they would slip away before he had his chance for the decisive battle that he—and his tabloid readers—craved. Custer had learned that his scouts had seen and been seen by Lakota or Cheyenne scouts and a surprise attack was now out of the question. If they knew that the soldiers were nearby, the Cheyenne and Lakota would try to escape, and Custer certainly didn't want that to happen.

Worst of all, Custer probably feared that if he delayed his attack for another twenty-four hours—as he had planned—then Gibbon would be a day closer and Custer would have to share this victory with him. America's great Indian fighter would have to make a bold decision.

With all of these concerns—and lack of concern—guiding (or clouding) his judgment, Custer made his decision. He would attack at once. His plan for this operation was to divide the command into three attack columns and one support column. Custer would lead the eastern column himself, while Major Reno took the center and Captain Frederick Benteen took the west. Reno had yet to see action against the Indians, but Benteen had been with Custer since the Washita. While Custer rode along the ridge above the Indian encampment in order to attack the northern end, Reno would attack from the south and Benteen would go wide to cut off any Indians who tried to escape the hammer and anvil of Custer and Reno.

W HEN the Lakota and Cheyenne pulled up their stakes at their Rosebud campsite of the June 17 battle, they moved north, crossing their earlier trail, to a place known as the Greasy Grass. It is here that the Little Bighorn River meanders erratically beneath a long ridge. They camped on the opposite side of the river from the ridge, each band pitching their tipis in a place relative to their place in the procession when it was moving. The Cheyenne and the Oglala were in the lead, so they were camped farthest to the north, or downstream. The largest Lakota band, the Hunkpapa, traveled last in the procession, so they were at the opposite, or southern, end of the huge encampment. The other bands were in camp circles between.

Measuring three miles in length, the camp was probably the largest that had been seen on the Northern Plains in the memory of most people who were there. Exactly how many were present will never be known, and in fact it probably wasn't known at the time. The big camp was made up of not only people who had been camped on the Rosebud, but others who had joined the gathering in the previous few days.

Portrait of One Bull, Sitting Bull's nephew, when he was twenty-seven years old. (*National Anthropological Archives*)

Countless studies have looked at the many and varied estimates of the Lakota and Cheyenne population of this huge camp that day at Greasy Grass. Dr. John Stephens Gray, one of the most thorough scholars to have looked at the events, approached the problem scientifically. He narrowed his data down to the most logically supported probabilities. Among other sources, he consulted the recollection of Wooden Leg, a Cheyenne warrior who was there, and who recalled the relative sizes of the six primary camp circles, as well as the work of Dr. Charles Eastman, who was mostly Lakota himself and who interviewed many who had a firsthand experience with the camp. Stanley Vestal, who interviewed White Bull, One Bull, and others who were there, estimated between 1,800 and 2,300 lodges, but Gray is more conservative. Based on his research, Gray feels that the maximum number of lodges at Greasy Grass would have been 1,216, but he rounds his "best" estimate to 1,000. With an average of five to six people per lodge, there could have been up to 7,000 people there according to Gray—or more than 12,000 based on Vestal's highest number.

Of these, the Cheyenne continent would have totaled, at most by Gray's calculations, 196 lodges, but probably 120. The Oglala maximum would have been 264, with a "best" estimate of 240. For the Minneconjou and Sans Arc, the ceilings would have been 186 and 131, with 110 and 120 tipis considered probable round-number estimates. In the combined Brulé, Oohenonpa (Two-Kettle), and Sihasapa circle, 177 would have been the maximum, and 120 tipis the "best" estimate. The Hunkpapa numbers range slightly from a ceiling of 262 tipis to a "best" estimate of 260.

In any case, one of the latter was the lodge that Sitting Bull shared with his two wives, Four Robes and Seen by the Nation. His nephew, One Bull, was camped on one side with his new wife, and his aged mother was in the tipi next door to the other side.

Four Robes and Seen By the Nation had become Sitting Bull's wives in 1872, because at that time, the great itancan and wikasa wakan had no wife. His first, Light Hair, had died in 1857, while his third, Red Woman, had passed away in 1871. He had grown disgusted with his second wife, Snow on Her—who had told lies about Light Hair, and who constantly harassed Red Woman—and had divorced her. As his fourth wife, Sitting Bull picked Four Robes, the sister of Gray Eagle, another Hunkpapa itancan. She had an older, widowed sister, Seen by the Nation, who also needed a husband, so Sitting Bull wound up with two new wives.

The ages of the sisters are difficult to determine. Wide conflicts exist in the 1888–1891 annual tribal censuses, in which Seen by the Nation's age in 1876 was either twenty-eight or thirty-seven, and Four Robes was either twenty-six or thirty-two. The data provided to me by Ernie and Sonja LaPointe gives their birth years as 1846 and 1848, respectively.

Living with them were two boys who had become Sitting Bull's step-sons when he married the sisters. Some sources say that they were the sons of Seen by the Nation, but were claimed by her youngest sister because of a Lakota tradition. Sonja LaPointe told me that they were the sons of Four

Robes and a man named Bear Louse. The stepsons were called Little Soldier and Refuses Them, but much later Little Soldier was known by the Christian name Henry, and Refuses Them was possibly known by several other names, including John and Louis. Estimates of their ages in 1876 vary, but Little Soldier is generally believed to have been born in 1868. Based on his age as given in the 1891 Standing Rock Census, Refuses Them would have been born in 1866.

Sitting Bull's natural children sharing his lodge that day included two daughters by Snow on Her, Many Horses, aged thirteen, and Walks Looking, aged eight, as well as his son by Four Robes, Crow Foot. Various sources disagree on the question of whether Crow Foot was a three-year-old at the time or less than a year old. Definitely a newborn in June 1876 was Sitting Bull's daughter Standing Holy. According to the LaPointes, she had been born to Seen by the Nation either at the Greasy Grass or around the time of the Sun Dance about ten days earlier.

A pair of twins, Left Arrow in Him and Runs Away From, are sometimes listed as having been at the Greasy Grass, but the family tree assembled by the LaPointes lists their birth year as 1878.

Also sharing Sitting Bull's lodge were his sister, Good Feather; Gray Eagle, the brother of his wives; and his nephew, White Bull. From the number of people in Sitting Bull's tipi, one can easily see how Gray's average of five to six persons per lodge is not an exaggeration.

Sitting Bull had probably been at his lodge around noon on June 24 when he first learned from Lakota scouts of the approaching wasichu soldiers. This was several hours before Custer got his first information about the likely location of the Indian camp. According to the old Hunkpapa stories related many years later by old men who were there as young men, Sitting Bull painted himself and crossed the Little Bighorn River that evening. He climbed the ridge and made an offering to Wakantanka, asking that the tribe be protected. He looked out over the vast camp as the sunset faded and the stars began to appear in the sky. He probably thought about the grasshoppers falling upside-down.

The following day, July 25, Sitting Bull is said to have dressed simply, and not for battle. He wore a buckskin shirt, leggings, and moccasins. He braided his long hair and wore, as usual, a single feather. He carried only his curved knife. Some accounts say that he went to the Hunkpapa council tent and had learned that two young Hunkpapa had contact with the soldiers early that morning. They had found a wasichu pack containing some hardtack and were sampling it when the soldiers appeared. The troopers killed one of the boys, but the other had gotten away.

Sitting Bull may or may not have known that Reno was a short distance from the Hunkpapa circle, and closing quickly. While the hills and ridges in the area were open grassland, the valleys and river banks were heavily wooded with deciduous trees, so it was impossible for Reno to see into the village until he was almost upon it.

At 2:10 p.m. local time Reno's three companies crashed into the southern end of the huge village. The battle was on. As he and his men raced forward at full gallop and got their first clear view of the encampment, they neither knew nor cared that these were Sitting Bull's band of Hunkpapa. They only cared that these were the Indians they had been planning to attack for the past month.

In his October 1877 interview with Jerome Stillson of the *New York Herald*, his first ever with a wasichu newspaper, Sitting Bull gave his own account of where he was when Reno's troops first attacked the camp. "I was lying in my lodge," he said through an interpreter. "Some young men ran in to me and said: 'the Long Hair' is in the camp. Get up. They are firing into the camp.' I said all right. I jumped up and stepped out of my lodge."

The reference to Custer is probably that in hindsight, Sitting Bull had learned that Custer was in command of the attack, although the scouts who had observed the troops earlier in the week may have identified Custer. In his interview with Stillson, Sitting Bull went on to confirm the location of his tipi as being in the Hunkpapa circle at the southern end of the camp.

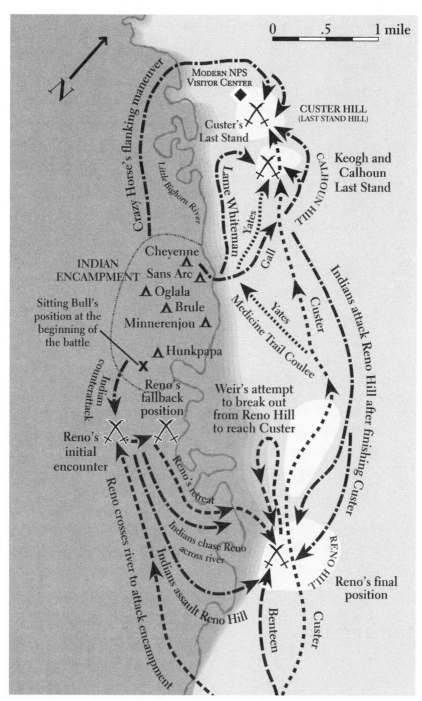

The battle of the Little Bighorn/Greasy Grass, June 25–26, 1876.

In the distance, he could see the dust of many mounted riders coming north at high speed. As he headed for his tipi to get his guns, warriors all around were mounting up to counterattack against the soldiers. The women and children were hurrying to get away, making a mass exodus toward the northern end of the camp. "The old men, the wives and the children were hurried away [to the other end of the camp]," Sitting Bull recalled. "Some of the Minneconjou women and children also left their lodges when the attack began."

Meanwhile, One Bull arrived with his horse and that of Sitting Bull. One Bull pulled his mother, Good Feather, aboard his horse and rode her to safety. Some accounts say that Sitting Bull did the same with his own mother, and others that he put her on a horse and sent her to a less exposed place within the camp.

Returning to the front lines within the Hunkpapa circle, One Bull went to join the fight, and Sitting Bull urged him on, saying "Fear nothing. Go straight in."

By all accounts, Sitting Bull then stood in the camp, shouting encouragement to the younger warriors who headed out to fight the wasichu soldiers who were a short distance away. Some accounts state that he did not enter the attack himself, although White Bull confirmed in his interviews with Stanley Vestal that he had seen his uncle firing at the troopers. Sitting Bull was armed with a Colt .44-caliber revolver and a .44-caliber Winchester Model 1873 carbine that day.

"We fell back, but it was not what warriors call a retreat," Sitting Bull said of the Hunkpapa's tactical withdrawal. "It was to gain time. It was the Long Hair who retreated. My people fought him in the brush." The reference to Custer is generic. It was actually Reno's contingent that had attacked the Hunkpapa. Custer was, at that moment, on the ridge high above the Greasy Grass, making his way north to attack the opposite end of the vast Indian encampment. When Stillson asked him whether the thought there were too many soldiers for the Hunkpapa to defend against,

Sitting Bull replied concisely: "Not at first; but by-and-by, yes. Afterwards, no."

As Sitting Bull watched, Reno's troopers themselves charged, withdrew, and then dismounted to take cover and shoot at the warriors from behind the cottonwood trees. It was cavalry doctrine at the time to dismount and form a skirmish line. Sitting Bull thought that this was a strange tactic, because by getting off their horses, they sacrificed all of their mobility. They were no longer fast, mobile cavalry, but fixed targets. The Lakota remained mounted and ran circles around the troopers.

Expecting to be chasing a scattering and fleeing enemy, Reno and his men were stunned to have faced a determined counterattack. As Sitting Bull watched, Reno ordered his men to halt. Sitting Bull thought that Reno should have continued his charge, but Reno feared being outflanked and cut off. As it turned out, his qualms were well founded. A group of Lakota attacked his left flank, and Reno ordered his men to move back upstream, where they could take cover in some trees near the river. As they formed their skirmish line, they were nearly overwhelmed. At about 2:55, realizing that their defensive position was untenable, Reno ordered the men to cross to the east side of the Little Bighorn and for higher ground on the ridge. With no organized covering fire, Reno's tactical withdrawal became a disorganized rout.

"They were brave men, [but] they were tired," Sitting Bull told Jerome Stillson when asked to characterize the 7th Cavalry troopers who fought with Reno.

> I tell no lies about dead men. These men who came with the Long Hair were as good men as ever fought. When they rode up, their horses were tired. When they got off from their horses, they could not stand firmly on their feet. They swayed to and fro—so my young men have told me—like the limbs of cypresses in a great wind. Some of them staggered under the weight of their own guns. But they began to fight at once; but by this time as I have said, our camp was aroused

and there were plenty of warriors to meet them. They fired with needle guns [single-shot Springfield carbines]. We replied with magazine guns—repeating rifles. It was so. Our young men rained lead across the river and drove the white braves back. . . and then they rushed across themselves. . . and then they found they had a good deal [more] to do.

Sitting Bull also compared the soldiers to the leaves of the quaking aspen tree common to eastern Montana, whose leaves quiver even in the slightest breeze. "Leaves that shake," Sitting Bull said. "Those were the Long Hair's soldiers. . . . They were tired. They were too tired."

Sitting Bull watched the standoff at the southern end of the camp until the soldiers were dislodged and sent scrambling across the Little Bighorn River and up the ridgeline beyond. They were overwhelmed by the Hunkpapa warriors and were in a full-fledged retreat up the slopes of what later became known as Reno Hill. Here, they would form a defensive perimeter. Panic had set in among the wasichu. They appeared to have abandoned all vestiges of unit cohesion and military discipline as each man struggled to save his own life. Both Wooden Leg and One Bull later recalled having personally killed several troopers as they fled.

As Sitting Bull surveyed the battlefield, strewn with Lakota and wasichu dead and wounded, he recognized Isaiah Dorman. An African American civilian employee of the U.S. Army at Fort Rice, where Sitting Bull had met him, he was married to a Hunkpapa woman. He had ridden with the 7th Cavalry in the campaign because he spoke Lakota and they needed interpreters. Badly wounded, he begged Sitting Bull not to count coup upon him. Sitting Bull knelt and gave the man a drink of water. A short time later, a group of Hunkpapa killed and mutilated Dorman.

Sitting Bull mounted up and rode north through the village. One Bull reported that his uncle crossed the river and rode into the hills, but did not participate in the battles that were raging all though the gullies on the side of the ridge. Sitting Bull was sure that the attack he had seen was not the only attack that the soldiers had planned.

Up on the ridge he could see another group of soldiers. They were mounted and also heading north as though looking for a place to attack the opposite end of the encampment. Sitting Bull could not know that the wasichu leading this contingent was Long Hair. Of course he wasn't wearing his hair long today, but it would have been hard to identify him at that distance even if it had been flowing long and yellow.

For more than a century, Sitting Bull and Custer have been identified with one another as the principal antagonists in one of history's most enduring dramas—but in fact, they never stood face to face. They never fought. This was the closest that the two men would ever come to one another—just a brief glimpse on a distant ridge.

As Sitting Bull was beginning his day within the Hunkpapa circle, Lieutenant Colonel George Armstrong Custer was a scant few miles away, consumed with fear. It was not the fear of battle, but the fear that his foe would elude him and cheat him out of the battle for which he longed. Shortly after eleven o'clock local time, Custer implemented his plan of attack, sending Reno up the center to strike first, while he went right and Benteen went left. The three attack columns advanced abreast into the valley, gradually extending their separation until they were no longer within sight of one another. As Reno had prepared for the initial strike, Custer and his column climbed the ridge along the east side of the valley.

At the time Reno attacked the village, his assault was clearly visible to Custer, high on the ridge and moving north. By now, the immense size of the village was also clear to Custer, who sent two messengers to find Benteen and ask him to come quickly—and to bring more ammunition. Custer was anxious to get into the fight, to take the pressure off Reno and to execute his own part of the battle plan.

As Reno's men were fighting for their lives amid the cottonwoods, Custer ordered Captain George Yates and his battalion to attack the

Indian camp by way of Medicine Tail Coulee, a broad, dry wash located approximately halfway between the point of Reno's attack and the northernmost part of the encampment. As Yates tried to cross the river, the Lakota and Cheyenne swept across, chasing the troopers back up the hill.

Referring to the attempted crossing at Medicine Tail Ford, Sitting Bull recalled, "That was where the big fight was fought. . . After the Long Hair was driven back to the bluffs [Reno Hill], he took this road [Medicine Tail Ford] and went down [to the river] to see if he could not beat us there."

By this description, Sitting Bull indicated that even a year later, he and the Lakota still believed that the camp had been attacked by a single contingent of soldiers. He assumed that the troops in Reno's attack retreated up the ridge, rode north and tried to attack a second time through Medicine Tail Coulee. In fact, Reno's battered force contingent retreated up the hill and stopped, while it was Custer's contingent, unseen by the Indians at the time of Reno's attack, who made the Medicine Tail Coulee assault after Reno had departed.

When Jerome Stillson asked him what happened in the "big fight," Sitting Bull replied simply: "Hell!"

"You mean, I suppose, a fierce battle?" Stillson asked.

"I mean a thousand devils."

"The village was by this time thoroughly aroused?"

"The wives were like birds; the bullets were like humming bees."

Custer forgot any further notion of offensive action and began looking to the high ground for a defensive position. Captain Myles Keogh, forming Custer's rear guard, took up a position north of Medicine Tail Coulee until Yates retreated. They probably then joined forces and moved uphill and farther north toward Custer, who had formed a defensive position on a knob of high ground that has been known ever since as Custer Hill—or Last Stand Hill. Indeed, Custer made his "last stand" in this place, with his brother Tom at his side, surrounded mainly by the men of Companies E and F, as the regimental headquarters flag fluttered above.

When asked whether he had witnessed the Custer Hill fight, Sitting Bull told Jerome Stillson that he had not, but that he had "heard of it from the warriors."

The soldiers still had some fight left in them. Sitting Bull went on to say that from his vantage point in the camp, he had watched the Cheyenne and Lakota attempt a frontal assault, "but afterward they found it better to try and get around him. They formed themselves on all sides of him except just at his back."

He continued, referring to his own experience in the Reno fight and what the warriors said of the Custer Hill action, to reflect upon how very tired the troopers were. "The trouble was with the soldiers. They were so exhausted and their horses bothered them so much that they could not take good aim. Some of their horses broke away from them and left them to stand and drop and die. When the Long Hair, the General, found that he was so outnumbered and threatened on his flanks, he took the best course he could have taken. The bugle blew. It was an order to fall back [to the defensive position atop Custer Hill]. All the men fell back fighting and dropping. They could not fire fast enough, though. But from our side it was so. . . . They could not stand up under such a fire."

Sitting Bull went on to tell Stillson, "They kept in pretty good order. Some great chief must have commanded them all the while. They would fall back across a coulee and make a fresh stand beyond on higher ground. . . . Every man [keep on fighting until the last], so far as my people could see. There were no cowards on either side." In his interview with Stillson, Sitting Bull was shown a map of the battlefield in which he confirmed the location of the "higher ground" as being Custer Hill.

As the survivors of Reno's command climbed atop the bluff now known as Reno Hill and began desperately to build a defensive position, Benteen got Custer's message to hurry to his aid. He reached Reno's position a half hour later. Major Reno ordered Captain Benteen to halt and assist him, and Benteen complied, rather than following Custer's orders and pressing forward. By now, however, the bulk of the Lakota were riding north to take part in the Custer Hill fight. Benteen took a contingent in that direction himself, but he was turned back before he had gone far enough to get a good view of Custer Hill.

"I have understood that there were a great many brave men in that fight," Sitting Bull said of the final moments on Custer Hill.

> And that from time to time, while it was going on, they were shot down like pigs. They could not help themselves. One by one the offi-cers fell. I believe the Long Hair rode across once from this place [where Tom Custer's company was wiped out] to this place up here [Custer Hill], but I am not sure about this. Any way it was said that up there where the last fight took place, where the last stand was made, the Long Hair stood like a sheaf of corn with all the ears fall-en around him. . . . He killed a man when he fell. He laughed . . . he laughed [and] he fired his last shot. . . . He rose up on his hands and tried another shot, but his pistol would not go off.

From the Greasy Grass, Sitting Bull watched the wasichu soldiers on the ridge. In his vision, he had seen many soldiers falling into the camp like grasshoppers. Now he was watching it actually happen. The troopers of Yates's command probably looked like they were falling as they swept down Medicine Tail Coulee toward the camp. They certainly looked like they were falling as Lakota warriors—including Sitting Bull's old friend Gall—attacked, shot, lanced, and kicked or threw them off their horses across the Little Bighorn. They were upside-down in the vision. They were upside-down now. Gall, especially, had reason to be angry. Some of the 7th Cavalry's Arikara scouts had just murdered his two wives and three children as they attacked the Hunkpapa camp.

Having routed Reno, Gall led his Hunkpapa warriors north through the village, across the Little Bighorn at Medicine Tail Ford and up onto the ridge through Medicine Tail Coulee. White Bull later recalled being part of this charge. Though he had a horse shot out from under him,

White Bull counted coup twice in hand-to-hand combat.

Near the top of the ridge, the Lakota clashed with Keogh's men. Keogh, a former Irish soldier of fortune and one-time papal guard, probably fought back fiercely. Meanwhile, a Cheyenne force led by Lame White Man blunted an attempt by Tom Custer's company to get off the ridge. Gall and Lame White Man then swept the ridge with a frontal assault that washed over the 7th Cavalry like a tidal wave.

The final and decisive blow was struck by Crazy Horse. He led the Oglala warriors in a bold encirclement from the north that outflanked Custer and his surviving troops on Custer Hill. It is not impossible—

Gall drove Reno's force across the river and to the bluffs. "It was like chasing buffalo," said Gall, "a great chase." (*National Archives*)

although it would be an improbable coincidence—that his was the last Indian face into which had stared the eyes of the man anointed by the tabloids as America's Great Indian Fighter. Also improbable is the myth—often reported in the nineteenth century—that Custer was the last man standing. Indian accounts, as well as recent archaeological evidence, indicates that after Custer and many others died, a number of Custer Hill survivors scattered, running for their lives in the draws and coulees. None of them made it.

Sitting Bull apparently did not visit Custer Hill that day, but rather rode through the camp urging people to prepare to break camp. "I started down to tell the women to strike the lodges," he explained. "I was then on my way up to the [southern] end of the camp, where the first attack was made on us. But before I reached that end of the camp where the Minneconjou and Hunkpapa wives and children were and where some of the other wives—Cheyenne and Oglala—had gone, I was overtaken by one of the young warriors, who had just come down from the fight. He called out to me. He said: 'No use to leave camp; every white man is killed.' So I stopped and went no further. I turned back, and by and by I met the warriors returning."

No wasichu lived to tell what happened on Custer Hill. As Sitting Bull later asked rhetorically: "Is there an American wife who has a husband left? Were there any Americans left to tell the story of that day? No."

White Bull recalled being on the hill as the battle ended and seeing Custer's body lying naked. He didn't know who it was, but a relative of his called Bad Soup pointed out that it was Custer. Bad Soup had been to Fort Lincoln and had seen him there. "I have talked with my people," Sitting Bull said. "I cannot find one who saw the Long Hair until just before he died. He did not wear his long hair as he used to wear it. . . . It was short, but it was of the color of the grass when the frost comes."

The prevailing story is that Custer, who was shot in the left temple and the left breast, was stripped but not, for some reason, mutilated. "My people did not want his scalp," Sitting Bull told Jerome Stillson. "I have said; he was a great chief."

Myles Keogh was also reported to have escaped mutilation, but nearly every other solder was scalped and/or mutilated—including Tom Custer. An oft-repeated tale relates that the Hunkpapa warrior Rain in the Face had once been insulted by Tom Custer, and that he told Custer he would one day cut out his heart and eat it. This may or may not have happened, but it is a fact that the two were both at the Battle of the Little Bighorn. Tom Custer died and was badly disfigured. Rain in the Face lived until 1905, reportedly taking credit for shooting Tom Custer, but always denying that he had eaten his heart.

Though Custer's 210-man command was a total loss, nearly 350 of the Reno and Benteen contingents had survived and were holed up about four miles to the south on Reno Hill. Custer Hill was out of their view, but they

Red Horse's drawing of dead cavalry and Indians at the Battle of Little Bighorn.
(*Manuscript 2367A 1881 National Anthropological Archives*)

recalled hearing the guns there fall silent around 4:30 local time. The warriors tormented and fired on Reno and Benteen through the night, but
made no full-scale attack. Dismissing the troops huddling on Reno Hill,
Sitting Bull recalled, "There were only a few soldiers there in those
entrenchments, and we knew they wouldn't dare to come out."

On the morning of June 26, the warriors picked up the tempo of the
harassment, but made no attempt to overwhelm the troopers. White Bull
took part in this action, but Sitting Bull did not. By the afternoon, he was
telling people that the soldiers should not be killed. They should be
allowed to live so that they could testify to all the wasichu of the power of
the Lakota and Cheyenne.

Late in the afternoon, the thirsty and exhausted wasichu atop Reno
Hill watched as the Cheyenne and Lakota packed their belongings, took
down their lodges and left the valley of the Greasy Grass. Four days later,
they celebrated their victory as the Gibbon and Terry columns arrived at

the battle site and began burying the bloating dead and assessing the enormity of the debacle.

As he rode away that summer day, Sitting Bull was troubled. He had been cautioned in his vision that the people should not mutilate and steal from the dead wasichu. Sitting Bull reportedly believed that the curse that would befall the Lakota for stealing from the wasichu at the Greasy Grass was that they would be addicted forever with a need for wasichu things.

Despite the victory, he now feared that time was running out—for the Lakota.

Fort Walsh in 1878. (*National Archives of Canada*)

4

THE FUGITIVE

THE BATTLE OF THE LITTLE BIGHORN QUICKLY ACHIEVED epic status as newspapers began referring to it as the "Thermopylae of the Plains." At Thermopylae in Greece, in 480 B.C., a Greek contingent held off a Persian army under Xerxes that outnumbered them by at least three to one. Ever since, the term "Thermopylae" has been used to refer to heroic opposition to much larger foe. The Little Bighorn, often under the name "Custer's Last Stand," would also achieve metaphor status.

The violent death of America's Great Indian Fighter ignited a media firestorm in the East within days. The newspapers who had created the myth of Custer as hero now worked overtime to craft the myth of Custer as martyr. There were a lot of myths to come out of the Battle of the Little Bighorn. It was widely rumored that Sitting Bull had personally killed Custer. When Jerome Stillson of the *New York Herald* asked Sitting Bull whether he had ever even met Custer, he replied: "No, [but] many of the chiefs knew him. He was a great warrior. He was a mighty chief." Even Sitting Bull had come to believe the Custer myth.

In the months after the battle, Sitting Bull was also widely reported by the wasichu media to have been in overall command of the Cheyenne and Lakota at the Little Bighorn. This long perpetuated myth continues to be repeated even today.

Was Sitting Bull in the wrong place at the wrong time?

A few years earlier, he had been virtually unknown outside this remote corner of the continent—which was the only corner of the continent that he cared about. By the summer of 1876, however, the same media that had made Custer a hero was starting to notice Sitting Bull. Every story that has a hero—especially a martyred hero—needs a villain. What better villain than the "great high chieftain of the savage Sioux"? Sitting Bull was in the wrong place at the wrong time, cast in a role that he neither deserved nor fit.

Sitting Bull, of course, was unaware how his name was being distorted on wasichu lips in the faraway East. He and his people just wanted to hunt buffalo and be left alone. However, as had been the case for more than a decade, the wasichu were crowding and pushing the Lakota more and more toward the point where neither of these things would be possible.

The number of dead at the Little Bighorn, while the equivalent of a few minutes fighting at Antietam or Gettysburg, was staggering for an Indian Wars engagement. Those east of the Mississippi who thought of Indians as an anachronism from a quaint and distant bygone era were stunned. How could this have happened? A groundswell of indignation over the perception that blood-thirsty, stone-age savages had butchered young American soldiers led to cries that Custer must be avenged.

There would be no hot pursuit of the Lakota and Cheyenne victors at the Greasy Grass. It would be an exaggeration to say that the wasichu were paralyzed with fear, but it would not be entirely untrue. Terry and Gibbon were still in the Powder River Country with their commands intact— except for the 7th Cavalry, of course—but they were numbed by what they had seen on the Little Bighorn. Crook, who did not know of the battle until July 10, was also stunned when he found out. Nobody really wanted to make a move until reinforcements arrived.

General Phil Sheridan quickly transferred the 5th Cavalry (then based in Kansas but operating out of Fort Laramie) to Crook's command, and by August 2, Terry had received two regiments of the reinforcements that he had requested. These included the 5th Infantry Regiment, led by the ambitious young Colonel Nelson Miles, who would play a much bigger role in the next phase of Sitting Bull's life than Custer had in the previous one.

General Nelson A. Miles. (*National Anthropological Archives*)

By the second week in August, nearly two months after the Lakota and Cheyenne had slipped away, Crook and Terry were on their trail. Rather, they were on their many, confusing trails. Operating independently, the two generals picked up and tried to follow the numerous Indian trails that criss-crossed the Powder River Country, finding that virtually all of them were at least a month old. There had been no hot pursuit, and there was barely a cold pursuit. The only great columns of warriors that Crook and Terry happened upon were those of one another!

Meanwhile, the last great concentration of Indians riding free on the Great Plains in the nineteenth century had broken up. Still largely intact since the Greasy Grass, they camped as a group for the last time near the mouth of the Powder River on August 9. From there, they went their separate ways. The Cheyenne went south, ascending the Powder River again. Crazy Horse and the Oglala returned toward the Black Hills, while Long Dog's Hunkpapa crossed the Yellowstone River at Glendive Creek and rode due north. Smaller bands scattered elsewhere. Sitting Bull's Hunkpapa moved northeast into Dakota Territory.

Military historians who have later tried to categorize the great concentration of 1876 as a mobile military command have questioned why so powerful a force would simple dissolve itself into smaller units and go off independently in different directions. Had they stayed together, they could have, as a "grand army," continued to fight and win against the wasichu soldiers. In fact, their actions can be understood by the fact that they did not consider themselves as a mobile military force, but rather a nomadic culture. They were just on the move as nomadic cultures have always been, and within nomadic cultures, groups frequently camp together one day and go their separate ways the next.

The combined Crook and Terry task force, numbering nearly 4,000 tired and dispirited troopers, reached the mouth of the Powder River a week after the Indians had dispersed. The U.S. Army had failed with a bang in June, and it had failed again with a whimper in August.

As the season was coming to an end, Sheridan ordered Terry to establish posts at the mouths of the Tongue River and Glendive Creek, and to leave troops on the Yellowstone River through the winter. Crook, meanwhile, took his column east toward the Black Hills. Though his rations were dangerously low, Crook had an almost quixotic determination to catch the enemy. The Battle of the Rosebud had not been the usually savvy old warrior's finest hour, but he was stooping to a new low.

Still working as a guide for Crook through this phase of the campaign was Sitting Bull's turncoat adopted brother, Frank Grouard. By now, Sitting Bull knew that Grouard had become his enemy and vowed to kill him if he ever caught him. However, the slippery Grouard would never let that happen. He would continue to offer his services to the U.S. Army as a scout until after Sitting Bull's death, but the two men would never meet again.

In 1894, Joe De Barthe published his glowing biography, *The Life and Adventures of Frank Grouard, Chief of Scouts, U.S.A.*, which served to assure Grouard's place in the history of the Old West. First published by the Combe Printing Company of St. Joseph, Missouri, the book has been widely reprinted since. In the book, the man whom Sitting Bull would have killed if he'd had the chance spoke often of him. Grouard did say, "There was nothing of the traitor about the man. . . . He did not hide his enmity." Sitting Bull, Grouard confirmed, told it like it was.

Grouard was also effusive in his praise, recounting Sitting Bull's sixty-three coups and noting, "No man in the Sioux nation was braver than Sitting Bull."

For a month after leaving the valley of the Yellowstone, Crook led his men on what came to be known as the "Starvation March." On September 8, as the soldiers were dining on the meat of their own horses, Crook decided to send Captain Anson Mills—the same man who he sent chasing wild geese on the Rosebud—into the Black Hills mining town of Deadwood to purchase food for the starving soldiers.

What happened the next day was a fitting end to the quirky summer campaign. A U.S. Army task force of unprecedented size had pursued an Indian congregation of unprecedented size without making contact. Now, at a place called Slim Buttes in western Dakota Territory, a fraction of a contingent of one side would meet a fraction of a contingent from the other side in the first and only battle of the campaign since the Little Bighorn.

Mills and his small detachment of supply shoppers stumbled across the Lakota encampment of American Horse—also known as Iron Shield. Bullets flew, and just as things started to get interesting, Crook arrived from one side and Crazy Horse—with more Lakota—from the other. It was almost like a replay of the Rosebud fight, although far less intense. The battle continued through the night and into the following day, but gradually Crook disengaged his hungry fighters in order to resume the search for food.

Sitting Bull and his band were camped in his old stomping grounds in the Grand River drainage when he received word that the Battle of Slim

Buttes was in progress. He led a contingent to the scene, but arrived as the fighting was winding down. An estimated fifteen Oglala died that day, including American Horse, who had been mortally wounded. Three of Crook's starving men were killed in action. Four days later, the soldiers linked up with a supply train and ate heartily at last.

As Crook limped back toward Fort Laramie, Crazy Horse and the Oglala returned to the Powder River Country, while Sitting Bull, Gall, and their Hunkpapa following headed for the Yellowstone to spend the winter hunting and trying to be left alone.

When Sitting Bull had signed the Fort Laramie Treaty in 1868, he took the wasichu at their word that the Powder River Country and the Black Hills would be Indian land forever. As he rode toward the Yellowstone that winter, the "unceded lands" in the Powder were being unilaterally "ceded," and the Black Hills were legally opened to wasichu settlement. Towns such as Deadwood, which were illegal under the treaty, had been legalized. The tide of wasichu that had seemed to be ebbing eight winters earlier was running like a tidal wave.

Just as Sitting Bull's vision of the soldiers falling down like grasshoppers had come to pass, so too would his fear that the Lakota would soon become inextricably bound to the largesse of the wasichu. In the wake of the Little Bighorn, the wasichu were getting tough. Sitting Bull had told the people to fear what might happen at the agencies and the reservations. Now the soldiers were going onto the agencies and the reservations and taking away the peoples' weapons and their horses so they could not become winter roamers. They also could not hunt without guns and horses. Soon, most of the demoralized Lakota would be reduced to eating the wasichu handouts.

Not so Sitting Bull, at least for the moment. As he went into the vast area of eastern Montana in the early winter of 1875, it was still unceded

Indian land. A year later, however, the U.S. Army was constructing out-posts along the Yellowstone River that would be permanently manned by troops. In this country and during this winter, Sitting Bull would meet Bear Coat Miles.

Sitting Bull had many opponents—from Crow to wasichu—but prob-ably only one true antagonist on the field of battle. Popular legend, although not historical fact, casts Custer as Sitting Bull's signature oppo-nent. The two never met and never did battle, though they were once on the same battlefield. The man whom historic reality casts opposite Sitting Bull is Colonel Nelson Appleton Miles. Sitting Bull would also have a true friend among wasichu officials—Major James Walsh—but that story would unfold the following year in the Grandmother's Country.

Born in Westminster, Massachusetts, on August 8, 1839, Miles was four months older than Custer. Unlike Custer, Crook and most of the com-manders who saw service in the Indian Wars, Miles was part of a new gen-eration of senior officers who had risen through the ranks during the Civil War, rather than beginning his career with a West Point commission. He had led troops at Antietam and Fredericksburg, and had earned a Medal of Honor for his heroism at Chancellorsville in 1863. As was the case with Custer, Miles ended the war as a brevet major general.

After the war, Miles became a colonel in the regular army and was assigned to command the 5th Infantry Regiment in the wars on the south-ern Plains against the Kiowa and Comanche. In this role, he became one of the stars in the U.S. Army's victory over the Indians in the Red River War in 1874. In the meantime, in 1868, Miles had married Mary Hoyt Sherman, the niece of both Ohio Senator John Sherman and Commanding General William Tecumseh Sherman. Eventually, Miles himself would hold the post of Commanding General of the U.S. Army (1895–1903).

As Sitting Bull and the Lakota were searching for buffalo in the Yellowstone Valley in early October, they first caught sight of the soldiers.

Johnny Brughière. (*National Archives*)

Miles and his 5th Infantry troopers—as well as Lieutenant Colonel Elwell Otis and the 22nd Infantry Regiment—were completing work on fortifications at the places where the Tongue River and Glendive Creek flow into the Yellowstone.

Twice, the Lakota attacked the Army's supply trains as they made their way toward the Tongue from Glendive Creek, the latter being the uppermost place on the Yellowstone that could be served by a steamboat in the low water of autumn. In the first attack, they managed to turn back the wagons, but in the second, the soldiers kept them at bay. Sitting Bull was not involved personally, but White Bull was hit in the left arm, breaking his humerus.

Sitting Bull was angry to find the wasichu running wagon trains through the country where he had come to hunt and be left alone. He wanted to send a message to the wasichu, and he decided to do it in their own language. It so happened that he had in his camp a man who could read and write the wasichu language. This man was the enigmatic Johnny Brughière (also spelled Bruguier), the son of a wasichu father and a Hunkpapa mother, who knew both languages. A sometime cowboy and sometimes agency interpreter, he was, like Frank Grouard, a member of that class of colorful drifters with a dubious past whose tales punctuate the grand story of the Old West.

Johnny Brughière was on the run from the wasichu lawmen when he crossed paths with Sitting Bull during the late summer of 1876. He had killed a man in a bar fight at the Standing Rock Agency and was wanted for murder when he sought sanctuary with the Hunkpapa. Sitting Bull took in this man whom the Lakota called "Big Leggings" because of his cowboy-style chaps.

As with Grouard, Sitting Bull found Brughière's ability to communicate in English to be useful. With the fugitive cowboy taking dictation, Sitting Bull composed a memo to the soldiers. This was attached to a sharp stake and dramatically planted in the wagon road where the wasichu would see it. Partly an ultimatum, and partly a dear friend letter, the memo read:

> I want to know what you are doing on this road. You scare all the buffalo away. I want to hunt in this place. I want you to turn back from here. If you don't, I will fight you again. I want you to leave what you have got here, and turn back from here.
>
> I am your friend, Sitting Bull.
>
> I mean all the rations you have got and some powder. Wish you would write as soon as you can.

In an exchange of communications with Otis, the standoff went from the officer saying that he was prepared to fight, to his agreeing to leave some bacon and other provisions along the trail for the Lakota to pick up. This transaction accomplished, Sitting Bull and the Lakota crossed the Yellowstone and headed north to hunt buffalo. The soldiers had scared away the herds south of the Yellowstone.

Otis had been willing to buy off the Lakota and keep going, but Nelson Miles was determined to find Sitting Bull. On October 20, after two days on the Lakota trail, Miles and his 449 officers and men located them on Cedar Creek about twenty miles north of the Yellowstone. Sitting Bull said that he wanted to talk to the 5th Infantry commander, whom the Lakota had dubbed "Bear Coat" because of his trademark heavy, bear-trimmed overcoat. That day, the two leaders were dressed more or less alike, as Sitting Bull wore his buffalo robe.

With Johnny Brughière translating, the two antagonists talked and talked. After all of the searching and campaigning that had taken place since the summer, the U.S. Army had finally found Sitting Bull, their

Indian "archvillain." After all that, it was a strange scene to have Miles and Sitting Bull sitting together and facing one another, throwing nothing more jagged than barbed comments.

Miles told Sitting Bull that it was inevitable that he would end up on a reservation, and that to do so sooner rather than later would save everyone a lot of trouble. Miles went so far as to promise Sitting Bull his own agency, and asked him where he would like it to be. According to Lakota witnesses later interviewed by Stanley Vestal, the old itancan actually seemed to consider going back to Dakota Territory and having an agency. Sitting Bull at one point told Bear Coat that "When I have made my hunt and when I think I have enough meat to carry me through, I will go straight back to the Black Hills and winter there. . . . In the Black Hills where Cottonwood Creek flows into the Spearfish [Creek] is a place we call the Water Hole. That is the place. Other Indians will of course pick out their own campgrounds, and where it is suitable to have an agency; we will all live in the Black Hills."

Miles and Sitting Bull seemed to be getting along amazingly well. They discussed hunting together north of the Yellowstone, and after that, going to the Black Hills. Miles reportedly said, "I'll come back with you. After that we'll go straight to the mouth of the Tongue. I'll get straightened out there, and then we'll go to the Black Hills, together."

The following day, October 21, as the parlay dragged on, their words turned contentious. When Miles demanded the mules that the Lakota stole from the Army wagon trains, Sitting Bull wryly demanded the buffalo that the soldiers had scared away.

The day before, Miles had chatted cordially with Sitting Bull about the Black Hills, and about Sitting Bull's dreams of happily living there in perpetuity. Miles should have known better. He knew full well that the Grandfather had already decided to turn the Black Hills over to wasichu settlement. In his State of the Union speech on December 5, just six weeks after Sitting Bull and Miles met, President Grant would call on

Congress to approve "ceding the Black Hills and approaches to settlement by citizens." It would become law in February 1877.

Though he probably should have seen it coming, Sitting Bull was not yet aware of this. But Miles was. He had listened to the musings of his opposite number and had cheerfully encouraged him. Overnight, however, Miles had apparently realized that he was only kidding himself—and Sitting Bull. The carrot of congeniality was replaced by the stick of pragmatism. Miles finally got down to business, telling it as it was. He insisted that Sitting Bull turn around and take his band of Lakota back to Dakota Territory. Miles ordered him to return to the Standing Rock Agency, near his birthplace west of the Missouri River, and surrender to the Grandfather's largesse. It was time, Miles insisted, that Sitting Bull accept a future as an "agency Indian."

Sitting Bull no doubt said, "Hiya-hansni" (absolutely not!). It is widely reported that it was during this discussion that Sitting Bull told Bear Coat that God had made him an Indian, not an *agency* Indian, and that he would die before he became an agency Indian. The conference broke up when Sitting Bull rose to his feet and walked out. The Lakota were already preparing to move camp when barbs turned into bullets.

The first shots of the Battle of Cedar Creek were fired by the 5th Infantry as the Lakota began riding away. With Miles in pursuit and the running battle in motion, Sitting Bull led his people downstream on Bad Route Creek to the Yellowstone, which they crossed on October 24. By this time, Bear Coat had finally broken off the chase. Lakota casualties were negligible, but they had been forced to abandon a large stockpile of supplies at Cedar Creek. As the first dry flakes of winter snow began to fall, Sitting Bull, Gall and the Hunkpapa went south into the Powder River Country to hunt.

THE cycle had come around again to the beginning of winter. As had happened every winter since the Fort Laramie Treaty had created the Great Sioux Reservation in 1868, the summer roamers came in from the Northern Plains to spend the winter at the agencies. The winter roamers, who were actually "all-year roamers," although the U.S. government did not use that term in its classification system, continued to roam—as people had done on the Northern Plains for centuries before the wasichu came.

In past years, ever since there had been two kinds of "roamers," there was a growing sense among all the Lakota that they were surrounded by wasichu, but those who roamed the open land of eastern Montana did so knowing that at least there, they were unlikely to cross paths with wasichu. The U.S. Army had generally avoided winter campaigns, especially on the Northern Plains. In March 1876, Crook came, got his nose bloodied, and went away. In the winter of 1876–1877, in the person of the tenacious Bear Coat Miles, the U.S. Army had come to stay all winter. The idea was to put the Indians on the run and keep them on the run.

Sitting Bull's dream of more or less peacefully not coexisting with the wasichu ended with the Battle of the Little Bighorn.

One of the most determined commanders that the Army had seen in the West in some time, Bear Coat Miles was able to keep up the relentless pressure on the Cheyenne and the Lakota throughout the winter because of the forts that had been established along the Yellowstone River.

It had become axiomatic since the Civil War that cavalry was better suited for such a task than infantry, but Miles disproved the axiom that winter. He was an infantry commander and he lived by an infantry doctrine. In his campaign, Miles demonstrated that infantry could be effective in operations against the Indians on the Plains. The U.S. Army's cavalry doctrine, which called for mounted troopers to dismount and form a skirmish line in a fight, erased the mobility advantage of having them on horses. Infantry could just as easily form a skirmish line—and every fifth man wasn't cancelled out by his having to hold the horses.

General Nelson A. Miles, center, in his trademark bearskin coat photographed on January 2, 1877, during his search for Crazy Horse's camp. (*National Archives*)

The cavalry could obviously cover more distance than infantry, but when it came to a fight—and after all, that was why the troops were there—Miles believed that his foot soldiers had an advantage over their mounted brothers.

Between Bear Coat's campaigning and the weather, the Lakota would have a hard winter. Sitting Bull went into the Powder River Country, then crossed back over the Yellowstone and went north toward the Missouri River. While Sitting Bull camped on Big Dry Creek, a tributary of the Missouri, many other people headed east toward the Great Sioux Reservation. By the end of October, his band numbered just thirty lodges, compared to around 260 in the Hunkpapa circle four months earlier at the Greasy Grass. The Minneconjou and Sans Arc who had ridden with Sitting Bull approached Bear Coat less than a week after Cedar Creek, and voluntarily asked to go to reservation. They went to the agency at Fort Peck on the Missouri to get food, but when some soldiers—bringing supplies for Miles—arrived, they got scared and left. Bear Coat traveled north from the Yellowstone to the Missouri, arriving at Fort Peck in mid-November.

Meanwhile to the south, General George Crook was in action in the same area where his winter campaign had run into trouble the previous March. Then, he had depended on the hapless Colonel Joseph Reynolds to lead the charge. This year, as Crook again headed north through the snow into the Powder River Country, his spearhead would be the energetic young Colonel Ranald Slidell Mackenzie.

About a year younger that Custer and Miles, Mackenzie had graduated from West Point in 1862 and had led troops at Second Bull Run, Antietam, and Gettysburg. After the war, he served as a regimental commander in the Apache Wars and alongside Miles in the Red River War. Like Miles, he was one of a new breed of dynamic officers that Sheridan had sent to command troops on the Northern Plains after the Little Bighorn.

Crook hoped to find Crazy Horse, who was wintering in the Powder River Country near where he had beaten Crook in June, but instead, his command discovered the large Cheyenne bands consisting of the followers of Little Wolf and Dull Knife, as they camped on the Red Fork of the Powder River. Mackenzie led a dawn attack on November 25, killing as many as forty Cheyenne while forcing the others to flee. As they prepared to torch the abandoned tipis and supplies, Mackenzie's men found a large number of items, including a flag bearing 7th Cavalry insignia, that had obviously been looted from the Little Bighorn battlefield exactly five months earlier.

As Crook and Mackenzie returned to winter quarters, Bear Coat Miles remained in action, still pursuing the Lakota and Cheyenne. He even succeeded in rounding up a number of smaller bands. At one point, Dull Knife himself, as well as several Lakota itancan, made surrender overtures to Miles. However, on December 16, as a group of itancan were coming to parley with Miles, some of Bear Coat's Crow scouts—lifelong enemies of the Lakota—attacked them. The survivors later joined forces with Crazy Horse.

By now, Bear Coat had achieved a major intelligence coup, when Johnny Brughière—like the shifty Grouard before him—switched sides. Once part of Sitting Bull's inner circle, he now provided Miles with inside information from the Hunkpapa itancan's own tent. Backed by this intelligence, Miles sent three companies of the 5th Infantry Regiment under Lieutenant Frank Baldwin to attack Sitting Bull. On December 7, Baldwin passed near the Hunkpapa camp on the Milk River, but mistook Hunkpapa sentries for his own scouts. Alerted to Baldwin's presence, Sitting Bull slipped his people across the frozen Missouri.

Ranald Slidell Mackenzie. (*Library of Congress*)

The continuous winter patrolling by Miles and his various units, such as Baldwin's battalion, served to keep the Lakota on edge, and this had the consequence of increasing Sitting Bull's appeal. Smaller bands, who were more fearful of the wasichu soldiers than they were hungry for wasichu supplies, sought out and joined Sitting Bull for mutual protection. In the six weeks following its nadir at the end of October, Sitting Bull's contingent had grown fourfold to 122 lodges.

Unlike the concentration of numbers at the Greasy Grass, however, these numbers did not constitute a critical mass that would benefit the Lakota. Rather, they included a large number of women and children that would compromise the fighting effectiveness of the warriors and the speed with which the Indians could move and maneuver. The Indians, however, had horses whereas the infantrymen were on foot.

While Miles probably made the best use of infantry in successful campaigning of any U.S. Army commander in the Indian Wars, there were times where the "walking soldiers" (as the Lakota called them) were at a disadvantage. Such was the case when it came to pursuit of an escaping foe. On December 18, Baldwin finally caught them camped on Ash Creek and attacked. Using improvised artillery, Baldwin created panic, but caused only one fatality—and the Indians got away.

Although he and his people managed to escape from Ash Creek relatively unscathed, the disaster for Sitting Bull was that when the Lakota fled, they abandoned mountains of dried meat, buffalo hides, and other provisions. The loss of all these supplies, vital for coping with the cold months ahead, created a terrible hardship for the Lakota as they headed south again to look for Crazy Horse.

After Christmas, Bear Coat Miles also turned his attention south into the Powder River Country. On January 7, he was campaigning with five companies of the 5th Infantry, plus two of the 22nd Infantry and an artillery detachment, when they turned the tables on an abortive Cheyenne ambush attempt near Deer Creek. Miles took a number of his opponents captive, and the Cheyenne were anxious to take them back. At this point, Crazy Horse and the Oglala joined the fray. The following day, as Bear Coat took up a defensive position near Wolf Mountain, a huge blizzard blew in, making Crazy Horse's objective difficult. This, combined with Beat Coat's artillery, finally made his task impossible, and he withdrew.

About a week after the Wolf Mountain fight, Sitting Bull found Crazy Horse. According to interviews with Eagle Shield, Fool Bear, Important Man, and Swelled Face that are preserved in the National Archives, this last great rendezvous between the two greatest itancan of the Plains took place on January 15, 1877, on Prairie Dog Creek in the headwaters of the Tongue River. Black Shield and Lame Deer of the Minneconjou were also there, as were Red Bear and Spotted Eagle of the Sans Arc and Black Moccasin of the Cheyenne.

Many of the people who attended this summit conference wanted to surrender to the wasichu sooner rather than later. Their people were tired and hungry, and this seemed like a good idea. Others did not want to surrender their guns and their horses to the wasichu. Of these who still refused to surrender to agency life, the Oglala and Cheyenne went west to hunt, and Sitting Bull led the Hunkpapa north.

It had been a very hard winter because of Bear Coat. The tenacious Miles had managed to do what was expected of him. He had kept both Sitting Bull and Crazy Horse on the run, but soon the running would be over.

As Sitting Bull turned north out of the Powder River Country for the last time in February 1877, Crazy Horse went south. On May 6, the Oglala itancan did the unthinkable: he surrendered with nearly nine hundred people at Fort Robinson in Nebraska, the military post adjacent to the Red Cloud Agency.

In late April, Red Cloud himself had gone to meet with Crazy Horse and had conveyed the notion that Crook would consider designating an agency for Crazy Horse, not in Dakota Territory with the others, but in the Powder River Country. Red Cloud was, like Crazy Horse, a respected Oglala leader, and he had once been—before the ascendancy of Sitting Bull—the most respected of all Lakota leaders. The people who traveled with Crazy Horse were hungry, and they were running short of ammunition with which to hunt and to continue the armed struggle against the U.S. Army. Red Cloud had counseled the younger man to come in, and Crazy Horse had finally acquiesced. He remained at a camp near the agency through the summer, waiting for the agency that never materialized.

Lame Deer remained at large, but not for long. On May 7, the day after Crazy Horse surrendered, at a side stream of the Rosebud called Little Muddy Creek, Bear Coat Miles executed a classic dawn surprise attack. It was the same sort of attack that Custer had planned for June 26, 1876, but never made. Lame Deer and his nephew Iron Star ran, but found themselves cornered. Hump, a Minneconjou Lakota scout for Miles, convinced them to come and parley with Bear Coat, and they did. Miles told them to put down their rifles, and they nervously complied, although they left them cocked and pointed forward.

As they began to talk, a scout made a false move and up came the rifles. Lame Deer fired at Miles, but he dodged and the bullet killed another trooper. A ferocious gun battle ensued and Lame Deer fell. When the smoke settled over Little Muddy Creek, Lame Deer's body had seventeen bullet wounds. Four troopers had been killed, along with more than a dozen Lakota.

By mid-April, as Red Cloud was conveying the wasichu promise of an agency to Crazy Horse, Sitting Bull was camped on Beaver Creek, about half way between the Missouri River and the Canadian border, beyond which Miles could not touch him. He told his followers that he would never give them up to the wasichu. He would take them into exile.

At almost exactly that same moment that Crazy Horse surrendered, Sitting Bull crossed over the "medicine line" with a following of 135 lodges. He had been in Canada before, on the occasional hunting trip, but this time he came to stay.

On May 7, as Lame Deer was holding his last council in the Powder River Country, Sitting Bull was having his first council with the wasichu in the Grandmother's Country. This was the Indian term for the British Dominion of Canada.

The actual "Grandmother" was Queen Victoria, the sovereign of the British Empire, just as the "Grandfather" was Ulysses S. Grant, or Rutherford B. Hayes, or whichever gray-bearded man happened to be president of the United States at the time. The two were also alternatively known to the Indians as the "White Mother" and "White Father."

The Dominion of Canada had been formed in 1867 when the British North America Act brought together a confederation of the four British

provinces of Ontario, Quebec, Nova Scotia,
and New Brunswick, as well as the vast,
barely populated lands on the Prairies that
formed the North West Territories. The
province of Manitoba was carved out of the
latter in 1870, and the British colonies of
British Columbia and Prince Edward
Island joined confederation in 1871 and
1873. The present provinces of Alberta and
Saskatchewan were not cleaved from the
North West Territories until 1905.

Major James Morrow Walsh.
(*National Archives of Canada*)

The Hunkpapa had already started
going north. Black Moon had taken fifty-
two lodges north of the border in December
1876, and Sitting Bull's uncle, Four Horns,
arrived in Canada with fifty-seven in March 1877. Grandmother's
Country was seen as a more hospitable place. Because the North West
Territories were less crowded with wasichu than the Montana and Dakota
Territories, they were proportionally more crowded with buffalo, which
was another inducement to settle here. For the moment, there was plenty
of good hunting for both the long-time Assiniboine residents and the
Lakota newcomers. There were wasichu there, but not very many, and
they were not as anxious to swarm into the vast open Plains as the wasichu
in the Grandfather's Country. They wasichu here used the same language
as the wasichu across the border, but the coats of their soldiers were red
instead of blue.

Sitting Bull's first official face-to-face encounter with a wasichu in red
was in the person of Major James Morrow Walsh, leading a detachment of
North West Mounted Police out of Fort Walsh in the southeast corner of
what is now Saskatchewan, and about two hundred miles west of Wood
Mountain, where the Lakota had camped. Walsh told Sitting Bull that the

Lakota could stay in Canada as long as they obeyed the rules. He also made it clear that, if the Lakota followed the Grandmother's laws, the red-coats would protect them from the bluecoats. At this point, Sitting Bull showed Walsh the King George III peace medal that his grandfather had been given at the time of the War of 1812. The family had a long history with the redcoats.

The North West Mounted Police, known as the "Mounties," were established in 1873 by Sir John Macdonald, the first prime minister of Canada, to assert Canadian sovereignty in the North West Territories. The Mounties were based on British cavalry regiments, and in the 1870s were the rough equivalent of the U.S. Army's cavalry regiments on the Plains. In 1920, they became the Royal Canadian Mounted Police (RCMP), functioning as a national police force in Canada, with law enforcement powers roughly analogous to the American FBI.

During the 1870s, the Mounties had a much better reputation for fairness among the Indians than did the American bluecoats. Part of this probably had to do with the fact that there was a lot more open space in Canada and a lot fewer wasichu. The North West Territories were less crowded in 1877 than Dakota Territory had been a generation earlier. The Canadian Pacific Railway's transcontinental line would not be completed until 1885, sixteen years after the first continent-spanning rails in the United States.

Walsh himself is recalled as having been a tough man, but a fair man, and generally respected by the Assiniboine, or Hohe, that were nominally under his jurisdiction. Born in Ontario in 1840, he was virtually the same age as the American military officers opposite whom Sitting Bull had earlier been cast. He was nine months younger than Nelson Miles and only five months younger than Custer. Assigned to establish a Mountie post in the Cypress Hills in 1875, he had been authorized to name it "Fort Walsh" after himself.

Over the coming months, a friendship developed between Sitting Bull and Walsh, whom the Lakota called "Long Lance" because of the largely ceremonial lances that the Mounties sometimes carried. Based on mutual trust and respect, their friendship was unlike any relationship that Sitting Bull had with any American wasichu—except perhaps Buffalo Bill, but that is a story that came in a later chapter of his life.

WHILE Sitting Bull and the Lakota breathed more easily in Canada, Bear Coat Miles was otherwise engaged south of the medicine line. During the autumn of 1877, he became involved in the climax of one of the most amazing Indian Wars of them all. Indeed it was one of the most astonishing chapters in the history of the American West. Though it involved neither Sitting Bull nor the Lakota, it is important to tell because it was the single most important example of Indian defiance to the will of the wasichu in 1877, and because Sitting Bull's sanctuary in Canada was its inspiration.

Since the middle of June, some of the most credentialed—if not the best—U.S. Army officers in the West had been leading their troops in an effort to catch a band of Nez Percé from Oregon who were trying, like the Lakota, to reach Canada. They were led by a man named Heinmot Tooyalakekt, who had taken the wasichu name Joseph. Regarded by his people with a respect and admiration that paralleled Sitting Bull's among the Lakota, Chief Joseph was one of the greatest and most charismatic Indian leaders of the nineteenth century.

The background of the affair was that the Nez Percé had been promised a reservation on their ancestral land in the Wallowa Country in Oregon, but this deal had fallen through. Tempers were frayed, and when killings of wasichu—that were unsanctioned by any Nez Percé leaders— occurred, the U.S. Army overreacted. As the Army closed in to force the Nez Percé onto an unacceptable reservation, Chief Joseph decided to take them all to Grandmother's Country.

For four months, Joseph's Nez Percé band, of whom nearly two-thirds were women and children, managed to outmaneuver or outfight troops under the command of officers from General Oliver O. Howard to Colonel John Gibbon—an alumni of the failed 1876 campaign against the Cheyenne and Lakota—in a chase that wound its way through Idaho, Montana, Wyoming, and Montana again. Bear Coat Miles finally got involved in late September just as Joseph's exhausted following reached the Bear's Paw (now called Bear Paw) Mountains in Montana, about forty miles from the Canadian border.

Having traveled over a thousand miles, and having defeated the U.S. Army in at least five major battles, the Nez Percé were finally beaten. A few people managed to slip away and reach safety, but most, including Joseph, did not.

One of the great epic tales of human history came to a tragic conclusion painfully close to the final goal. In surrendering to Miles on October 5, Joseph delivered one of the greatest of the many speeches that are remembered from the words of the famous Indian orators. It concluded with those truly eloquent words, "I am tired. My heart is sick and sad. From where the sun now stands I will fight no more forever."

There has long been speculation that the Lakota at Wood Mountain had planned to cross the border to come to the aid of the Nez Percé in their final battle with Miles. While there is no official record of such a move, a memo by James Walsh, among his personal papers that are preserved in the Manitoba Provincial Archives, gives a detailed account of his having convinced Sitting Bull not to intervene. To have done so would have clearly jeopardized the status of the Lakota people in Canada, because using Grandmother's Country as a base of operations for raids into the United States was unquestionably breaking one of her rules.

EVEN more than watching Bear Coat Miles crush the Nez Percé dash for freedom, another event south of the medicine line must have made Sitting Bull feel as though the walls of the wasichu world were closing in on him.

He had last seen Crazy Horse in the deep snow of February 1877 as the Oglala and Hunkpapa parted company in the Powder River Country. Crazy Horse could have followed Sitting Bull to Canada, but he chose not to. Three months later, Crazy Horse and his hungry followers had ridden into Fort Robinson, Nebraska, as much compelled by the condition of the people with him as lured by the promise of an agency of his own. Later, when the pledge of a "Crazy Horse Agency" faded like so much prairie dust on the horizon, he admitted that he wished he had followed Sitting Bull.

Crazy Horse remained at a camp near the Red Cloud Agency through the summer, making everyone—from the soldiers at nearby Fort Robinson, to the agents, to the other chiefs—nervous. For someone conditioned to spending his summers hunting in the hills and valleys of the Powder River Country like Crazy Horse, this was an alien way of life. Only a year before, he had led Oglala warriors at the Rosebud and the Little Bighorn in two of the biggest victories over the wasichu ever achieved by the Lakota. Now he was pacing around at Red Cloud's agency, growing angry and nervous. He was invited to go to Washington to meet President Hayes, but he refused. Crazy Horse saw what Red Cloud and Spotted Tail looked like as "agency Indians" and he didn't like what he saw.

In August, news of the Nez Percé exodus, and of Chief Joseph's masterful eluding of the U.S. Army, reached the Red Cloud Agency. It was exciting to see this. It reminded many warriors of the previous year when the Lakota and the Cheyenne had eluded the U.S. Army all summer after the Little Bighorn. However, it reminded others of the futility of riding against the bluecoats. The fact that they were all sitting at the agency was evidence of that futility.

When the U.S. Army started to recruit Lakota for its corps of scouts and for service against the Nez Percé, this infuriated Crazy Horse. He imagined that such scouts could, and would, be used against Sitting Bull. Crazy Horse could not contain his anger, and he became especially restless. On September 2, General George Crook, who happened to be at Fort

Robinson, got wind of this. He feared that Crazy Horse might leave his camp near the Red Cloud Agency and cause trouble, so he ordered that Crazy Horse be arrested. Crook then departed, leaving Lieutenant Colonel Luther Bradley, Fort Robinson's commander, in charge.

The arrest did not go forward until additional troops arrived from Fort Laramie two days later, and word of the impending action reached Crazy Horse before the soldiers. With advance warning, he dispersed the warriors in his entourage and unsuccessfully attempted to elude arrest. On September 5, Crazy Horse agreed to surrender to Lieutenant Jesse Lee of the Spotted Tail Agency, who brought him to Fort Robinson. Here, he was turned over to Captain James Kennington, commander of the guard at the fort.

As he was being escorted to the stockade, Crazy Horse recognized a familiar face among the Indian Agency police at the fort. It was Little Big Man, a fellow Oglala with whom he had once ridden. To Crazy Horse, this was an immense indignity. As Crazy Horse was about to be locked up in the stockade at Fort Robinson, he bolted. He saw that in this place there were men in leg irons and this was not for him.

There are several stories in circulation regarding the events that took place next. What is known for certain is that there was a scuffle and Crazy Horse suffered a stab wound. Whose blade was responsible has long been debated. Some say that it was a bayonet wielded by Private William Gentles on the order of Captain Kennington. Others say it was Little Big Man, possibly in response to Crazy Horse pulling his own knife in an attempt to escape.

John Gregory Bourke, in his autobiography *On the Border with Crook*, said that he later talked with Little Big Man, who insisted that Crazy Horse pulled two concealed knives, one of which was made from a U.S. Army bayonet. Little Big Man went on to say that he saw Crazy Horse pull a knife and feared that the soldiers would use this as a pretext for shooting Crazy Horse. In order to prevent this, Little Big Man tried to subdue

Crazy Horse himself. During the tussle, according to Bourke's interview, the bayonet slipped and stabbed Crazy Horse. Little Big Man told Bourke that he and Kennington concocted the story that Gentles was responsible as a deliberate cover-up to prevent a reprisal against Little Big Man.

The wounded Crazy Horse was treated by Dr. Valentine Trant McGillycuddy, who had served as a surgeon on several of Crook's campaigns and who was then assigned to Fort Robinson. However, the wound was mortal, and the doctor pronounced the thirty-five-year-old warrior dead around midnight. Like the unnecessary deaths of John Grattan and Conquering Bear at Ash Hollow in 1854—and so many such incidents—the death of Crazy Horse was entirely avoidable. It was a case of nervous men behaving impulsively.

A month later, many of the Oglala who had been part of Crazy Horse's band left the agency to join Sitting Bull in Canada. Still others would follow them north in the spring of 1878.

The death of Crazy Horse occurred almost exactly one month before Joseph's memorable speech in the Bear's Paw Mountains, and news of the two events probably reached Sitting Bull in the space of a couple of weeks. This also coincided with the death, due to sickness, of a young son who had been born to him and third wife Red Woman in about 1868, three years before her death. No one would have faulted Sitting Bull for feeling a bit melancholy. He had a lot on his mind.

Just as he was pondering these turns, Sitting Bull received word that the bluecoats were coming.

MAJOR Walsh may have been happy to have his new friend Sitting Bull remain in Canada indefinitely, but Grandmother's government in Ottawa—and indeed in London—was nervous. They didn't particularly like having the "great villain" of the "Custer Massacre" living under their roof—even if he was nearly two thousand miles west of Ottawa in the middle of nowhere and behaving himself.

Almost as soon as Sitting Bull dismounted to pitch his lodge in Canada, Her Majesty's diplomats in Washington undertook to negotiate with the government of Rutherford B. Hayes to cut some sort of deal with Sitting Bull that would allow him to return to Dakota Territory. It was suggested that perhaps he could keep his guns and horses, but the United States rejected such a concession as being favoritism. Other Lakota "chiefs" had not been allowed to do so, and why should Sitting Bull be any different? For the time being, the U.S. government was happy to have Sitting Bull remain in Canada as Her Majesty's guest *and* Her Majesty's problem.

However, in August 1877, the Hayes government finally agreed to send a delegation to Fort Walsh to negotiate with Sitting Bull. The team would be headed by none other than Brigadier General Alfred Terry, the same officer who had, the summer before, commanded the eastern wing of the campaign that climaxed in the Little Bighorn disaster. Custer's former boss was going west again, this time to try to do with words what Long Hair had failed to with bullets.

Sitting Bull said that he wanted nothing to do with the Terry Commission, but Walsh went to Wood Mountain personally to coax him back to Fort Walsh. The timing could not have been worse. The Lakota had just heard the news of Miles subduing the Nez Percé, and here Walsh was trying to convince the Lakota leaders to voluntarily sit down in the same room with another bluecoat general.

Despite his reluctance, Sitting Bull trusted Long Lance Walsh, and he finally agreed to come, accompanied by a contingent of about twenty others, including Rain in the Face, and Spotted Eagle of the Sans Arc. Walsh's superior, Lieutenant Colonel James Macleod, added his own voice to assure that Terry was not coming to attack the Lakota.

The Terry Commission departed St. Paul on September 14, while Miles was still in pursuit of Joseph, and reached Fort Walsh less than two weeks after Joseph's surrender at the Bear's Paw Mountains. Terry and his

secretary, Lieutenant Colonel H. C.
Corbin, were accompanied by A. G.
Lawrence, a civilian government official
from Rhode Island with diplomatic experience, and stenographer Jay Stone. They
crossed the border on October 15 and were
greeted personally by Lieutenant Colonel
Macleod and a North West Mounted Police
contingent who escorted the Americans for
the final forty-five miles to Fort Walsh.

Also traveling with Terry were journalists
Jerome Stillson of the *New York Herald* and
Charles Diehl of the *Chicago Times*. Since

Brigadier General Alfred Terry
photographed during the Civil
War. (*Library of Congress*)

the Little Bighorn, Sitting Bull had become
a prominent figure in the image that the
outside world had of the Plains Indian. As interest in him had grown, the
national media was anxious for more information about the enigmatic
"Indian Chief who had defeated Custer." Thanks to these journalists, the
council was reported for posterity. At the same time, there was considerable media curiosity about Walsh, who seemed to be the only wasichu
who had ever exercised any influence over Sitting Bull.

In his first report, dispatched by telegraph and published by the *New
York Herald* on October 22, Stillson gave credit to Walsh for making the
meeting possible:

> We must really regard Major Walsh as the only man in the Dominion
> of Canada who could, in the first place, have induced such deter-
> mined enemies of the white man as Sitting Bull and his followers to
> come on and interview the United States Commission, and, in the
> second place, to have enticed these wild and suspicious savages to
> bide a delay of considerable extent and await the approach of the
> Commissioners. The wild and romantic stories told of Major Walsh

in the Canadian and United States newspapers have led some people to question whether he really exercises the influence which it is claimed he possesses over the Indians of the Northwest. . . . Nobody, however, would think of doubting Major Walsh's control over his savage wards after being at this post [Fort Walsh] for one hour. I must characterize him, from what I have seen and heard, as one of the bravest and most remarkable diplomats of his day.

We hasten to note that Stillson's use of the term "savage" was by way of a definition no longer used today. He did not mean it as a synonym for "barbaric" or "sadistic," but in the nineteenth century context to mean "untamed," in the sense of not possessing the characteristics of Euro-American culture.

Stillson also reported the story, widely repeated later on, of Walsh reprimanding White Dog of the Assiniboine for stealing some horses. In the incident, which had occurred earlier at Sitting Bull's camp, Walsh simply told White Dog to return the horses. When White Dog asked what Walsh would do if he didn't, Walsh just told him that he'd be under arrest. White Dog, observing what Stillson described as Walsh's "quiet determination," had apologized and complied. He then "retired from the Major's presence a wiser man."

As for the actual meeting with Terry, which was held on October 17 in one of the buildings at Fort Walsh, Stillson recounted the dramatic entrance of the Lakota delegation. "At 3 o'clock, Sitting Bull entered, followed by Spotted Eagle and the rest," Stillson said, awed by the drama of the moment. "Now for the first time was visible to white men since the beginning of the Indian Wars the most noted Indian of the period, and now was made real [James Fenimore] Cooper's often derided vision of an Indian's face. . . . His features, like Goethe's, made music to the senses. He wore a quiet, ironical smile. His black hair streamed down along his beardless and swarthy cheeks over clean cut ears, not burdened with ornaments."

Stillson described how Sitting Bull seated himself on a buffalo robe near a wall and quietly lit his pipe. His opening comment, issued through an interpreter, was "This commission that has come to interview me can go to the devil."

Terry, seated with Lawrence at a table, avoided confrontation, telling Sitting Bull that "the President has instructed us to say to you that he desires to make a lasting peace with you and your people. He desires that all hostilities shall close and that all the people of the United States shall live together in harmony. He wishes this not for

Spotted Eagle. (*Denver Public Library*)

the sake of the whites alone, but for your sake as well, and he has entrusted us to say that if you will return to your country and hereafter refrain from acts of hostility against its government and people a full pardon will be given to you for all acts committed in the past."

Terry went on to insist that in order to avail himself of a pardon and of the opportunity to live in peace south of the border, Sitting Bull would have to abide by the conditions that the U.S. government demanded of all the Indians. He would have to give up his guns and horses. This was obviously a deal-breaker. Sitting Bull made a remark about it being preposterous for Terry to demand that he walk a thousand miles back to Dakota Territory on foot.

Terry whined that "the President cannot and will not consent that you return to your country armed, mounted, and prepared for war." According to Stanley Vestal, Sitting Bull pointedly explained that the United States had not been good for the Lakota, but the British had. "For sixty-four years [since the end of the War of 1812] you have kept me and my people and treated us bad," Sitting Bull told Terry.

What have we done that you should want us to stop? We have done nothing. It is all the people on your side who started . . . making trouble. We could go nowhere else, so we took refuge here. It was on this side of the line that we first learned to shoot, and that's why I came back here again. I would like to know why you came here. I did not give you my country, but you followed me from place to place, and I had to come here. . . . Look at me. I have ears, I have eyes to see with. If you think me a fool, you are a bigger fool than I am. This house is a medicine house. You come here to tell us lies, but we do not want to listen to them. I don't wish such language used to me, nor any such lies told to me in my Grandmother's house. Don't say two more words. Go back home where you came from.

"Sitting Bull's stage management of this council was admirable; he overlooked nothing," wrote Stanley Vestal of the encounter. "One of the most effective speakers was a woman, whom he brought in to present the case of the Sioux mothers: she was The One That Speaks Once, the wife of Bear That Scatters. Said she: `I was over in your country. I wanted to bring up my children there, but you did not give me time. I came here to raise my family and have a little peace. That's all I have to say. You go back where you came from. These Red Coats are the people I am going to stay with, and raise my children with.'"

The council had been an opportunity for Terry to show some understanding of Sitting Bull's position, but he apparently did not want to understand Sitting Bull. As an attorney, he might have displayed some negotiating skills rather than behaving merely as a courier carrying a message from Rutherford Hayes. Terry left Fort Walsh the next day, having allowed an opportunity to cut a deal with Sitting Bull slip through his fingers, but at least he had told the Lakota itancan the truth. Terry might have told Sitting Bull that he could keep his guns, that he could ride back to the Grand River country and keep his horses, but that would have been a lie.

Of course, perhaps Terry was smarter than he appears in the history of the encounter. Perhaps his true purpose was not to succeed, but to fail to lure Sitting Bull back. Perhaps he succeeded by allowing Sitting Bull to remain with the Grandmother. After all, it certainly did not hurt to have Sitting Bull remain as Her Majesty's guest. If he did cause trouble, as the U.S. government expected he would, he would be Her Majesty's problem and not that of the Hayes administration.

If Terry failed—or appeared to fail—to grasp an understanding of Sitting Bull as a man and as an important figure among the Lakota, Jerome Stillson did not.

The popular view of Sitting Bull in the wasichu press was of an Indian head of state or at least of an Indian general, a Napoleon or a Robert E. Lee. However, from his observations, Stillson quickly figured out how Sitting Bull figured into Lakota society. Stillson correctly deduced that in Lakota society, the traditional wasichu image of an "Indian chief" did not exist. "He has never been either a chief or a warrior and yet his influence over his tribe is stronger than that which he would exercise in either of these capacities," Stillson wrote. Of course, Sitting Bull had been a warrior, but Stillson correctly deduced that being a leader within the Lakota was not the same as being a wasichu governor. "That his position may be clearly understood you should comprehend the real and peculiar organization of his people."

Stillson went on to demonstrate a grasp of Indian military organization that continues to elude most wasichu to this day. "In time of battle there is no chief warrior who exercises the same authority as that of a general in a European army over his troops," Stillson explained. "Even in the fight with Custer, it is alleged by the chiefs who participated in that memorable and sanguinary struggle that no one among them controlled the rest or exercised any authority or command. They all acted in perfect concert, but in a sort of federal [united, but autonomous] direction."

In retrospect, we are lucky for the sake of posterity that Stillson had come to the windswept Canadian prairie during October 1877. We are also indebted to Major Walsh for the way he arranged for the reporter to spend the evening of that auspicious day.

IT was on the evening of October 17, 1877, that Sitting Bull gave his first ever interview to a wasichu journalist, when he sat down with Jerome Stillson of the *New York Herald* in the quarters that Stillson had been assigned at Fort Walsh. The interview was published in the paper nearly a month later, on November 16, three weeks after Stillson's first dispatch concerning the Terry conference.

It was Major Walsh himself who arranged the meeting, having told the wary Lakota itancan that Stillson was "a great paper chief who talked with a million tongues to all the people in the world. This man is a man of wonderful medicine; he speaks and the people on this side, and across the great water people open their ears and hear him. He tells the truth; he does not lie. He wishes to make the world know what a great tribe is encamped here on the land owned by the White Mother. He wants it to be understood that her guests are mighty warriors."

In reexamining this interview, we learn a great deal about Sitting Bull from Walsh himself. Walsh had clearly taken the time to get to know Sitting Bull, and he was very perceptive in his understanding of the Lakota itancan and his role in Hunkpapa society at that moment in history.

Sitting Bull finally agreed to come, but only after dark, and on the condition that nobody would be present except himself, Stillson, Major Walsh, two interpreters, and a stenographer. The latter probably did an accurate job of recording what was said, and it is likely that in his haste to file his story, Stillson only lightly edited the content of the transcription. Therefore, Sitting Bull's historic "first interview" comes down to us reasonably intact.

At 8:30 that evening, according to Stillson, "the most mysterious Indian chieftain who ever flourished in North America was ushered in by Major

Walsh, who locked the door behind him. . . . Here he stood, his blanket rolled back, his head upreared, his right moccasin put forward, his right hand thrown across his chest." This was, as Stillson pointed out "the first time that Sitting Bull had condescended, not merely to visit but to address a white man from the United States. During the long years of his domination he had withstood, with his bands, every attempt on the part of the United States government at a compromise of interests. He had refused all proffers, declined any [en]treaty." Indeed, Sitting Bull had always declined consistently to be interviewed for the record.

Stillson arose and approached him, holding out both hands, which Sitting Bull grasped cordially. Stillson described the itancan as "about five feet ten inches high. He was clad in a black and white calico shirt, black cloth leggings, and moccasins, magnificently embroidered with beads and porcupine quills. He held in his left hand a foxskin cap, its brush drooping to his feet. . . . His eyes gleamed."

After exchanging greetings, the first thing that Sitting Bull told Stillson was "I am no chief."

"You are a *great* chief," Stillson told Sitting Bull, "but you live behind a cloud. Your face is dark; my people do not see it. Tell me, do you hate the Americans very much?"

"I am no chief," Sitting Bull insisted. "I am," Sitting Bull said slightly nodding and smiling satirically, when Stillson asked him what he was, if not a chief, "A man." At this point, Stillson turned to Major Walsh for clarification.

"He means to keep you in ignorance of his secret if he can," said Walsh. At this point in the conference, Walsh demonstrated that he probably understood Sitting Bull's role among the Lakota far better than any wasichu who had yet written about him. "His position among his bands is anomalous," Walsh tried to explain, giving us a clear insight into Hunkpapa society.

His own tribes, the Hunkpapa, are not all in fealty to him. Parts of nearly twenty different tribes of Sioux, besides a remnant of the Hunkpapa, abide with him. So far as I have learned, he rules over these fragments of tribes, which compose his camp of 2,500, including between 800 and 900 warriors, by sheer compelling force of intellect and will. I believe that he understands nothing particularly of war or military tactics, at least not enough to give him the skill or the right to command warriors in battle. He is supposed to have guided the fortunes of several battles, including the fight in which Custer fell. That supposition, as you will presently find, is partially erroneous. His word was always potent in the camp or in the field, but he has usually left to the war chiefs the duties appertaining to engagements. When the crisis came he gave his opinion, which was accepted as law.

Stillson then foolishly asked Walsh whether Sitting Bull was a "medicine man," the wasichu term for wikasa wakan. "Don't for the world," replied the major anxiously, "intimate to him, in the questions you are about to ask him, that you have derived the idea from me, or from any one, that he is a mere medicine man. He would deem that to be a profound insult. In point of fact he is a medicine man, but a far greater, more influential medicine man than any I have ever known."

Stillson was trying to grasp the magnitude of this man who now seemed more of an enigma that he had before he entered the room. It was typical of the way most wasichu approached Sitting Bull and have always approached Sitting Bull. The caricature was easy to grasp, but the reality was mysterious. Stillson turned to Sitting Bull to try again for an answer. "What, then, makes the warriors of your camp, the great chiefs who are here along with you, look up to you so?" he asked. "Why do they think so much of you?"

"Oh, I used to be a kind of a chief," Sitting Bull replied, his lips forming into a proud smile. He obviously understood that his role as an active

Hunkpapa leader had diminished by his being in exile, hundreds of miles from the heart of Hunkpapa territory. "But the Americans made me go away from my father's hunting ground."

"You do not love the Americans?" Stillson asked as Sitting Bull's lips curled. "I saw today that all the warriors around you clapped their hands and cried out when you spoke. What you said appeared to please them. They liked you. They seemed to think that what you said was right for them to say. If you are not a great chief, why do these men think so much of you?"

"Your people look up to men because they are rich," Sitting Bull said disdainfully. "Because they have much land, many lodges, many women?"

"Yes," Stillson said, probably with a somewhat sheepish expression.

"Well, I suppose my people look up to me because I am poor. That is the difference." Sitting Bull had meant to say that his voluntary vow of poverty was highly respected among the Lakota, but Stillson took the answer as mere evasiveness.

When Stillson asked, "What is your feeling toward the Americans now?" Sitting Bull merely touched his hip where his knife was. "Listen," said Sitting Bull, not changing his posture but putting his right hand on Stillson's knee. "I told [the men of the Terry delegation] today what my notions were—that I did not want to go back there. Every time that I had any difficulty with them they struck me first. I want to live in peace. . . . They asked me today to give them [surrender] my horses. I bought my horses, and they are mine. I bought them from men who came up the Missouri in mackinaws. They do not belong to the government; neither do the rifles. The rifles are also mine. I bought them; I paid for them. Why I should give them up I do not know. I will not give them up."

Playing diplomat, Stillson asked, "Do you really think, do your people believe, that it is wise to reject the proffers that have been made to you by the United States Commissioners? Do not some of you feel as if you were destined to lose your old hunting grounds? Don't you see that you will probably have the same difficulty in Canada that you have had in the United States?"

"The White Mother does not lie."

On the theme of prevarication and misrepresentation, Stillson raised this issue of the many far-fetched stories about him that were told in the wasichu tabloids. "Great lies are told about you," Stillson said with no overstatement. "White men say that you lived among them when you were young; that you went to school; that you learned to write and read from books; that you speak English; that you know how to talk French?"

"I have heard some of these stories," Sitting Bull laughed. "They are all strange lies. What I am I am. . . . I am a man. I see. I know. I began to see when I was not yet born; when I was not in my mother's arms, but inside of my mother's belly. It was there that I began to study about my people."

At this point, Stillson touched Sitting Bull on the arm. Walsh obviously thought that the reporter wanted to change the subject, just as Sitting Bull was about to open up on the topic of Lakota cosmological beliefs. "Do not interrupt him," said Major Walsh urgently. "He is beginning to talk about his medicine." Stillson paused to let the Hunkpapa leader continue.

"I was," repeated Sitting Bull, "still in my mother's insides when I began to study all about my people. God [at this point, Stillson noted that Sitting Bull waved his hand to express a `great protecting genius'] gave me the power to see out of the womb. I studied there, in the womb, about many things. I studied about the smallpox, that was killing my people—the great sickness that was killing the women and children. I was so interested that I turned over on my side. The God Almighty must have told me at that time [and here Sitting Bull unconsciously revealed his secret] that I would be the man to be the judge of all the other Indians—a big man, to decide for them in all their ways."

"And you have since decided for them?" Stillson asked.

"I speak. It is enough."

"Could not your people, whom you love so well, get on with the Americans?" Stillson suggested, changing the subject and failing to follow up with a deeper exploration of Lakota cosmology.

"No!" Sitting Bull said emphatically.

"Why?"

"I never taught my people to trust Americans. I have told them the truth—that the Americans are great liars. I have never dealt with the Americans. Why should I? The land belonged to my people. I say never dealt with them—I mean I never treated with them in a way to surrender my people's rights. I traded with them, but I always gave full value for what I got. I never asked the United States government to make me presents of blankets or cloth or anything of that kind. The most I did was to ask them to send me an honest trader that I could trade with and I proposed to give him buffalo robes and elk skins and other hides in exchange for what we wanted. I told every trader who came to our camps that I did not want any favors from him that I wanted to trade with him fairly and equally, giving him full value for what I got but the traders wanted me to trade with them on no such terms. They wanted to give little and get much. They told me that if I did not accept what they would give me in trade they would get the government to fight me. I told them I did not want to fight."

"But you fought," the reporter countered.

"At last, yes; but not until after I had tried hard to prevent a fight," Sitting Bull explained, trying to make it clear that the Lakota were responding to transgression. "At first my young men, when they began to talk bad, stole five American horses. I took the horses away from them and gave them back to the Americans. It did no good. By and by we had to fight."

Stillson saw this as an opening to ask Sitting Bull about the topic that was probably most on his mind during the interview, the Battle of the Little Bighorn. Only 16 months had passed since the battle, and it was still fresh in the minds of the readers of the New York Herald, so Stillson was certainly doing his job to raise the subject. "It was at this juncture that I began to question the great savage before me in regard to the most disastrous, most mysterious Indian battle of the century—Custer's encounter with the Sioux on the Bighorn—the Thermopylae of the Plains," Stillson wrote for his New York readership, using the term "savage" in its nineteenth-century context.

In Sitting Bull's descriptions of his perspective on the battle—which are included in our discussions in the previous chapter—Stillson showed Sitting Bull a generally accurate map of the battlefield. Using this, Sitting Bull confirmed various points of fact about the geography of the conflict, including his own location in the encampment at the time of the initial attack, the point of Reno's attack, and the place on Custer Hill where the last large concentration of men from Custer's detachment made their last stand.

Sitting Bull also conveyed the long-held misconception on the part of the Lakota and Cheyenne that the contingent that initially attacked at the southern end of the camp (Reno's command) were the same group of soldiers that later attacked at Medicine Tail Coulee and wound up making the last stand on Custer Hill and the adjacent ridges (Custer's command).

The discussion of the Battle of the Little Bighorn apparently was an obvious ending point in the conversation, for Sitting Bull rose to leave the building. As he started to leave, Stillson asked him "whether he had the stomach for any more battles with the Americans."

"I do not want any fight," he answered.

"You mean not now?"

Here Stillson noted that Sitting Bull "laughed quite heartily."

"No," Sitting Bull laughed. "Not this winter."

"Are your young braves willing to fight?"

"You will see," Sitting Bull replied ominously, perhaps with a grin still on his face.

"When?"

"I cannot say."

"I have not seen your people," Stillson said, obviously making a pitch for a follow-up conversation. "Would I be welcome at your camp?"

"I will not be pleased," Sitting Bull responded after gazing at the ceiling for a few moments. "The young men would not be pleased. You came with this party [a reference to the United States commissioners] and you can go back with them. I have said enough."

Having denied Stillson permission to visit the Hunkpapa camp, Sitting Bull wrapped his blanket around himself, gracefully shook hands with the reporter, and probably Walsh as well, strode to the door. Here, he placed his fox-skin cap on his head, and the reporter bade him "adieu."

Sitting Bull's first encounter in which his words were recorded for posterity by a wasichu journalist had come to an end.

For the moment, Sitting Bull could congratulate himself on his having stood his ground with Terry. It had to seem that for the second time since the military campaign the previous summer, the Lakota had denied Terry what he sought. In so doing, the Lakota had achieved a diplomatic success.

If the summit conference had been a victory for Sitting Bull, it had been a defeat for Canadian foreign policy. They were arguably more troubled by Terry's failed mission than the Americans. Walsh and Macleod had told Sitting Bull that he was welcome in Canada, but Her Majesty's government really did not want a Lakota leader of such notoriety as Sitting Bull within its borders.

In the wake of Terry's mission, Nelson Miles proposed that the U.S. Army simply defy the border and ride up to Wood River and capture Sitting Bull. A precedent for such an operation existed in the May 1873 cross-border incursion by Colonel Ranald Mackenzie's 4th Cavalry against a large Kickapoo encampment near the town of Remolino in

Mexico. However, neither Terry, nor U.S. Army Chief of Staff General William Tecumseh Sherman, had any desire to have Miles involved in an international incident involving the North West Mounted Police. Canada would certainly have protested such a raid in the strongest of terms, although the Canadians probably would have breathed a secret sigh of relief had Miles succeeded.

Both sides were especially sensitive to the way that the media was portraying the genuine friendship that was developing between Major Walsh and Sitting Bull. Walsh was spending as much time at the Lakota camp as at his own headquarters, and news reports were starting to refer to the Mountie Major as "Sitting Bull's Boss." Long Lance was cast in a heroic light as the man who had tamed the celebrated Lakota "chief," and the two men were seen as exemplifying a great detente on the Prairies.

Meanwhile, Sitting Bull was the man of the hour among the Lakota. By the spring of 1878, nearly 600 lodges were located at his camp, to which were added nearly 250 lodges from among the Oglala who had once camped with Crazy Horse and a few dozen from among the Nez Percé who had managed to slip north of the medicine line when Joseph surrendered.

However, the greater the Lakota presence grew, the more they came into competition with the tribes previously living in Canada for scarce resources. The arrival of the Lakota put a strain on that staple of all Plains tribes, the buffalo. The Lakota now hunted the same land as the Assiniboine, the Cree, and the Blackfeet (Siksika, pronounced as sheek-sheek-awah). The latter consist of three major branches, the Blood, the Piegan, and the Blackfeet proper. Then, as now, they lived on both sides of the medicine line in the lands immediately east of the Rocky Mountains. The more the Lakota came into competition with the Canadian tribes, the more potential trouble there was for the Mounties. Monitoring the cross-border traffic was always a complex job for the North West Mounted Police.

In the beginning, the Lakota treated the medicine line as though it were a real thing. However, just as the Blackfeet moved across the medicine line as though it was not there, eventually, so too did the Lakota. The buffalo didn't understand that the 49th parallel, 49 degrees north latitude marked a division between two worlds, and neither should those who hunted them. By 1879, the Lakota were riding south into the Milk River drainage north of the Missouri River on regular hunting expeditions. Walsh had admonished Sitting Bull not to use Canada as a base of operations for attacks against the United States or its citizens, but crossing into Montana Territory to hunt buffalo was not an attack against Americans. Indeed, it became routine, and this was a source of worry for Walsh.

If Bear Coat Miles and the U.S. Army happened to catch Sitting Bull on American soil, there was nothing Walsh, as his protector, could do to help him, or the other Lakota hunters whom the Americans often referred to with matter-of-fact hyperbole as "hostiles." The term was used at that time to identify not people who were being specifically antagonistic, but rather Indians who were technically in violation of orders that they confine themselves to an agency or to the Great Sioux Reservation. A more precise term might have been to call them fugitives, given that Miles was authorized to use force to detain them.

Though unobserved by American authorities, forays into the United States by the celebrated exile were often reported in the American press by those who had seen him. The March 5, 1878, issue of the *Bismarck Tribune*, for example, noted that Luther S. "Yellowstone" Kelly, the trapper and mountain man who served as Chief of Scouts for Nelson Miles from 1876 to 1878, had told its reporter that "Sitting Bull has most certainly been on this side of the line this winter." The paper went on to say that Kelly

> thinks he [Sitting Bull] is now probably north of the line but that
> there is a large hostile [Lakota hunting] camp on Woody Creek, and
> one on Frenchman's Creek. The most authentic information leaves

little doubt that there are hostiles [Lakota hunters] on this side, in the Milk River country, and General Miles is determined to investigate the question Canada has no right to allow these hostile camps to remain on her border a constant menace to this country and the result of General Miles expedition, will be to bring the question too a settlement one way or the other. Whatever hostiles he finds on this side he will either kill, capture or drive over the line, and he will probably remain in the Milk River Country with his command until the question is settled. If Sitting Bull determines to cross [to] this side he must fight on the threshold.

When the penalty for crossing the border was articulated thusly, it is no small wonder that Sitting Bull was reluctant to surrender voluntarily to the American authorities.

By the summer of 1879, however, Miles had failed to find Sitting Bull, although many of his countrymen and at least one big city reporter had. On June 16, Stanley Huntley of the *Chicago Tribune* caught up with Sitting Bull in Montana, within earshot of the Big Bend of the rushing Milk River. Huntley had accomplished his rendezvous through the intercession of Walsh, who introduced him to a mixed-race Canadian trader who did business with the Lakota at Wood Mountain.

The scene that Huntley described was as colorful as anything that could have been conceived in Hollywood a couple of generations later. "It was about noon when the Sioux appeared on the ridge above the camp," Huntley wrote from his vantage point within a hunting camp as he awaited Sitting Bull's arrival.

> The very air trembled with their yells. . . . Suddenly there came a wild, unearthly shriek, and down the side of the hill, the horses of the Little Bighorn poured in a resistless stream. The half-breeds were paralyzed, not with fear, but with admiration. A more magnificent and grander sight never started human eyes. As the column rushed down, charging here and there, as their horses were quick or slow, they

turned the valley into a kaleidoscope, the colors shifting swiftly into a thousand forms, barbarous, yet beautiful. The horses were covered with foam, and urged to their utmost. Without warning the whole column turned into flames, and the mountain shook with the crash and roar of their arms. The brilliant colors flashed through the smoke, and the cloud of dust to and from the ground, caused by the hurrying hoofs, was scattered by the fire that poured from their rifle barrels.

After that spellbinding entrance, Huntley was introduced to Sitting Bull, who eyed him suspiciously and accused him of being a spy.

"You are an American," Sitting Bull insisted. "What do you want? You are a spy."

"I am an American, but not a spy," Huntley insisted. "My people think your heart's bad. They hear stories about your cruelty to their brothers. They are told that it is you and your people who steal their horses. . . . The chief of the paper that talks to white men has sent me to ask you if this is true. . . . My chief does not feel unkindly toward you, but he does not know your heart."

Sitting Bull replied that he was tired of the lies that were told about him in the wasichu newspapers, and Huntley promised to tell his readers only what Sitting Bull said.

"I have not stolen their horses, but your people sent the long knives against me. Why do you do that?"

"Because they have believed the stories they have heard," Huntley tried to explain. "Do you not hate Americans?"

"I hate them," Sitting Bull replied succinctly, "because I and my people have always been deceived by them. They asked us to go to the gift-houses [at the agencies] and said they would care for us and feed us. Many of my people went. They believe what the Americans said to them. They were there but a short time, and then they were told they must farm. . . . I never wanted to go to a gift-house, and I never will. They want my people to farm. I will not farm."

Sitting Bull went on to articulate legitimate reasons to distrust—even to hate—the U.S. government. "They found their rations were short," Sitting Bull said of the people who had acquiesced to life in the gift-houses only to have corrupt Indian agents cheat them. "It is not many years ago your people said they would give us the country of the Black Hills. They said our children should have it and own it . . . that it should be our hunting ground. As soon as they found there was shining dust [gold] there, they drove us from there and told us the country did not belong to us. . . . It is for that I dislike Americans. It is for their conduct toward me."

Indeed, the corruption among the Indian Agents who stole, pilfered, and watered down the rations is one of the most long-lived and outrageous scandals of the nineteenth century. As for the Black Hills, the 1868 Fort Laramie Treaty had clearly stated what Sitting Bull said that it had. The fact that the gold discoveries caused the U.S. government to unilaterally abrogate the treaty is inexcusable.

"You want us to live in houses and give you our guns and horses," Sitting Bull said, reminding Huntley of the long-standing United States government demand. "The Crow are at a gift-house, but you let them have guns and horses, let them hunt, let them go to war."

Sitting Bull made a point of underscoring this hypocrisy when it came to the Crow, a long-time rival of the Lakota and a tribe that had supplied the U.S. Army with numerous scouts during its campaigns against the Lakota.

"Are you willing to live in the [Grand]Mother's country at peace with the Americans if they let you alone," Huntley asked.

"When we went into the White Mother's land, I told the Lances [Mounties] that we had left behind us all the bad we had ever done; that I had been hounded in my own country, and had come to find a place where I could sleep sound. I was told that there were laws, and strict laws, that I had to obey. I asked to hear what these laws were. When I heard them, I said I would obey them, and I was told I could remain there in peace. I stayed there for two years and slept sound."

Thanks to his friend Long Lance, Sitting Bull slept sound in Canada. However, south of the border, Bear Coat Miles had seven companies of the 2nd Cavalry, plus another seven of mounted 5th Infantry, in the field. He was itching for a decisive confrontation.

More than two years into Sitting Bull's exile, Miles finally got his wish. On July 17, 1879, a contingent of two companies of troopers and fifty-four scouts—including some Crow—under the command of Lieutenant William Clark were riding as the advance guard of Miles's force when they came upon more than one hundred Lakota. These people, most of them women, were butchering a recent buffalo kill on Beaver Creek near the Milk River about fifty miles south of the border. Sitting Bull was among them.

The solders and scouts attacked, and the Lakota returned fire. In the midst of the shootout, a Crow scout named Magpie reportedly rode forth to challenge Sitting Bull personally to a man-to-man fight, and Sitting Bull shot him. Soon, both sides were reinforced. About sixty Lakota warriors who had left the scene with Bear Cap after the buffalo kill were about two miles away, and they rode back at the sound of the gunfire. On the opposing side, Miles arrived with the main body of his troops, as well as some artillery. Finally, the two sides broke off the fight.

Miles went on to frame the fight as a prominent victory in his campaign against Sitting Bull and the hostile Sioux, although he greatly overestimated the number of enemy present at the battle.

Three month later, the October 31, 1879, issue of the *Bismarck Tribune* carried an article supported on interviews of people who were actually there, including two of Miles's scouts, Chris Gilson and Oliver Brisbo, whose mother was Nez Percé. Before signing on with Miles to serve as a scout, Brisbo himself had been one of many people to have crossed paths and spoken with Lakota hunting parties in the country between the Missouri River and the Canadian border. As the newspaper summarized their background, "Both Gilson and Brisbo are well acquainted with the hostile Sioux. They have been to Sitting Bull's camp several times during the past season." Based on the eyewitness accounts of the scouts, the paper concluded that "The reported great fight of Miles with the hostile Sioux last summer was a farce."

In its report on the July 17 battle, the *Bismarck Tribune* stated,

> Brisbo saw Sitting Bull in the distance accompanied by two Nez Percé and two Sioux. They were waving their hands which signified the desire to talk with Miles. The Crow scouts with [Lieutenant William] Clark wanted to fight and began firing. Sitting Bull turned away and joined his band on the ridge. There were only 12 braves with their women and children with Sitting Bull, the main band being on [its way back to Canada]. They wanted to get their women and children to a place of safety so they showed fight. Selecting a favorable location, they began to fire back, the women and children retreating in haste. One woman and child had already been killed by the scouts, who kept up incessant firing. The 12 warriors held off the 54 scouts until the two companies came up. They then retreated, several of the scouts following them closely.

Magpie's fatal encounter with Sitting Bull, as told by Brisbo to the *Bismarck Tribune*, was a great deal less heroic than in other accounts. In Brisbo's version, Magpie had been shooting at Sitting Bull repeatedly without hitting him when Sitting Bull turned and said: "You want to kill me do you? Die you dog." With that, Sitting Bull shot off the top of his head.

As Brisbo explained, the sixty warriors who had been with Bear Cap "returned and showed fight simply to give the main band a chance to get the women and children away. Had the Indians wanted to fight they could have taken Miles's whole command. They were armed and lacked nothing in number. They knew if they fought they could not return across the British line."

Indeed, one of Walsh's most important rules given to Sitting Bull had been not to use Canada as a base of operations for offensive action within the United States. Conversely, the Lakota frequently complained that the U.S. authorities did not punish the Crow who sneaked into Canada to steal Lakota horses.

Major Walsh met with Miles along the border on at least two occasions that summer in an effort to explain that the Lakota hunting expeditions should not be considered aggression. However, Miles was still intent on fighting Sitting Bull whenever and wherever he caught him.

By this time, the perception within the Canadian government was that Walsh's friendship with Sitting Bull was clouding his judgment. Even Prime Minister Sir John Macdonald, who had been instrumental in the establishment of the Mounties, was displeased with the detente between the major and the itancan. Canada saw Sitting Bull as an unsettling nuisance, and as a liability to its program of pacifying the Indians within its boundaries. In an article in the February 1998 issue of *Wild West* magazine, Ian Anderson wrote that Macdonald "had become convinced that Walsh was being too sympathetic to Sitting Bull, that his sympathy was encouraging the Sioux chief to remain in Canada. According to R. C. Macleod, Macdonald believed 'Walsh was deliberately keeping the Sioux in Canada because he enjoyed the publicity his association with Sitting Bull brought him. In November 1879, Macdonald confided his suspicion to the Governor General.'"

In July 1880, at Macdonald's direction, Walsh was transferred to Fort Qu'Appelle, Saskatchewan. Sitting Bull was reportedly devastated by the loss of the man who had been perhaps the only wasichu of prominent rank to yet befriend him. Walsh told his friend that he would be going to Ottawa, and that he would speak to Macdonald on his behalf. He promised to discuss the establishment of a reserve, the Canadian equivalent of a reservation, for Sitting Bull and the Lakota — even though Walsh himself saw Sitting Bull as too restless to be tied down in such a way.

Meanwhile, there was a perception within the United States government that food was running short for the Lakota north of the border, and it was only a matter of time before Sitting Bull returned—and that steps should be taken to encourage and manage this process. From the American side, the point man was Major David Brotherton, the commanding officer at Fort Buford, located in Dakota Territory near the point where the Yellowstone River flows into the Missouri River. Late in 1880, Brotherton undertook to open a dialog with Sitting Bull, using as his intermediary Edward Allison, a Lakota-speaking scout and trader who had been active in the upper Missouri River country for years.

The November 19, 1880, issue of the *Bismarck Tribune* carried a report from Allison, who had recently visited the hungry people at Sitting Bull's camp and posted his memo to the newspaper on November 13. "There are in Sitting Bull's camp about 900 Indians, and I took with me a small load, barely enough to give them a feast without appearing contemptible," wrote Allison. "My interview with Sitting Bull was entirely satisfactory. He had made an agreement with Maj. Walsh not to make a treaty with anyone until Maj. Walsh returned from the east. . . . Maj. Walsh at the time of the agreement was an officer and representative of the British government, and he, Sitting Bull, feels under obligation to keep his promise. . . . Sitting Bull says that any of Gen. Miles's scouts may visit him without fear, but that he has no confidence in them, and he will make no reply to what they say to him."

From this, one might grasp an insight into Sitting Bull's sense of honor regarding his commitment to Walsh. A cynic, however, might interpret Sitting Bull as "playing" the reporter, although reports of Sitting Bull's feelings with regard to Walsh are consistently respectful. Certainly, his distrust of the bluecoats remains evident in the piece.

In any case, it was now deemed inevitable that Sitting Bull would return to the United States, and Walsh hoped that, as a last act of their friendship, he could help make such a transaction go as smoothly as possible. However, the prime minister declined Walsh's request to officially send Walsh to Washington, D.C., to plead Sitting Bull's case with the

Indian Bureau. The United States already had a plan in place for Sitting Bull's return, and it involved accepting his surrender, not welcoming him back to an agency of his own.

Sitting Bull himself, meanwhile, faced the increasing isolation of being generally ignored by Major Leif Crozier, Walsh's successor. Sitting Bull was left to spend his last winter in exile without the kind paternalism of Long Lance.

"Do you expect to live here by hunting?" JEROME STILLSON had asked in his October 17, 1877, interview with Sitting Bull. "Are there buffalo enough? Can your people subsist on the game here?"

"I don't know," the Lakota itancan answered thoughtfully. "I hope so."

"If not, are any part of your people disposed to take up agriculture? Would any of them raise steers and go to farming?"

"I don't know."

Stillson might have known that Sitting Bull abhorred the thought of agriculture, of seeing his people tied to a single finite plot of ground, when for centuries they had lived as though the land and the buffalo were infinite.

"What will they do, then?"

"As long as there are buffalo that is the way we will live."

"But the time will come when there will be no more buffalo."

"Those are the words of an American," Sitting Bull said with growing anger.

"How long do you think the buffaloes will last?" Stillson persisted.

At this point, Sitting Bull stood up. Stillson's insistent line of questioning had pushed his subject to the limit. Their interview was over.

"We know that on the other side [of the international frontier] the buffaloes will not last very long," Sitting Bull said, extending his right hand with what Stillson would later describe as an impressive gesture. "Why?

Because the country there is poisoned with blood—a poison that kills all the buffaloes or drives them away." As Stillson recalled, Sitting Bull continued his commentary with a "peculiar" smile.

"It is strange," Sitting Bull said. "That the Americans should complain that the Indians kill buffaloes. We kill buffaloes, as we kill other animals, for food and clothing, and to make our lodges warm. They kill buffaloes— for what? Go through your country. See the thousands of carcasses rotting on the Plains. Your young men shoot for pleasure. All they take from dead buffalo is his tail, or his head, or his horns, perhaps, to show they have killed a buffalo. What is this? Is it robbery? You call us savages. What are they? The buffaloes have come North. We have come North to find them."

Indeed, as Sitting Bull knew well, the era of the buffalo—the tatanka— as a ubiquitous presence on the Plains and Prairies of North America was already coming to an end. Sitting Bull also knew that as the buffalo faded away, so too would the Plains Indian way of life which depended on them. He knew that the buffalo were no longer infinite, nor was the world of the Lakota. The decline in the tatanka was like a time bomb, and Sitting Bull could hear it ticking.

In his lifetime, Sitting Bull had witnessed the collapse of this cornerstone of the Lakota world. The end of the line for the buffalo would be the end of the line for the lifestyle of the Plains tribes as they had known and enjoyed it for centuries.

What he had said about the dramatic decline in the numbers of buffalo was painfully true. The ravenous non-Indian appetite for hides would upset the balance forever between 1870 and 1880. These hides that became the robes that kept the Plains Indians warm were very much in demand for wasichu winter coats and hats, and the market was not only on the East Coast of the United States, but abroad in Britain and continental Europe as well. Since buffalo were still so vast in number, even as late as the 1860s, it would have been hard—even impossible—to imagine

that they would be pushed to the precipice of extinction within a generation, but they were.

By about 1800, the small buffalo herds that had existed east of the
Mississippi River were gone. The last buffalo was seen in Pennsylvania in
1801. Buffalo may have been killed to protect livestock and farmlands in
that region, and they were probably hunted for meat. With the westward
expansion of the American frontier, systematic reduction of the Plains
herds began around 1830, when buffalo hunting became the chief industry on the Plains.

Letters to and from Ramsay Crooks and other officials and agents of the
American Fur Company—that are in the collection of the New York
Historical Society—paint a picture of an enormous trade on buffalo robes
during the 1830s, when Sitting Bull was a young man. Indeed, the har-
vests were so huge that there was a glut in the market. Pierre Chouteau,
the American Fur Company agent in the upper Missouri River country,
shipped 51,000 in 1838 though there was still a surplus of 23,000 from the
previous year. Crooks insisted that Chouteau ship no more than 30,000 in
1839 and he grudgingly complied. Hunting was so good the following season that Chouteau shipped 67,000 in 1840.

Organized groups of hunters were shooting buffalo for hides and meat,
often killing up to 250 buffalo a day. In 1850, 100,000 buffalo robes
reached St. Louis en route to the East. In the spring of 1854, Sir George
Gore made a hunting trip into Montana that netted 2,000 buffalo.

The construction of the railroads across the Plains in the middle years
of the nineteenth century further hastened the depletion of buffalo popu-
lations. In 1857, Kansas City alone processed 70,400 robes and 55,000
pounds of meat.

The wasichu were not alone as participants in the slaughter of buffalo.
Many Plains Indians recognized that a profit was to be made in the lucra-
tive trade in buffalo hides. In his *The Hunting of the Buffalo*, E. Douglas
Branch points out that in the 1820s, the Pawnee and Osage deliberately

drove buffalo herds away from the Santa Fe Trail, so that they could control the trade and sell the meat and hides to the Santa Fe traders at higher prices. In "Historians Revisit Slaughter on the Plains," a November 16, 1999, article in the *New York Times*, Jim Robbins quoted Dr. Dan Flores, a professor of Western history at the University of Montana. "Indians were involved in the market," Flores told Robbins. "They were cashing in on buffalo in the 1840s as their principal entree into the market economy, and very few species are able to survive when they become a commodity."

The most famous of wasichu buffalo hunters was William Frederick "Buffalo Bill" Cody. Though he is best remembered for his Wild West show, where we revisit him in a later chapter, Cody literally made a name for himself as a buffalo hunter. In 1867, he was hired by the Goddard Brothers, who had a contract to supply meat for construction crews on the Kansas Pacific division of the Union Pacific Railroad. In just eighteen months, Cody alone supplied 4,280 animals. This total would, however, be exceeded by many other hunters. It was Cody's flair for self-promotion that placed his name in the history of the great animal that became his namesake.

"When in the West in 1872, I satisfied myself by personal inquiries that the number of buffalo being then annually slaughtered for their hides was at least one million per annum," wrote William Blackmore, the famous British hunter in the preface to *Plains of the Great West* by Colonel Richard Dodge, published in 1877. "In the autumn of 1868, whilst crossing the plains on the Kansas Pacific Railroad for a distance of upwards of 120 miles, between Ellsworth and Sheridan, we passed through an almost unbroken herd of buffalo. The Plains were blackened with them, and more than once the train had to stop to allow unusually large herds to pass. A few years afterwards, when traveling over the same line of railroad, it was a rare sight to see a few herds of from ten to twenty buffalo."

After the transcontinental railroad lines were completed in 1869, it became remarkably easy to ship buffalo hides and buffalo meat to the

Shooting buffalo along the line of the Kansas–Pacific Railroad from the June 3, 1871, issue of *Frank Leslie's Illustrated Newspaper*. (*Library of Congress*)

East. Based on railroad shipping records and other data, 3,158,730 buffalo were killed by wasichu, and 405,000 by Indians in Kansas alone between 1872 and 1874. The hides sold for an average of two dollars each, but that was good business. During the winter of 1872–1873, the peak season for hide shipments, one firm reported handling 200,000 hides, tons of meat, and $2.5 million worth of bones. Buffalo bones were shipped to Eastern cities, where they were ground up for use as phosphorous fertilizer or bone char. After the early 1870s, when refrigerator cars became available, it was possible to ship buffalo meat to the East year-round. According to E. Douglas Branch in *The Hunting of the Buffalo*, the Atchison, Topeka & Santa Fe Railroad alone carried 424,000 hides in 1872 and 1873, and the Union Pacific and Buffalo Bill's Kansas Pacific brought the total to 1.25 million for just three companies.

But buffalo were not only slaughtered for money. There were so many buffalo and the country was so huge and so new that no one could imagine the killing could do any harm to their unimaginable numbers, much less their very existence. Thus they were often slaughtered needlessly. Hunting from train windows was advertised widely, and passengers shot them as the buffalo raced beside the trains. People came from Europe, as well as from the eastern United States, to hunt the buffalo purely for the sport. The irony was that these animals were hardly dangerous, and so large that little skill was needed to fell one with a bullet from a gun. As Sitting Bull correctly pointed out, many sport hunters killed a buffalo and took only its tail, head, or horns.

The darkest side of the buffalo slaughter was that many wasichu advocated the eradication of the buffalo as a means of taking away the livelihood and well-being of the Plains Indian people and forcing them into submission. Columbus Delano, who served as Secretary of the Interior from 1869 to 1875 during Ulysses S. Grant's administration, is notorious for have advocated such a policy. In 1872, he theorized that Indians could be forced to turn to agriculture for their subsistence if the buffalo herds were destroyed.

As the Kansas herds were depleted, the hunters moved north into Montana and Dakota Territory. From 1874 through 1877—the last years that Sitting Bull and his Hunkpapa were hunting in Montana's Powder River Country—the wasichu shipped an average of 90,000 robes annually from Fort Benton on the Missouri River alone. In 1882, about 200,000 hides went east from Montana and Dakota Territory by rail, but only two years later, the last carload left Dakota Territory because there were now too few left to make commercial hunting viable.

Just as estimates of the original number of buffalo on the Plains range from 30 to 75 million, so too do the estimates of their numbers at various points during their decline. In *"Introduction to Social Mathematics,"* a 2005 paper published at the Illinois Mathematics and Science Academy, Bernard C. Hollister cites Interior department data, noting that "In 1865 [there were] approximately 15 million bison and only ten years later their numbers [had] fallen to less than two million."

What is not in dispute is that the buffalo population declined rapidly in the 1870s and even more rapidly in the 1880s. In 1886, zoologist William T. Hornaday wanted specimens of the Plains buffalo for the National Zoological Park in Washington, D.C. He knew that the buffalo were becoming scarce on the Plains, but in eight weeks' time, he collected only twenty-five buffalo in Montana, an area that had supported tens of thousands just a few years earlier. His thorough search demonstrated that the species was indeed in danger of imminent extinction.

In 1889, Hornaday published what is probably the first scientific study to contain reasonably accurate population data. By this time, it was almost too late. In his *The Extermination of the American Bison*, published by the Smithsonian Institution, he calculated that only 1,091 buffalo remained on the Plains. Other estimates show that the total sank to fewer than 1,000 during the 1890s. The U.S. Fish and Wildlife Service estimates that there were fewer than 300 buffalo remaining in the wild in the United States at the turn of the century.

Meanwhile, though, many buffalo survived in herds that were collected and preserved by individuals who recognized the value of not letting this great signature animal of the Plains go extinct. One such effort was the deliberate preservation project undertaken by ranchers Michael Pablo and Charles Allard in Montana's Flathead Valley on the western side of the Rocky Mountains during the 1880s. The federal government also got into the preservation business. Yellowstone National Park, created in 1872, was the first public land where killing buffalo was totally banned, although poachers and predators took their toll, and a census 1894 found only twenty buffalo in the park. Congress then rushed to pass the National Park Protective Act, which increased the fines and even threatened imprisonment for buffalo poaching.

In 1905, the American Bison Society was formed, with Hornaday as president and Theodore Roosevelt as honorary president. Roosevelt persuaded Congress to establish preserves, and, with the help of a cadre of private buffalo owners, the society was able to stock a number of preserves and parks. Ranchers and breeders, recognizing the economic potential of the animal, expanded their efforts to preserve and reestablish the buffalo. The buffalo was finally pulled back from the abyss in about 1910, as the census topped 2,000 and continued to rise slowly.

A 1929 inventory counted 3,385 buffalo and, although the count was not precise, it was encouraging enough that the society discontinued its programs and activities in 1930. By 1951, there were 12,158, and by 1989, there were 98,000. At the turn of the twenty-first century, the Fish and Wildlife Service estimated that the buffalo population in the United States had surpassed a sustainable population of 200,000, with their numbers increasing rapidly.

Today, the vast majority of buffalo are in private herds, and buffalo meat is once again on the menu, widely enjoyed by both wasichu and Indian alike throughout the northern Plains, the Mountain West, and elsewhere. However, even as the buffalo population approaches a half million, the days of them being the cornerstone of a way of life for the inhabitants of an area the size of Western Europe ended within Sitting Bull's lifetime and will never return.

When the great Crow leader Alaxchiiaahush (Plenty Coups or Plenty Achievements) was interviewed by Frank B. Linderman for his 1930 book *Plenty-Coups: Chief of the Crows*, he said, "When the buffalo went away the hearts of my people fell to the ground, and they could not lift them up again. After this, nothing happened." This statement, better than any other, completely describes the effect upon the Plains culture of the end of the buffalo as a viable source of subsistence. The culture was devastated. As Plenty Coups put it, afterward nothing happened. It was like the end of time, the end of the history of a people.

Even by 1879, the Lakota had found that the buffalo were growing more scarce in southern Canada than south of the border, and they were compelled to risk arrest to fill their bellies. "The buffalo have come down

By 1903, only a handful of buffalo remained in the federally protected herd in Yellowstone National Park. (*Library of Congress*)

here, and we follow them," Sitting Bull told Stanley Huntley in June 1879, when the Chicago journalist interviewed him at his hunting camp in Montana. "We want meat. Our women and children are hungry. There is nothing for us but wild game. . . . The buffalo have left us. We have followed them. . . . I am a hunter, and will hunt as long as there is wild game on the prairie. When the buffalo are gone I will send my children on the prairie to hunt mice."

As the Lakota looked south across the "medicine line" from the Grandmother's Country during the bleak winters of the 1870s, they saw a country poisoned with blood. They saw the end of an era. The buffalo had left them in Canada, and soon the buffalo would be gone—period.

"You must not think that the Great Spirit does not watch me as closely as he watches you," Sitting Bull told Huntley in 1879. "I know that he is watching me, and he will never leave me to starve. When the buffalo are gone he will give me something else. The Americans must think the Great Spirit thinks of them alone." He may have hoped and prayed for such a thing, but Sitting Bull had to have known that it was wishful thinking. It was hard for the Lakota to conceptualize a future without the tatanka. It was like trying to conceive of a future without sunlight. Presaging Alaxchiiaahush's perspective in the 1930s, some Lakota even began to fear that the end of the tatanka would mark an end to the people themselves.

Sitting Bull wore an elaborate feather headdress during his appearances with Buffalo Bill's Wild West, although he probably never wore more than two feathers during his years on the Plains. A white feather represented his first coup, and a red one his first injury in battle. This headdress represented the image that audiences expected of an "Indian chief." This photograph was part of the August 1885 session at the studio of William Notman & Sons in Montreal. (*Library of Congress*)

5

THE CELEBRITY

As Sitting Bull sat at Wood Mountain, contemplating his own half-century mark during the winter of 1880–1881, he recognized that his life was changing. Men such as Jerome Stillson and Stanley Huntley, men that Long Lance Walsh called "great paper chiefs who talk with a million tongues to all the people in the world," had established Sitting Bull's name as a household word among the wasichu.

However, even as this was happening, his status as an itancan among the Lakota was diminishing. Once he had been seen as the foremost defiant voice of opposition to the wasichu. Now, many of the Lakota living on the Great Sioux Reservation in Dakota Territory and elsewhere saw him as having abandoned them to run away to Grandmother's Country. In Canada, meanwhile, the Lakota were slowly abandoning Sitting Bull, encouraged by Major Crozier of the North West Mounted Police, who used every opportunity to undermine Sitting Bull's authority.

Those who had traveled north to Canada with him in 1877, as well as those who streamed north in 1878 to be with him, had started to filter back across the medicine line to stay. In the fall of 1880, Spotted Eagle and Rain in the Face went back. In January 1881, Gall followed them. Then his own family, including Jumping Bull and Gray Eagle surrendered. Even Sitting Bull's own daughter, Many Horses, had gone south with her new husband, Thomas Fly.

From an estimated eight hundred lodges at one time, Sitting Bull's encampment at Wood Mountain had shriveled to about sixty-five lodges, or around 125 families, by the spring of 1881.

The decision to go back to the Grandfather's country was not an easy one for Sitting Bull, and he changed his mind several times. In April, he promised the North West Mounted Police that he would leave, but he remained. Crozier's impatience grew, as he was under increasing pressure from Ottawa to make it happen. Unlike Walsh, Crozier saw Sitting Bull not as a friend, but as a predicament to be eliminated.

In May 1880 and again nearly a year later, Sitting Bull had sent his nephew—and adopted son—One Bull to Fort Buford to look things over. As he reported, the conditions there were not pleasant, as the post was crowded with more than a thousand returning Lakota. Some of the more prominent leaders had been arrested. North of the border, conditions were also deteriorating. As their numbers declined, Sitting Bull's people were under pressure from neighboring tribes who had been less inclined to bother the mighty Lakota a few years earlier when they had a strong presence. The Cree were stealing horses, and all the Canadian tribes were competing with the Lakota for buffalo.

In April 1881, when Sitting Bull impulsively decided that he would make a brief trip up to Fort Qu'Appelle to visit his friend James Walsh, Crozier ordered his second in command, Captain Alexander Macdonnell, to accompany Sitting Bull, and to function as the North West Mounted Police point man in facilitating Sitting Bull's return to the

United States. The captain would remain with or near Sitting Bull for the remainder of his tenure in Canada, and would also be in communication with Major Brotherton at Fort Buford.

In early May, Edgar Dewdney of the Canadian Indian Commission came to meet with Sitting Bull. His was a carrot-and-stick approach. He first took Sitting Bull to task for breaking his promise to Crozier to return to the United States, and next promised rations to Sitting Bull on his journey south to the border if he would change his mind and leave Canada once and for all.

Meanwhile, the American and Canadian press were abuzz with rumors of Sitting Bull's pending surrender. Would he or wouldn't he? Finally, a journalist from the *Bismarck Tribune* managed an interview with Macdonnell, who was traveling with Sitting Bull. The correspondent wrote in the May 6 issue that he had learned from Macdonnell that "Sitting Bull had concluded to surrender."

"The circumstances leading to such a resolve are as follows," the correspondent continued, giving us an excellent insight into Sitting Bull's situation and that of the Lakota in Canada as he grappled with the decision.

> First, he is starving; second, the continual desertion of the several . . . bands from his camp have left him so weak [from a security standpoint] that he is afraid to leave Wood Mountain to hunt, there being so many enemies on the watch for him. Third, Low Dog, one of his chiefs, left Wood Mountain a short time ago with 20 lodges or 30 families, and came over to Poplar River [a U.S. Army post in Montana] to surrender. This last desertion was the straw that broke the camel's back. Capt. McDonald [sic] has Kyo Morra, interpreter and three hostiles with him, they having been sent over to Buford with a letter to the soldier chief [Brotherton]. In this letter to Maj. Brotherton, Sitting Bull says "I am ready to surrender unconditionally." He asked that provisions be sent out to meet him, and that the Indians who are already at Fort Buford be held there until his arrival.

In council at Wood Mountain Sitting Bull said that he would have
sent his son [to Fort Buford] with Capt. McDonald as an evidence of
good faith if the boy [five-year-old Crow Foot] had been old enough
to ride a horse. He told [Major] Crozier that he was going to take his
advice and go over and peacefully surrender to the American authorities. He will move this way as soon as the snow gets off and travel is
practicable.

There had also been speculation in the media that the Canadian government was in opposition to the return of Sitting Bull to the United
States—as Walsh had been. In his *Bismarck Tribune* interview, when
Macdonnell was asked about this, he explained "that the reports of
Canadian police interference with negotiations for Sitting Bull's surrender are untrue; that the policy of the police has been in favor of surrender." Macdonnell went on to say that "Crozier has done all he could to
break Sitting Bull's influence in the [Lakota] camp, and he had continu-
ally advised the other chiefs to go over and surrender." The walls were
closing in.

Would he or wouldn't he? He said he would, but he changed his mind.
He said wouldn't, but he changed his mind. Sitting Bull was unsure of
what to do, because he was unsure what would happen to him in
American custody. Would he be executed? Would he be jailed? He had
received word that his daughter Many Horses had been shackled with leg
irons when she reached Fort Buford. This story, which he would later
learn to be untrue, troubled him greatly. He was in a quandary, but as we
learn in the *Bismarck Tribune* article, forces were in motion to take the
decision out of his control.

During this time, one of Sitting Bull's closest confidants was Jean-Louis
LeGaré, a French Canadian trader who was active around Wood
Mountain, and whom Sitting Bull had known since he had come to
Canada. LeGaré had long been trusted by the Lakota, and Sitting Bull was
inclined to trust him now. In April, the trader had made Sitting Bull a

standing offer to lead a supply-laden train of his own wagons and Red River carts to take the Lakota down to Fort Buford. At last, Sitting Bull agreed.

Sitting Bull changed his mind several more times, not sure if he should go to Buford or back to Wood Mountain, but on July 10 the journey finally began. LeGaré escorted him and nearly 187 of his followers, three-quarters of them women and children, south toward the medicine line.

They were met at the international border on July 17 by a U.S. Army supply train led by Captain Walter Clifford. As Clifford recalled in an interview with the *Bismarck Tribune* published on August 5, it was from him that Sitting Bull first heard that the stories of Many Horses having been shackled were untrue. "What is the reason they put my daughter into irons?" Sitting Bull asked Clifford. "What has she done? What will they do to me?"

"The United States government has no reason to lie to you," Clifford replied, having told Sitting Bull the truth about Many Horses. "What would I gain by lying to you? It was in the spirit of mercy that you were sent for; they wish to settle this great question forever. I put a knife in your hands, and if I am lying to you, you may kill me."

"I don't believe you," Sitting Bull replied.

He later discovered that his daughter was fine.

Sitting Bull and his group entered Fort Buford on July 19. Many accounts, including Stanley Vestal's, state that the arrival was at "high noon," but Clifford recalled in the *Bismarck Tribune* interview that it was at 2:30 p.m.

His formal surrender took place the following day in the office of Major Brotherton at Fort Buford. According to Clifford, Sitting Bull, through his interpreter, was careful not to use the word "surrender." A sizable number of Lakota, as well as U.S. Army officers, were present, and Captain Macdonnell rode down from Canada for the occasion. Crozier no doubt wanted a first-hand confirmation that the elusive Sitting Bull had actually given up.

In what amounted to a surrender, despite his intentions, Sitting Bull relinquished his prized Winchester carbine, handing it to his five-year-old son, Crow Foot, who in turn handed it to Brotherton. Crow Foot apparently impressed the people who were assembled there that day. Like his father, the little boy had a presence that people remembered. Nine years later, he was mentioned in his father's obituary as "bright as a dollar with eyes that fairly snap like whips."

It is widely reported that Sitting Bull made a statement which included a phrase to the effect of "Let it be recorded that I was the last man of my people to lay down my gun." He may or may not have said this. One Bull, who was seated next to Sitting Bull at the time, later told Stanley Vestal that Sitting Bull remained silent. Clifford recalled that Sitting Bull told Brotherton that he came and yielded to the wishes of the U.S. government "not on my own account, but because my women and children were starving."

We can get a snapshot of the Dakota Territory to which Sitting Bull and his family returned in a short article on Indian demographics that appeared in the June 3, 1881, issue of the *Bismarck Tribune*.

Dakota has no less than 27,550 Indians," the paper reported, not mentioning that the number was 20 percent of the wasichu population of the territory. "Of these 27,550 Indians only 10,223 have assumed the ways of civilized people, and wear citizen's dress. There are engaged in civil pursuits 2,903, nearly all being agriculturists. They have 21 day schools and eight boarding schools. There are 3,773 children of a schoolable age, and of these 648 girls and 417 boys attend school. The average daily attendance is 826, which compares favorably with any white schools. The whole number of Dakota [Territory] Indians who can read is set down at 1,305, of which 103 have learned to read within the year. The number of Indians who have died [within the territory in the preceding year] was 389, and the number of children born was 530, showing an increase in the

Dakota tribes of 130. The amount of land held in reserves by these Indians amounts to the enormous body of 41,999,456 acres [44 percent of the territory], of which over 5,000,000 is good farming land. The Indians only cultivate 16,150 acres of their land. Last year they raised 24,172 bushels of wheat, 75,401 bushels of corn, 2,452 bushels of barley, and 62,593 bushels of vegetables. The Dakota Indians own 24,193 head of horses, 6,781 head of cattle, and 632 swine.

When one gets past the disturbing nineteenth-century ethnocentrism and paternalism, the data provide a useful look at the how many Indians were living in the territory at the moment when Sitting Bull surrendered—the last significantly large group of Lakota that were living outside the confines of wasichu "civilization." Obviously, most Lakota still lived beyond wasichu influence, but that would change within a generation.

By way of comparison, six of the largest reservations that exist in the area that once comprised the Great Sioux Reservation—Cheyenne River, Crow Creek, Pine Ridge, Rosebud, Standing Rock, and Yankton—now have an area of 9.2 million acres. Their total population, according to the 2000 census, is 51,435 people living within the reservations or on associated trust land.

THE U.S. government's plan for Sitting Bull as he returned officially and finally to the United States was that he should be sent to the Standing Rock Agency, adjacent to the U.S. Army's Fort Yates on the Missouri River in the center of Dakota Territory. The agency's area of jurisdiction coincidentally contained the section of the Grand River where Sitting Bull is believed to have been born.

The name is derived from a natural stone that is seen to resemble a woman with a child on her back. Lakota legend holds that there was a woman who became jealous of her husband's second wife and refused to travel with the tribe when it moved camp. When her husband's brothers returned to retrieve her, they discovered that she had turned to stone. This rock, considered to be wakan, or sacred, was carried with the people for many years, and eventually erected on a pedestal at the Standing Rock Agency.

Many of Sitting Bull's closest followers were already at Standing Rock when he returned from Canada. So too, were Gall and Rain in the Face, as well as Sitting Bull's daughter Many Horses and her husband. On July 29, Sitting Bull left Fort Buford aboard the steamboat *General Sherman*, heading south on the Missouri. He was accompanied by his wives and seven of his younger children, as well as his sister Good Feather and his uncle Four Horns. Bone Tomahawk, High as the Clouds, Scarlet Thunder, and White Dog were also noted to have been with Sitting Bull's entourage. Edward Allison accompanied him as his interpreter. Two days later, as the steamer docked in Bismarck, he had his first look at an American city, and wasichu city folk had their first look at him. He was feted as the celebrity that he had become. The *Bismarck Tribune* (then a weekly) devoted the entire front page of its August 5 issue to his arrival in the city on the last day of July, and added additional pages of coverage of the continuation of his journey to Standing Rock. The paper reported him "jovial and not at all despondent," as his mood at Fort Buford had been reported.

Much of the later confusion about Sitting Bull's birth date may be traced to interviews he gave to various *Bismarck Tribune* reporters that week. One news story stated that he "looks older than 50, but is only 47." Another reported that "He commenced by stating that he is 44 years old." These items would seem to be a source of the birth dates of 1834 and 1837 that appear in some references to Sitting Bull. Of course, these discrepancies may be errors in translation or errors in reporting. Later, conflicting data in the 1888–1891 annual tribal censuses would further complicate the calculations by suggesting birth dates of both 1832 and 1834. Today, it is generally accepted that he was born in the Winter That Yellow Eyes

Danced in the Snow, or 1831. This would mean that Sitting Bull was exactly fifty when he made his first visit to Bismarck.

The same reporter who reported him as forty-four said that Sitting Bull identified the place of his birth as Willow Creek, just below the mouth of the Cheyenne River, which is more than sixty miles south of the mouth of the Grand River, where most sources claim as his birthplace.

He took a great interest in a Northern Pacific locomotive that was near the riverboat landing, and asked to see it moved. B. D. Vermilye, the private secretary to Herman Haupt, the general manager of the Northern Pacific, was among the dignitaries on hand to greet Sitting Bull, and he readily obliged. Sitting Bull was impressed, but when Vermilye offered to give Sitting Bull a ride to the planned reception at the Sheridan House Hotel, he said he'd rather walk. A government ambulance wagon was made available, and Sitting Bull and part of his entourage were driven to the Sheridan House. Here, as dozens of wasichu crowded around to catch a glimpse of them, Sitting Bull and several of his companions, including Allison, sat on the floor of a "spacious parlor" and passed what the newspaper described as a "pipe of peace."

The newspaper reported that Sitting Bull was scantily dressed, purposely so, no doubt, so as to impress white men with his poverty.

> He is below medium height, sits erect and displays a well developed arm. . . . he wore a pair of smoked glass goggles. . . . He had on a pair of blueish leggings and wore about him a blue blanket. His feet were covered with a pair of moccasins of expensive pattern richly studded with porcupine quills. He had what was once a fine laundried shirt, but little the worse for wear, and a noticeable feature was the absence of ornaments, in striking contrast to his associates. Streaks of war paint ornamented the shirt sleeves and the neck, face and scalp at the hair parting were covered with bright red paint. His hair is jet black, reaches below his shoulders, and hangs in three braids, the center one being pendant from a round part at the crown of his broad head, encircled at the parting with a bright streak of red.

The mention of his wearing goggles would seem improbable were it not for the fact that he was photographed that same day at the Merchants' Hotel by Bismarck photographer Orlando Goff. Reportedly, Goff paid Sitting Bull for the privilege of taking his picture. During his brief stay in Bismarck, Sitting Bull was also paid by several people for his autograph, as he had by now learned to write his name in the wasichu cursive script.

Goff's was the first known portrait photograph ever taken of Sitting Bull, and the second time that his image is known to have been recorded on film. The first was in a photo taken at Fort Walsh in 1878 by George Anderton. It is a general view of the fort in which a number of people are pictured. One man wrapped in a blanket is identified as Sitting Bull.

The reason for his wearing the smoked-glass goggles, and whether they were worn as a vision aid, remains a mystery, although there are several references to them. Other Indians were also photographed during this period with such eyewear.

After a half hour at the Sheridan House, Sitting Bull and his party were driven to the Merchants' Hotel where a luncheon was planned. The *Bismarck Tribune* was effusive in its praise of the affair, noting that the proprietors,

> Messers. Marach and Wakeman had spread themselves in this respect, and everything was served as it would be to the queen of England, with the exception that the whole bill of fare was put before each Indian. They laughed at the printed bills of fare, and at the names of some of the dishes, which were explained to them by interpreter Allison. To the surprise of the scores of people who were peeping in at the windows, and the servants within, each Indian handled his knife and fork as graceful as the most cultivated. Sitting Bull ate very slowly, stopping quite often to fan himself. When desert was served the Indians marveled much at the ice cream, and remarked that they could not see how the white men could cook victuals so cold. At the conclusion of the feast, Sitting Bull presented Capt.

The first photographic portrait of Sitting Bull was almost certainly taken on July 31, 1881, at a hotel in Bismarck, Dakota Territory, by local photographer Orlando Goff. According to Stanley Vestal, Sitting Bull and his entourage were dining at the hotel and agreed to be photographed for a fee. The reason for the smoked-glass goggles, and whether they were worn as a vision aid, has never been established. (*Library of Congress*)

Batchelor with his pipe, and gave his glasses to Mr. Vermilye, which event was duly celebrated a few moments after by the uncorking of wine bottles, to the delight of the friends of the above named gentleman [Sitting Bull]. After finishing dinner Sitting Bull registered in his own name on the register, and the party started for the river. A month earlier, he and his people had been camped at Fort Qu'Appelle, running short of food. Now he was seated in one of Bismarck's finest hotels, enjoying a sumptuous meal—not to mention the marvel of ice cream, which he relished.

Rather than spending the night at one of the Bismarck hotels, Sitting Bull and his party reboarded the *General Sherman*, which departed Bismarck at 6:00 p.m. Ten miles downriver, the vessel tied up for the night and the Indians went ashore to camp. The following day at about noon, the steamer disembarked its 190 Lakota passengers—including four dozen children—at Fort Yates.

A brief reception was held in the cabin of the ship, at which, again as in Bismarck, curious wasichu crowded around to catch a glimpse of the Lakota itancan. According to the *Bismarck Tribune* reporter, comments included "Why, he does not look at all like I expected, he don't look as savage as I thought he would," and "Can that be the instigator of the Custer Massacre?"

The report went on to say that "the great chieftain was very gracious to the ladies, as indeed he was on the entire trip [from Fort Buford], and would show them attentions and furnish them his autograph free of charge, while he either refused entirely or demanded one to five dollars [nearly $100 in current dollars] from the gentlemen."

Many Horses was unable to meet him because she had recently been moved from Fort Yates to a place on Standing Rock that was about two miles from the Missouri River. Perhaps she was not told of the time that her father would be arriving. Perhaps too, it had something to do with her father's reported displeasure with her having eloped to marry Thomas Fly while Sitting Bull was at Fort Qu'Appelle a few weeks earlier. His disapproval of this marriage has long been a point of controversy. It is simply not known how he took it. Perhaps it was a case of his being initially unhappy about it, and later coming to accept it. In any case, within the next couple of years he would sit for a photograph with Many Horses and her son, Thomas Fly, Jr.

Sitting Bull sat on the shore in the "hot noonday sun," and smoked his pipe as the others left to accept their new life at Standing Rock. As the *Bismarck Tribune* recalls, "Only a few years ago Sitting Bull had a following of 10,000 people, including nearly 5,000 good fighting warriors. He rambled at his leisure and adorned his belt with many a scalp. He planned the Custer massacre and defied the government. At this moment he is looked upon with jealousy by nearly all other chiefs, his spirit is broken and he sits on a sandy river bank surrounded by civilization, with his last 200 followers calmly awaiting the pleasure of Uncle Sam to change his camp or invite him to partake of pork and beans."

In the space of a couple of weeks, Sitting Bull had gone from life as a mysterious exile to that of a celebrity—or that of a curiosity, depending upon one's perspective. The man known to most wasichu only by his reputation had now been seen by hundreds of average wasichu. Many even had his autograph.

In its August 5 coverage of this transition, it is jarring to read the phrase "He planned the Custer massacre" in the pages of the *Bismarck Tribune*. The Battle of the Little Bighorn had not, of course, been planned by the Indians—who reacted defensively—nor had Sitting Bull been involved in the action on Custer Hill that left the "boy general" dead. However, his being the archvillain of the fight was part of the Sitting Bull myth that the wasichu accepted, just as they accepted without question that he had two eyes and two feet. We can take the reporters who interviewed him to task for not getting such a salient fact right, but by 1881, it was so widely accepted as true that it probably occurred to no one to question it.

Sitting Bull's role at the Little Bighorn played no small part in his notoriety. In the years immediately following, the Little Bighorn had become the signature event of the Indian Wars. It is still regarded as such. There is little wonder that its "archvillian" should have attracted immense curiosity and publicity.

For Sitting Bull, the ice cream and attention he received in Bismarck must have been amusing and pleasant, but there is a downside to being viewed by the world as an archvillain. He had been promised that he would be taken to a gift-house at Standing Rock, but this was, as Sitting Bull would have put it, a lie. In September, barely a month after he reached the agency, Secretary of War Robert Todd Lincoln, the son of the great emancipator, decreed that the man who killed Custer should be incarcerated as a prisoner of war at Fort Randall.

Abraham Lincoln's son, now a cabinet secretary in the new government of "White Father" James A. Garfield, had succumbed to pressure from those who still considered Custer a martyr. Only five years had passed and memories were still fresh. So too were the tireless public relations efforts by Elizabeth Bacon "Libby" Custer to ensure her late husband's status as a member of the most hallowed pantheon of American heroes. In the minds of the wasichu who refused to let go of their animosity, the Lakota itancan was the dark reverse side of the shining Custer coin.

Sitting Bull was understandably furious. As the *Bismarck Tribune* reported on September 9, 1881, "He protested against the removal [when informed on September 6], and carried on at a great rate during the night. This morning he proposed to hold a council with the commanding officer [Colonel Charles Gilbert]. This being refused he assumed an attitude of defiance and swears that he will never go to Randall alive. He says he wishes to die as Crazy Horse did."

Gilbert then ordered Company H of the 17th Infantry Regiment to round up everyone at Sitting Bull's camp and escort them to the boat landing at Fort Yates to await the steamer that would take them away. The *Bismarck Tribune* described Gilbert as "a man who will allow no trifling, and his action to-day will have a wholesome effect on all."

Sitting Bull's fate was no longer his own to decide. His only choice was to allow them to kill him—and let him die like Crazy Horse—or to do as he was told. After much protestation, he decided upon the latter course. On September 9, he once again boarded the *General Sherman*, ironically named for the U.S. Army's commanding general, under guard.

Coincidentally, Robert Lincoln's boss, President Garfield, was shot and killed on September 19, just two days after Sitting Bull stepped off the steamer at Fort Randall. Robert Lincoln was with him when he died. A recurrent myth from American folklore holds that both Lincoln's father and President Garfield were victims of a curse. It was placed on the American Presidency in 1811 by the Shawnee leader Tecumseh or by his brother Tenskwatawa, the "Shawnee Prophet," after General William Henry Harrison defeated the Shawnee at the Battle of Tippecanoe. Essentially, the curse stated that Harrison would be elected president, but that he would die in office and everyone elected to the office in twenty-year increments thereafter would die in office. Harrison was elected in 1840 and he died in office. Two decades later in 1860, Abraham Lincoln was elected and he too died in office. Thereafter, the presidents elected in 20-year increments, including 1880, 1900, 1920, 1940, and 1960, all died in office. Because these years were the only presidential election years during that time frame that ended in zero, the curse became known as the "Zero Year Curse." Had only Harrison died in office, it would have been a coincidence. However, the fact that the pattern continued for 120 years kept the myth of the curse alive.

In a further strange coincidence, Robert Lincoln was also present when President William McKinley, elected in 1900, died after being shot by an assassin. Having been present at the death of his own father in 1865, Robert had been at the sides of *three* presidents as they died in office from gunshot wounds.

Life at Fort Randall, while humiliating, was not altogether disagreeable for Sitting Bull. The post commander, Colonel George Andrews, treated the prisoner of war as a respected guest. Andrews, unlike those who pulled Robert Lincoln's strings, knew what had really happened at the Little Bighorn. In contrast to the way many Indian leaders had been—and would be—treated by the U.S. Army, Sitting Bull was hardly a prisoner at all. Many others had been shackled and thrown in jail cells for months or years. Sitting Bull camped as he had at Wood Mountain, or at many other places before that. He was with his family and many of the people that he knew. His wives and children were there, and so too was his mother, Her Holy Door, who had been part of his household since her husband was killed a quarter century before.

The winters were cold, and at first life at Fort Randall was boring, but there were no shackles. The Lakota were not allowed to hunt—but neither were they allowed to go hungry.

Sitting Bull submitted quietly, albeit not happily, to his life at the post. He certainly knew that things could have been worse. The Fort Randall complex—more a campus than a stockade—was his forced residence, but ironically it gave him his first-ever known, fixed address. Because of this, Sitting Bull suddenly started receiving fan mail. Bags of it began arriving from all over the world. Having learned to write his name in wasichu script, he relished signing autographs for people who wrote to him, or who made their way up the Missouri to visit him.

Just as there were two sides to the Little Bighorn coin, there were two sides to the wasichu perception of Sitting Bull. Just as the "archvillain of the Little Bighorn" was greeted in Bismarck with ice cream rather than a hangman's noose, so too did many wasichu regard Sitting Bull as a mysterious and interesting man rather than as the cold-blooded killer as claimed by Libby Custer and the die-hard devotees of her husband's heroic myth.

Sitting Bull drawing of him in a fight with an Assiniboine warrior. (*Manuscript 1929B. Sitting Bull pictographic autobiography, 1882. National Anthropological Archives*)

While at Fort Randall, Sitting Bull and his wives, Four Robes and Seen by the Nation, as well as many of his children and other family members, were photographed several times by the studio of Bailey, Dix & Mead, and by William DeGraff of Bismarck. In these photographs, Sitting Bull seems relaxed and at ease. In some of the photographs, he is posed with officers at the post, as well as their wives and family members. Sitting Bull was also visited by Rudolph Cronau, an illustrator for the German magazine *Die Gartenlaube*, who came to Dakota Territory to view and paint the Lakota.

During his time at Fort Randall, Sitting Bull sat down to re-create many of the images from his 1846–1870 Hieroglyphic Autobiography, which had gone missing in about 1870, and on which he had never resumed work. Using graphite, colored pencil, and ink, Sitting Bull completed twenty-two drawings on 8 1/2 x 13 1/2-inch leaves of a bound volume of ruled paper. Shortly after Sitting Bull did them, the drawings came into the possession of Lieutenant Wallace Tear, who sent them to General John C. Smith in April 1882. How this happened is uncertain. Perhaps

Sitting Bull gave them to Tear. Perhaps not. Preserved today by the National Anthropological Archives, Sitting Bull's portfolio is inscribed on the inside front cover "For Gen'l J.C. Smith, No 250 West Van Buren St, Chicago, Ill," and "Fort Randall, DT, April 14, 1882."

In the meantime, back in 1870, his uncle Four Horns had re-created copies of many pages from Sitting Bull's Autobiography as well as some pages from that of Sitting Bull's adopted Assiniboine brother Jumping Bull. Using colored pencils, ink, and watercolor, he completed fifty-five drawings on fifty-four blank backs of seven-by-ten-inch loose-leaf printed roster sheets originating with the 31st Infantry Regiment and dated 1868. Of the fifty-five, fifteen represent Jumping Bull's accomplishments, while the remainder are Sitting Bull's. Sitting Bull signed his drawings with wasichu cursive, but Four Horns used Sitting Bull's seated buffalo pictograph as a signature on his pictures. In 1882, Sitting Bull deliberately omitted images of him battling the wasichu soldiers—which would have been awkward to do under wasichu eyes at Fort Randall—but Four Horns had not.

These well-known pictographs were not the only ones that Sitting Bull did at Fort Randall. As William John Armstrong wrote in the January-February 1995 issue of *Michigan History* magazine, Sitting Bull also made some drawings for the family of Captain Horace Quimby, who was a regimental quartermaster at Fort Randall in 1881–1882. His wife, Martha Quimby, their daughter Alice, and Martha's sister Maggie Smith became friendly with Sitting Bull and his family. As Armstrong wrote, "During one of their visits to the Lakota encampment, Martha noticed some sketches Sitting Bull had drawn for the Indian agent. She asked him if he would draw some for her. He agreed. Sitting Bull was particularly fond of children and he especially liked Alice. She may have been one of the reasons he agreed to Martha's request. After acquiring a ledger book from the Indian agent's headquarters, Sitting Bull went to work."

Pursuing his research during the 1920s and 1930s, Stanley Vestal had access to many people, both Indian and wasichu, who had known Sitting

Bull. Among them was Lieutenant Colonel George Ahern of the 25th Infantry Regiment, who got to know the "very remarkable man" when he was supervising Sitting Bull's mail at Fort Randall. His recollections provide an enlightening insight into Sitting Bull's character and personality. "He would visit me in my quarters when I failed to show up in camp," Ahern told Vestal. "He would enjoy leaving his card; in fact it was my card which I had left purposely in his tipi, and he would return it with his own name written on the reverse side. The nearest he came to being jovial was when he dropped the card on my table with a smile and a twinkle in his eye. . . . Even then I had become acquainted through older officers with some of the great wrongs done the Indian, and I marvelled at the Indian's patience and forbearance!"

In May 1883, after nineteen months at Fort Randall and countless petitions to Washington by wasichu and Indian sympathizers, Robert Lincoln finally changed his mind and ordered Sitting Bull released. On the tenth of that month, he and 171 other prisoners of the U.S. Army stepped off the steamer at the Fort Yates boat landing. One hesitates to say that Sitting Bull disembarked a free man, but at least he was no longer officially a prisoner. He was now back at Standing Rock, the place where a wasichu gift-house would be his home for the rest of his life.

As we have seen through the example of Sitting Bull, the plight of the Plains tribes in the 1880s was a pitiful one. With the buffalo all but exterminated, the way of life that had sustained a civilization for centuries was simply gone. Given this painful reality, the role of the U.S. government's Office of Indian Affairs—referred to as the "Indian Bureau"—was to do something about the deplorable condition of the people who had surrendered themselves to its care. The near-term solution, as had been practiced by way of the Indian Agencies for the preceding decade, was to provide rations. Originally, the Indian Bureau provided rations so that the

Indians wouldn't have to leave the reservation to hunt. Now the rations had to be provided because they couldn't hunt.

The long-term solution to the plight of the Plains people was seen in "assimilation." The idea behind this buzzword was to dismantle native cultural traditions and reshape the Indians as members of wasichu society. In the vernacular of the day, the idea was to "civilize" the Indians. Today, one might use the word "mainstreaming." Children were given haircuts and uniforms and sent to boarding schools, many of which were back East, in an alien world thousands of miles from their homes. Back on the reservations, hunters were to be retrained to plant and harvest grain and vegetables.

At the time, assimilation was seen as the road to prosperity for a destitute subculture. Today, the doctrine of assimilation is seen in retrospect by some as having been a form of cultural genocide. When one recalls the horror of Lakota children being taken away from their families, and of their being beaten by their schoolmasters for speaking Lakota instead of English, it is hard to disagree with the cultural genocide argument.

What must be remembered, however, is that the assimilation policy of the late nineteenth century had its origins not in a lust for genocidal cruelty, but in a well-intentioned paternalism. Many wasichu believed that this was good for the Indians. Their lives as they had known them were gone forever, and the sands of time could not be reversed. They could not go back, it was reasoned, so they must go forward. It was hoped that within a generation or two, the people whose way of life had reached extinction would become happy and prosperous members of the dominant wasichu society.

Hand in hand with the paternalism of public policy, there was a growing wasichu fascination with the Indians. When the Indians ceased to be objects of fear, they became objects of interest. When we look at the wasichu perception of Indians in eighteenth- and nineteenth-century America, we can see it going through three phases: fear, fascination and empathy. In the East, it had progressed from fear to fascination much sooner than in the West. The memory of "massacres" such as Brookfield (1675) and Deerfield (1704) once terrorized New Englanders, but when generations come and go without conflict, emotions fade and memories become abstract. Today, American tourists born since 1975 flock to Vietnam to enjoy sandy beaches.

By the 1880s, the emotions inflamed by the press coverage of the Little Bighorn cooled. After Sitting Bull's well-publicized "surrender," conflicts with Plains Indians seemed resigned to the past. The wasichu mood, even in the West, had gradually turned from one of fear to one of fascination. We can see this in the way that Sitting Bull was received in Bismarck and later, in St. Paul and beyond. He was greeted by autograph seekers rather than a lynch mob.

As public opinion in the West changed, the mood in the East turned from fascination to empathy. Newspaper pages that once carried news of conflict now carried reports of corrupt Indian Agents and the mistreatment of the Indians by the government. There had always been an interest in Indian rights, especially among religious groups, notably the Quakers. Indeed, during the 1870s, the Grant Administration had worked with various church groups to supply staffing for some of the Indian agencies.

By the 1880s, the trend toward the empathy phase saw the gradual rise of what can best be described as an Indian civil rights movement. Inspired by an increasing interest by the media in the perceived and real injustices suffered by the people on the reservations, a number of social activist civil rights organizations sprang up among the wasichu in the East. These included the Indian Protection Committee, the Indian Rights Association, the National Indian Defense Association, and the Women's National Indian Association.

Unfortunately, this growing empathy took the form of paternalism, embracing the idea that the best thing for the Indians was for them to become "civilized." When Mary Bonney and Amelia Stone Quinton

started the Women's National Indian Association in 1879, they were outraged by the wasichu encroachment on the Plains, but felt that the Indians
should react to this by becoming assimilated into wasichu culture. If you
can't beat them, the women theorized, then the Indians should join them.

Like many of the rights groups, the Indian Rights Association advocated the strict paternalism of the demanding headmaster rather than the
compassion of the kindly father figure. According to one of the organizations 1882 founding documents, now in the manuscript collections of the
Historical Society of Pennsylvania, the stated objective was to "bring about
the complete civilization of the Indians and their admission to citizenship." It is ironic that the very people who most empathized with the
Indians felt that they could be saved only by eliminating the essence of
their unique language and culture, their "Indian-ness."

By the 1880s, assimilation became national policy. The "wise" paternalism of the civil rights organizations had convinced the government that
what was best for the Indians as individuals trumped the survival of their
culture. The children were taken from the "wild" and put into schools not
only to learn the essence of wasichu culture, but to be made to forget the
culture of their ancestors.

Once there had been cries to "kill the Indians." Now the cry was to save
these poor people by killing the "wild" Indian within each of them — or at
least within each of their children.

In 1882, Sitting Bull arrived at Standing Rock and met his new boss, a
man who would, much more than Walsh, fill that role.

Born in Ontario in 1842, two years after Walsh was born in the same
province, James McLaughlin had become a U.S. citizen at twenty-three
and worked as a civilian blacksmith for the U.S. Army for several years
before applying for an agent's position with the Indian Bureau. In 1876,
he was assigned as the agent for the Devils Lake Agency in eastern Dakota

Sitting Bull dedicating the "standing rock" for which the Standing Rock Reservation is named, in 1886. Indian Agent at Standing Rock, James McLaughlin, is to the right of the monument. His interpreter Louis Primeau is leaning on a post. (*Denver Public Library*)

Territory. In 1881, he arrived to replace Father Joseph Stephan, a Catholic missionary priest, as Indian Agent at Standing Rock. The same year that Sitting Bull surrendered, McLaughlin began his fourteen-year tenure in the post.

Like the old boss, whom the Lakota called Long Lance, the new boss, whom the Lakota called White Hair, had a reputation for being strict. Unlike many other agents of the previous decade, he was strict with himself, and was neither corrupt nor dishonest. McLaughlin had acquired an understanding of Indian people and the ability to be somewhat conversant in their language from his wife, who had a Mdewakanton Dakota grandmother. Marie Buisson McLaughlin also often functioned as an interpreter for her husband.

Though his wife was ethnically part Indian and he could speak an Indian language, James McLaughlin counted himself among the paternalists who believed that the best way to relive the genuine suffering of the Plains tribes was to assimilate them into wasichu society. This was the way that he approached his job as the agent at Standing Rock.

When Sitting Bull met the new boss on the day after he returned to Standing Rock, his was a much different conception of the way things were to be. For the first thing, Sitting Bull imagined that he, not White Hair, would be the new boss. He had accepted Walsh as boss in Grandmother's Country, but Standing Rock was Lakota country.

The press had treated Sitting Bull as a "great chief," and he assumed that he was regarded as such by the White Grandfather in Washington. McLaughlin explained that neither he nor the White Grandfather shared the perception of Sitting Bull's greatness. Sitting Bull would, like other Lakota, have to start from scratch. McLaughlin treated Sitting Bull as a strict father would treat a headstrong teenager, telling him that in order to achieve a position of prominence at McLaughlin's agency, he would have to earn it by working hard to assimilate.

Unfortunately, Sitting Bull's attitude rubbed McLaughlin the wrong way—and certainly vice versa—so the two got off to a bad start that was to permanently characterize their relationship.

McLaughlin had organized the Standing Rock Agency into agricultural zones and had gotten the Indians started in the process of farming their land. Sitting Bull and his family too, began farming, and reportedly did quite well for awhile. As for the Indian schools, however, Sitting Bull refused to send his own children, thus setting an example that many followed. This made McLaughlin furious.

Meanwhile, the Grandfather was unilaterally considering changes to the Great Sioux Reservation. Chester Arthur's administration had formulated a scheme to subdivide the reservation into separate reservations for each of the agencies contained within it. This would have been merely an administrative exercise were it not for the fact that one slice of the pie, rather than being assigned to an agency, was to be sliced off and opened for wasichu settlement. Congress, in its wisdom, refused to ratify the scheme on a technicality, that being the plan would, under the Fort Laramie Treaty that created the reservation, require an 80 percent vote of approval by the Lakota men living on the reservation.

To sort things out, the U.S. Senate sent a select committee out to the Great Sioux Reservation to hear what the Lakota actually had to say. Senator John Logan of Illinois was part of the group, as were Angus Cameron of Wisconsin, John Morgan of Alabama, and George Vest of Missouri. The chairman was Senator Henry Laurens Dawes of Massachusetts, champion of what he perceived as the best interest of the Indians. When the committee arrived at the Standing Rock Agency in August 1883, Sitting Bull had his first opportunity to make his voice heard by wasichu from Washington.

Before he did, however, the Washington men got an earful of McLaughlin's voice. He explained to them that Sitting Bull was a liar, a troublemaker, an obstacle to assimilation, and an adversary of civilization. Most of all, he told them, that contrary to what they may have read in the newspapers about Sitting Bull's importance, he was not a great chief and should not be recognized as such.

Finally, there was a public meeting, and Sitting Bull had a chance to speak for the Washington men to hear. His words are preserved in the Congressional Record (48th Congress, 1st Session; Senate Ex. Doc. No. 70; Senate Reports 148 through 348).

"I am here by the will of the Great Spirit, and by his will I am a chief [itancan]," Sitting Bull explained, according to the translator who interpreted his words for the Congressional Record. "My heart is red and sweet, and I know it is sweet, because whatever passes near me puts out its tongue to me; and yet you men have come here to talk with us, and you say you do not know who I am. I want to tell you that if the Great Spirit has chosen anyone to be chief of this country, it is myself."

The chairman, who had previously told Sitting Bull that he saw no difference between him and the other Indians at the agency, let the Lakota itancan continue.

"If a man loses anything and goes back and looks carefully for it he will find it, and that is what the Indians are doing now when they ask you to give them the things that were promised them in the past," he continued, underscoring the displeasure that many Lakota felt regarding broken promises. He had done his part by surrendering, and he wanted to see the United States government do its part. "I do not consider that they should be treated like beasts, and that is the reason I have grown up with the feelings I have. . . . Whatever you wanted of me I have obeyed, and I have come when you called me. The Grandfather sent me word that whatever he had against me in the past had been forgiven and thrown aside, and he would have nothing against me in future, and I accepted his promises and came in; and he told me not to step aside from the white man's path, and I told him I would not, and I am doing my best to travel in that path."

Next, he revisited the long-simmering irritation that many Lakota still felt regarding the seizure of the Black Hills, despite the provisions of the Fort Laramie Treaty.

"I feel my country has got a bad name, and I want it to have a good name. It used to have a good name, and I sit sometimes and wonder who it is that has given it a bad name," he said. "You are the only people now who can give it a good name, and I want you to take good care of my country and respect it. When we sold the Black Hills, we got a very small price for it, and not what we ought to have received. I used to think that the size of the payments would remain the same all the time, but they are growing smaller all the time. I want you to tell the Grandfather everything I have said—that we want some benefit from the promises he has made to us. And I don't think I should I be tormented with any talk about giving up more land until those promises are fulfilled. I would rather wait until that time, when I will be ready to transact any business he may desire. I consider that my country takes in the Black Hills, and runs from Powder River to the Missouri, and that all of this land belongs to me. Our Reservation is not so large as we want it to be; and I suppose the Grandfather owes us money now for land he has taken from us in the past."

Finally, Sitting Bull turned the tables on the issue of assimilation, taunting the senators for the policy of trying to remake the Lakota in the wasichu mold.

"You white men advise us to follow your ways and therefore I talk as I do," Sitting Bull said. "When you have a piece of land, and anything trespasses on it, you catch it and keep it until you get damages, and I am doing the same thing now. . . . I am looking into the future for the benefit of my children, and that is what I mean when I say I want my country taken care of. . . . I sit here and look about me now and I see my people starving. . . . Our rations have been reduced to almost nothing, and many of the people have starved to death. Now I beg of you to have the amount of rations increased so that our children will not starve."

At the conclusion of Sitting Bull's remarks, Senator Logan seized on his statement that "by the will of the Great Spirit . . . I am a chief." Said Logan, "Appointments are not made that way."

The senator went on to explain to Sitting Bull that the government was feeding him and he ought to appreciate that, and accept the authority of the Indian Bureau and its agent, McLaughlin. In so doing, Logan paraphrased everything that Sitting Bull had heard from McLaughlin. Echoing McLaughlin, Logan had looked down at Sitting Bull and told him that he was not a chief, deliberately intending to cut the celebrated man down to size and put him in his place.

However, the men from Washington went away empty-handed. They retired without getting the approval they needed to subdivide the Great Sioux Reservation. The issue was moribund, but only for the time being. It would be revisited again, five years later, under a new presidential administration.

What the senator had tried to do in a cutting remark before leaving for Washington was even then evolving into the personal crusade for White Hair. McLaughlin had come to Standing Rock with a reputation for honesty and fairness, but his growing jealousy and animosity toward Sitting Bull would consume him.

THOUGH he had the contentious McLaughlin to deal with, life for Sitting Bull at Standing Rock was different than it had been at Fort Randall. The main thing was that he was no longer a prisoner. While it was no longer possible to ride over to the Powder River Country to hunt buffalo, McLaughlin would occasionally allow Sitting Bull to leave the reservation to take advantage of invitations by the wasichu to make public appearances. One of his first such excursions after taking up residence at Standing Rock was most puzzling.

After the Fort Laramie Treaty of 1868 granted the Plains Indians more or less unfettered autonomy in the Powder River Country—albeit briefly—the wasichu had persisted in building the Northern Pacific Railroad. Its main line would run through eastern Montana parallel to the Yellowstone River, which was at the northern edge of the unceded Powder River Country. The Indians were understandably displeased, and Sitting Bull himself had led a memorable skirmish against the U.S. Army escort of a railroad survey party near Pryor's Fork of the Yellowstone in August 1872. This was the encounter where Sitting Bull had famously sat on the battlefield casually smoking his pipe while the fight raged around him.

A year later, when the railroad went bankrupt in the Panic of 1873, Lakota opposition to its steel rails had become a moot point. The railroad simply stopped at Bismarck. However, in 1881 Henry Villard pulled it out of bankruptcy and resumed work on the uncompleted section between Bismarck and the Pacific Northwest. The golden spike marking the completion of the railroad was driven on September 8, 1883, at Gold Greek, Montana, but the city of Bismarck jumped the gun by commemorating the event three days earlier.

On September 5, Bismarck celebrated the Northern Pacific, as well as its own selection as the capital of Dakota Territory (superseding Yankton, which had held the honor since 1861). As part of the festivities, Sitting Bull was invited up to Bismarck to ride in the parade. According to Stanley Vestal, Sitting Bull carried the flag at the head of the parade. A photograph

by David F. Barry in the collection of
the State Historical Society of North
Dakota shows a parade that may have
been this one. A number of Indian men
are pictured, but Sitting Bull cannot be
positively identified among them.

It was around this time, or perhaps
as late as 1885, that he went into Barry's
studio in Bismarck for the first of a
series of portraits that are today among
the most widely reproduced images of
Sitting Bull. He probably visited Barry's
studio on several occasions over the
next several years.

The thought of Sitting Bull helping
to celebrate the completion of a railroad he had once opposed demon-
strates to what extent he had come to
accept—despite words to the contrary—the wasichu and their form of
civilization.

This photograph is perhaps the best
of the memorable series of photographs taken by David F. Barry of
Sitting Bull holding a tomahawk as a
prop. The session occurred at Barry's
Bismarck studio in either 1884 or
1885. (*Montana Historical Society*)

A few months later, Sitting Bull was away from Standing Rock on yet
another trip, this time to an even larger city. At his own insistence, Sitting
Bull, along with his nephew One Bull and one of his wives, accompanied
McLaughlin on an official visit to St. Paul, Minnesota. So too did Marie
McLaughlin and their son.

The party traveled on the Northern Pacific—the same entity that the
Lakota once bitterly opposed—arriving in the Minnesota capital on
March 14. As in Bismarck, Sitting Bull was a topic of great interest, and
again, as on his previous visits to Bismarck, Sitting Bull sat for a portrait
photographer. In the studio of Palmquist & Jurgens, a dozen plates were
made of Sitting Bull alone, and one of him with One Bull.

Probably to the chagrin of McLaughlin, who sought to downplay his importance, Sitting Bull was being treated as a visiting dignitary. As a result of the visit, however, McLaughlin began noticing a curious transformation in the Lakota wikasa wakan. This was his growing fascination with the trinkets, machines, and accoutrements of wasichu civilization. He toured a grocery warehouse and a printing plant, he watched a pair of shoes being made for him in a factory, and he marveled at firemen in a firehouse sliding down a pole. He saw electric lights and he flicked the switch that made them go off and on.

McLaughlin happily interpreted this as Sitting Bull's process of conversion from the "wild" to the "wasichu." In McLaughlin's mind, this meant assimilation.

WHILE Sitting Bull was in St. Paul, he attended a show that featured a young sharpshooter who went by the name of Annie Oakley. Born Phoebe Ann Mosey, she was twenty-four, although she stood only five feet tall and looked much younger. She was an attractive young lady, but it was her uncanny shooting skills that left audiences in slack-jawed amazement. Having started hunting as a child to help feed her family, she had honed her skills to the point where she could split a playing card edge-on at ninety feet, then put a half dozen holes in it before it reached the ground. She began her career as an exhibition shooter in Cincinnati in 1881 with the Baughman & Butler shooting act when experienced marksman Francis E. "Frank" Butler bet $100 that he could outshoot any local marksman. Annie took the bet and won. Butler lost the bet, but won the heart of young Annie. During their forty-four-year marriage, which began the following year, Frank and Annie were constant companions on the show circuit and he served as her manager.

When Sitting Bull saw Annie shoot in St. Paul, he was so taken with her that he sent $65 to her hotel room along with a request for her photograph.

She declined the cash, but she agreed to meet with him, and he got his autographed picture. The two would cross paths again the following summer.

Seeing Annie Oakley perform was Sitting Bull's introduction to the wasichu stage. Just as he was captivated with Annie, he was smitten with the idea of show business. When the opportunity presented itself, he decided to try it himself. There had been several queries dating back to Sitting Bull's time at Fort Randall, but the first man to put together a serious proposal for such a thing was Father Joseph Stephan, the Catholic missionary priest

Annie Oakley. (*Denver Public Library*)

who had preceded McLaughlin as Indian Agent at Standing Rock. He now headed the church's Bureau of Catholic Indian Missions, and it is hard to imagine someone in such a position putting on a traveling show starring a famous, non-Catholic Indian. Apparently he was a man of many interests. Father Stephan had gone so far as to secure the approval of the Department of the Interior and the Indian Bureau for such a project and had communicated the details of the undertaking to McLaughlin at Standing Rock.

One can imagine McLaughlin's first reaction when the proposal reached his desk. In any case, his next reaction was that if Sitting Bull was to become a showman, Father Stephan was not the right promoter. Instead of approving the priest's request, McLaughlin diverted the project to an acquaintance, Alvaren Allen. The owner of the Merchant Hotel, where McLaughlin and Sitting Bull had stayed while in St. Paul, Allen was a promoter and a former mayor of St. Anthony, Minnesota (which had been incorporated into Minneapolis in 1872). It is unclear whether he had the idea for putting Sitting Bull on the stage independently of Father Stephan's brainstorm, or whether McLaughlin took the priest's idea and gave it to Allen because he didn't think it was a task for which Stephan was suited. In any case, it was Allen who was responsible for the beginning of Sitting Bull's career in show business.

With McLaughlin's aid, Allen—sometimes given the title Colonel—put together an ensemble cast that would feature Sitting Bull as its head-liner. Also in the troupe would be Crow Eagle, Flying By, Gray Eagle, Long Dog, and several others. The show, billed as the Sitting Bull Combination—in those days, "combination" was a synonym for "reperto-ry company"—would showcase the Lakota simply sitting around smoking and doing household chores. The idea was for people in the East to see "wild" Indians doing what "wild" Indians did. This was the "fascination" phase of the wasichu perception of Indians.

The show premiered on September 15, 1884, at the Eden Musée in New York City, where it received passing notice from the theater critic of the *New York Times*.

The June 1964 issue of *American Heritage* magazine carried a story about a young Lakota named Standing Bear. A student at the famous Carlisle Indian School in Pennsylvania, the sixteen-year-old happened to stop by the Eden Musée to see the Sitting Bull Combination. He had read an advertisement that reportedly referred to Sitting Bull as "the murderer of Custer."

Standing Bear heard Sitting Bull tell the audience in Lakota that he had seen many wasichu and what they were doing, and that he was glad to know that some day his children would be educated. He also said, as he had so often, that the buffalo were all gone, as were the rest of the game, and that he was going to shake the hand of the Grandfather in Washington, and tell him these things. In turn, Standing Bear heard Sitting Bull's remarks translated as a description of the bloody defeat of

Custer and the 7th Cavalry. The only person in the audience who understood Lakota, Standing Bear was stunned as the people around him hissed
at Sitting Bull.

Colonel Alvaren Allen may have put coins in Sitting Bull's pocket—
coins that he readily doled out to street urchins—but he had not represented him honestly. Fortunately, the two men parted company for good, and
Sitting Bull would come under the wing of another promoter who knew
enough to treat Sitting Bull, and other Indian showmen, with the respect
he knew they deserved.

The 1884 tour had not been an altogether bad thing for Sitting Bull.
He had seen a lot, and he was quite intrigued by the prospect of seeing
even more of what lay in the wider wasichu macrocosm. Nor was the 1884
tour a bad thing from McLaughlin's perspective. He probably had a great
many misgivings when Sitting Bull went east with the Colonel, but his
fears had not been realized. In retrospect it seems strange, but perhaps it
should come as no surprise that McLaughlin was becoming an enthusiastic supporter of Sitting Bull's new career. He reasoned that the more
Sitting Bull saw of wasichu civilization, the more he would be anxious to
abandon his "uncivilized" ways.

What happened to Standing Bear? Ironically, he went on to a career in
show business himself. After the turn of the century, he moved to
Hollywood and starred in a dozen Western movies between 1916 and
1935.

A natural showman, Buffalo Bill Cody eventually became what Larry
McMurtry has called "probably the most famous American of his day . . .
easily more famous than any president." He came to epitomize the Wild
West, a concept that he played an important part in creating. He was the
predecessor of the movie and television cowboys of the middle twentieth
century. Unlike them, however, he was the real deal.

Born on a farm in rural Iowa in 1846, William Frederick Cody was an excellent horseman while still a boy, and like many young men of his generation, he was captivated by the lure of the frontier. With this in mind, he went west to seek his fortune. Even before he had reached his mid-twenties, Cody had a resume that established the credibility upon which he would base his later career as a showman. Having served with the 7th Kansas Cavalry as a teenager during the Civil War, he worked as a cowboy on cattle drives, and he trapped, hunted, and signed on as a scout and wagon master for wagon trains going west. As noted in an earlier chapter, he was extraordinarily skilled with a rifle and earned his nickname for his work as a buffalo hunter for the Kansas Pacific Railroad. He styled himself as a frontiersman in the mold of Kit Carson, but unlike the quiet-mannered Carson, Buffalo Bill was flamboyant and extroverted, and he would ultimately find his niche in show business.

Cody's bona fides as an "Indian fighter" were established when he was hired as a civilian scout by the U.S. Army between 1868 and 1872, and he also rode with them in later occasions, notably in the summer of 1876. He served with various regiments, but it was with the 3rd Cavalry that he received the Medal of Honor, the United States' highest award for valor. In April 1872, when a band of Minneconjou rustled some horses belonging to the Union Pacific Railroad, Cody led the patrol that found them and bested them in a bitter firefight.

His most famous encounter with the Plains Indians occurred on July 17, 1876, three weeks after the Little Bighorn. Cody was scouting with the 5th Cavalry under Colonel Wesley Merritt when his patrol engaged a Cheyenne raiding party near Hat Creek in northwestern Nebraska. Cody was the first to make contact, finding himself face to face with the Cheyenne leader Yellow Hair, better known to wasichu as Yellow Hand, who was riding in the vanguard of his party. It was, as this author has noted on previous occasions, one of those real moments in the folklore of the West that seems so unreal as to have been created by Hollywood. Cody, who was an excellent marksman, shot Yellow Hair's horse out from under him, but at that moment, Cody's own horse stumbled and fell.

The two armed men stood facing one another, man to man. Armed with a Winchester repeating rifle and clad in buckskins, Cody faced Yellow Hair, who was armed with a Colt revolver, and—if the stories are true—wearing an enormous headdress of the type that was so dearly loved by the costume managers of classic Western filmmaking. Cody got off two shots, killing Yellow Hair with the second. He then took out his knife and lifted Yellow Hair's scalp, declaring it the "First scalp for Custer."

In the coming years, this encounter at Hat Creek, now known as Warbonnet Creek, would be embellished as a legend and replayed thousands of times. Charles M. Russell, the greatest Western artist of them all, even created an oil painting of the event in 1917 that is now in the Sid Richardson Collection of Western Art in Fort Worth.

Cody's "heroism" would also soon be the subject of many dime novels and even stage shows. Yet before his 1876 encounter with Yellow Hair, Buffalo Bill Cody was no stranger either to the news rack or the theater. He had been performing his shows for several years in theaters before Warbonnet Creek, encouraged by dime novelist Ned Buntline, who recognized his talent for the stage. In 1872, Buntline convinced him to portray himself as the heroic plainsman that he more or less really was, with great success. The following year, Cody actually formed a melodramatic repertory company, touring with such notable Western "characters" as James Butler "Wild Bill" Hickok and John Baker "Texas Jack" Omohundro.

The idea for the large-scale extravaganzas for which Cody is best known, originated somewhat later. Apparently he had discussions in New York in 1882 with actor-producer Nate Salsbury about a big arena show with cowboys and Indians as well as horses and cattle—and even buffalo— that would give spectators a feel for what it was like "out West."

A few weeks later, Buffalo Bill was back in North Platte, Nebraska, where he lived, when the city fathers approached him to put on a show for the town's Fourth of July celebration. Known as the Old Glory Blowout, this event succeeded brilliantly. It is today seen as the earliest precursor of modern rodeos as large spectator events, and it was also an opportunity for him to test his ideas for a large, spectacular show.

Buffalo Bill Cody unveiled his Wild West in the spring of 1883. There had been such productions before him, but nothing so well organized, nor on such a grand scale. In addition to being a natural showman, Cody was also a remarkable organizer—though not quite so good when it came to managing a business. During his first season, which opened in Omaha on May 17, Cody toured in partnership with marksman William Frank "Doc" Carver, but the two parted company and Bill teamed up with Nate Salsbury, a more skillful businessman, for the 1884 season. If Buffalo Bill made the show, it would be Salsbury's business acumen that made it profitable for both men.

The production was purposely called "Buffalo Bill's Wild West," rather than "Buffalo Bill's Wild West Show." Cody wanted to imply authenticity. Though the action was obviously contrived, he aimed for more than just an implication of authenticity by using real cowboys and real Indians rather than actors.

Initially, the Indians used in the show were mainly Pawnee whom he recruited from Indian Territory (now eastern Oklahoma), but Cody later began using Lakota. Eventually, as more "Wild West" shows appeared, many of these imitators had a reputation for cheating and abusing their Indian employees, and occasionally leaving them stranded far from home. It should be remembered that Cody always paid his Indians employees fairly, didn't deduct their room and board from their salaries, and sent them home at the end of the season with a new suit of clothes which he provided. They, in turn, were loyal to him, and many, such as Red Shirt and Iron Tail, returned season after season. Contrary to the image suggested in his constant replay of Warbonnet Creek, Buffalo Bill was predisposed to both like and respect Indians, and they responded favorably to him. Iron Tail and others even went on hunting trips with Cody in the off-season.

The posters used to advertise Buffalo Bill's Wild West emphasized the popular stereo-type of the "warpath Indian," but in the shows, the action featured actual Plains Indians. (*Library of Congress*)

Even before Sitting Bull went on the road with Alvaren Allen's Sitting Bull Combination, Cody had thought about signing him for the Wild West. McLaughlin may have been cool to the idea in 1884, but when Buffalo Bill contacted him for the 1885 season, he readily signed off on the idea. Sitting Bull, too, was agreeable. On April 29, 1885, having secured endorsements from military officers such as Generals Phil Sheridan, Nelson Miles, and Alfred Terry, Cody sent his formal request to the Interior Department. Lucius Quintus Cincinnatus Lamar, who had just been named as Secretary of the Interior by the recently inaugurated President Grover Cleveland, replied with "a very emphatic No."

Undaunted, Cody wired former Commanding General William Tecumseh Sherman, who twisted a few arms in Washington on his behalf. Lamar, a former Confederate diplomat, was unwilling to stand up to a U.S. Army officer with Sherman's unmistakable Civil War credentials, and on May 18, he sent a telegram to McLaughlin. In essence, the message wished Sitting Bull a happy season with Buffalo Bill's Wild West.

ONE of the most enduring visual images of Sitting Bull is that of him with Buffalo Bill Cody. Between the two of them, they represented the wasichu conception of the Wild West. They were both household names, and among the biggest there were in the late 1880s and for a generation thereafter. The impact of their presence—and of their legacy—was even more indelible because of the fact that they were authentic. So indelible is that image of the two of them that it is hard to realize that they were together for only a single season.

It is also remembered that Sitting Bull's contract with the Wild West permitted him to sell autographed photographs of himself at each of the stops during the tour. Cody not only permitted this but encouraged it, and he took no percentage of the proceeds. In turn, Sitting Bull gave away much of his cash to the beggars whom he encountered in American cities. He was confused that such people could exist in a society as prosperous as that of the wasichu.

Sitting Bull was paid $50 a week, more than $1,000 in today's dollars. The five Lakota men who traveled with him each received $25 per month, and William Halsey, his interpreter, was paid $60 per month. Of the salary, Sitting Bull received $100 as an advance, plus a signing bonus of $125. Cody and Salsbury, certainly with the acquiescence if not the urging of their tireless publicist, Major John M. Burke, also agreed to pay all the expenses incurred by Sitting Bull's entourage from Standing Rock to join the show, and all expenses from the show to Standing Rock after four months on the road.

After securing the government's approval, Sitting Bull and his Lakota entourage first joined Cody on June 12, 1885, during the Wild West's round of performances in Buffalo, New York, and remained with the show as it wound its way through a forty-city tour that included New York City, Philadelphia, and Washington, D.C.

It was also during the 1885 season that Annie Oakley and Frank Butler joined Buffalo Bill's Wild West. She and Sitting Bull got along famously, and at the end of the season, he gave her an extraordinary endorsement, dubbing her "Little Sure Shot," an appellation that would be widely used in future advertising.

According to Richard Walsh in his 1928 book, *The Making of Buffalo Bill*, Sitting Bull remarked upon his first visit to the nation's capital at the end of June, "I wish I had known this when I was a boy. The white people are so many that if every Indian in the West killed one every step they took the dead would not be missed among you."

During the visit to Washington, Sitting Bull and some of the Lakota visited the White House, where they may or may not have actually met Grover Cleveland. The *Washington Post*, which called Indians in the show "Howling Savages," does not mention whether they went to the White House. The paper did note their visit to U.S. Army headquarters, where Sitting Bull deliberately snubbed the Commanding General, his old nemesis General "Little Phil" Sheridan.

Describing Sitting Bull as a "Renowned Sioux Chief," Cody gave him top billing in posters and advertising, making his name only slightly less prominent than "Buffalo Bill's Wild West." Cody also made a point of not identifying Sitting Bull directly with Custer's death. Nevertheless, the wasichu public was so used to this erroneous conclusion that for many, merely the name "Sitting Bull" was thought of as synonymous with the "murder" of the "boy general."

So pervasive was this image of Sitting Bull that it led to a very contentious encounter between him and representatives of the Indian Rights Association. When the Wild West was performing in Philadelphia during 1885, some gentlemen from this organization visited Sitting Bull in his tent. Nate Salsbury, who was present, later recalled the verbal exchange in

a May 18, 1891, letter to Herbert Welsh that is preserved in the collection
of the South Dakota State Historical Society in Pierre. "Ask Sitting Bull if
he ever had any regret for his share in the Custer massacre," they said to
the interpreter, having earlier said that Sitting Bull should "flee from the
wrath to come," meaning divine punishment, for the sin of murdering
Custer.

At this question, Sitting Bull became furious with these self-important
men whom Salsbury later described to Welsh as "worthy cranks." "The old
fellow sprang to his feet," Cody's partner remembered. "Thrusting his long
lean fingers into his questioner's face he shouted, 'Tell this fool that I did
not murder Custer; it was a fight in open day. He would have killed me if
he could. I have answered to my people for the dead on my side. Let
Custer's friends answer to his people for the dead on his side.'"

The tour included mainly cities in the eastern United States, but the
itinerary also reached into Canada. While the Wild West was in Montreal
in August, Cody and Sitting Bull stopped at the photography studio of
William Notman & Sons to sit—and stand—for portraits. Of the series
that were taken that day, four included both of the showmen, these being
the only photos taken of the two iconic figures together.

For these photographs and least one of him alone taken during the
same session, Sitting Bull wore the elaborate feather headdress which he
wore during his appearances in the show. He probably never wore more
than two feathers at any one time during his years on the Plains. A white
feather represented his first coup, and a red one his first injury in battle.
The headdress came to represent the image that audiences expected of an
"Indian chief," but this was in large part because this was how the public
saw such men portrayed in the wild west shows.

After successful runs in Detroit, Saginaw, and Columbus, Buffalo Bill's
Wild West concluded the 1885 season with a series of performances in St.
Louis that wrapped up on October 11. A million people had seen the once
enigmatic Sitting Bull, and they had seen him as a man, not as an ogre.

Sitting Bull poses with William F. "Buffalo Bill" Cody at the studio of William Notman & Sons in Montreal. This was part of a series of four photographs taken in August 1885 of the two men together. (*Library of Congress*)

Relaxing with reporters at his hotel in St. Louis, he explained that he had enjoyed show business, but that he was ready to go back to the quiet of the Plains.

As Sitting Bull departed the Wild West for the real wild west, Cody gave him a broad-brimmed western hat, much like Cody's own, and made a gift of the horse that Sitting Bull had ridden in the show. Cody even paid to have the animal shipped to Standing Rock. This splendidly trained, light gray steed would remain one of Sitting Bull's most prized possessions until the day that he died.

His legacy as a "Show Indian" can be measured by the number of other Lakota who followed in his footsteps with Buffalo Bill's Wild West and the imitators that it inspired. Theirs would be a mixed lot. Many had enjoyable careers, saw the world, and pocketed some money, while others were not so lucky, having signed with disreputable performers.

Buffalo Bill's Wild West continued as a successful enterprise until after the turn of the twentieth century. In 1887, Buffalo Bill took the Wild West to London, where it was an immense success. In order to attend a Wild West performance at Earl's Court, Queen Victoria officially ended more than two decades of public withdrawal into which she had gone after her husband's death. She later asked for a royal command performance at Windsor Castle. The show toured Europe in 1889 and 1890, and when in Rome, Cody enjoyed an audience with Pope Leo XIII.

In 1893, the year that they played the Columbian Exposition in Chicago, the Wild West was seen by two million people. By then, Buffalo Bill himself was perhaps the most recognized man in the world. As Larry McMurtry put it so well, both Cody and Annie Oakley became entertainment superstars, perhaps the "first American superstars."

After the turn of the century, as interest in the big arena shows began to wane, Buffalo Bill Cody turned to the new medium of motion pictures, forming his own production company to produce an ambitious film about the Indian Wars. Sadly, he was not as successful in his new entertainment venture as he had been with the Wild West—and not so by a very wide margin. Had it not been for the money lost to the bad investments in Arizona mines that he made during the later years of his life, Buffalo Bill would have been a very wealthy man at the time of his death in 1917. Had his movie ventures succeeded, they might have reversed Cody's fortunes. They were a gamble, and he knew it, but he had taken risks all his life. However, it was not in his character to ignore the possibilities offered by the new technology of the twentieth century.

AFTER his tour of major American cities in 1885, Sitting Bull returned to Standing Rock with his eyes having been opened. Such symbolism was as common among Indians as it was among the wasichu. Sitting Bull had seen the wasichu world, and the wasichu world had seen him.

James McLaughlin had hoped that this would convert him to becoming an "agency Indian," but he was wrong. Sitting Bull had now seen too much to be convinced that the wasichu sun rose and set on the whims of the Standing Rock agent. Sitting Bull had been celebrated in the wasichu cities by wasichu of far greater importance than McLaughlin.

The agent had failed on two counts. The experiment of sending him out into the world had not had the effect of "civilizing" him, and it had the unintended effect of undoing all of McLaughlin's efforts to make Sitting Bull insignificant. After his having received top billing in Buffalo Bill's Wild West, there was no way that the wasichu world would believe that Sitting Bull was *not* important. Unfortunately for Sitting Bull, McLaughlin grew ever more bitter and resentful.

According to Stanley Vestal, who spoke with One Bull and White Bull, who were around Sitting Bull in the 1880s, Sitting Bull compared McLaughlin to his resentful former wife, Snow on Her. "Once I had a jealous woman in my lodge," Sitting Bull laughed. "This agent reminds me of that jealous woman."

Ironically, the magnitude of Sitting Bull's significance among the Lakota, especially the Hunkpapa, is perhaps best illustrated by McLaughlin's continual insistence on denying and belittling his influence among his people.

It wasn't that Sitting Bull rejected wasichu civilization out of hand. He had seen too much to do that. He was just unwilling to see his people totally abandon their own culture to accept another. As Stanley Vestal learned, Sitting Bull was rather open-minded. He once asked a missionary, "What does it matter how I pray, so long as my prayers are answered?"

His response to wasichu medical solutions could have been taken straight from twenty-first-century holistic doctrine. Said he, "The main thing is to cure the patient; any method that works is a good one."

Much has been said about James McLaughlin's unwillingness to recognize Sitting Bull as a "great chief." The fact that the agent went out of his way to reiterate such on numerous occasions indicates that this assertion needed to be repeatedly underscored in the face of the overwhelming belief that Sitting Bull was, in fact, a "great chief." The wasichu press certainly believed it, and so too did many Lakota. Senator John Logan represented those among wasichu officialdom who agreed with McLaughlin that the perception of Sitting Bull's greatness could be undone by repeatedly denying his greatness—but they were in the minority.

Much has also been said about James McLaughlin's unwillingness to recognize any Lakota as a "chief," but this view is untrue. Those Lakota who cooperated with McLaughlin curried his favor, and he was willing to give them prominent administrative roles at Standing Rock. One such man was John Grass. A leader from among the Sihasapa Lakota living at Standing Rock, Grass had earlier been known as Charging Bear, but changed his name after being baptized either by Father Pierre-Jean De Smet or by Father Joseph Stephan, McLaughlin's predecessor at Standing Rock. The *Dictionary of American National Biography* recalls that his "willingness to cooperate marked him as 'progressive,' and he was named

chief justice of the Court of Indian Offenses
for the Standing Rock Agency, a position he
held until his death" in 1918. The wasichu
media sometimes went as far as to speak of
Grass as the "premier" of the "Sioux
Nation."

McLaughlin also undertook to incorpo-
rate Lakota warriors into a tribal police
force. Many men signed on for this role, cut
their hair and put on blue uniforms not
unlike those of the U.S. Army troops against
which they had once fought.

John Grass. (*National Archives*)

Grass became a leading exponent of
assimilation during the 1880s, and in
McLaughlin's view, a useful counterbal-
ance to Sitting Bull's considerable influence, especially among the
Hunkpapa Lakota at Standing Rock. Indeed, his willingness to cooperate
with the government led McLaughlin to name him "head chief of
Standing Rock." He is often referred to in contemporary newspaper
accounts as "Chief" John Grass.

John Grass had long since signed on to the notion of accepting the
inevitability of the wasichu way of life. He had also signed on to the concept that the paternalistic wasichu had the best interest of the Lakota at
heart. Certainly many actually did, even if they frequently had strange
ways of showing it. One such wasichu was Senator Henry Dawes of
Massachusetts, the chairman of the Senate's Indian Affairs Committee,
who had chaired the Senate commission that had come west to Standing
Rock in 1883.

Dawes had embraced the concept of assimilating Indians into mainstream society through individual private ownership of land. This, on the
face of it, sounded quite noble, but where would the land come from? The

Dawes Act, or General Allotment Act of 1887, provided for land that was owned collectively by tribes to be subdivided into individual plots that would be owned by individual tribal members—and potentially sold to nontribal members. The idea was that each head of household would have 160 acres assigned to him, a figure based on the 160-acre allotment given to wasichu homesteaders under the Homestead Act of 1862. According to the wise paternalism of the federal government, what was best for the Indians as individuals trumped the survival of their land in the configuration they had known for centuries.

In 1888, Congress followed the Dawes Act with the Sioux Act, which called for implementing the scheme of 1883 to subdivide the remaining 22 million acres of the Great Sioux Reservation into separate reservations for each of the agencies contained within it—while slicing off a sizable piece for wasichu settlement. It should be recalled that the *Bismarck Tribune* article of 1881 cited an area of 42 million acres, and that the six major reservations in the area today comprise 9.2 million acres. The 22 million-acre figure did not, of course, include the already confiscated Black Hills.

The plan was to open 11 million acres, or half the tract, to settlers at fifty cents per acre. Section 17 of the bill also called for a million-dollar cash payment. Adjusted for inflation, the fifty cents offered is the equivalent of approximately ten dollars in current dollars. Today, acreage in this part of the country, especially in the Black Hills, can easily go for much more than two hundred times the adjusted rate. The million dollars would today be worth $20 million.

As in 1883, the U.S. government sent a commission to Standing Rock to elicit approval for the dissolution scheme. This time, the group included Indian Commissioners John V. Wright; Captain Richard Henry Pratt, founder of the Carlisle Indian School in Pennsylvania; and the Reverend William Cleveland, the second cousin to President Grover Cleveland who had earlier served as a missionary in Dakota Territory.

Arriving in late July 1888, they asked the tribal leaders to sign color-coded ballots indicating acceptance or rejection of the Sioux Act. Numerous conferences were held, all with the same result: almost nobody signed. John Grass was opposed, and even McLaughlin was skeptical. That was how poorly the commission was received.

During the first round of talks, Sitting Bull boycotted the commission, and when he finally did show up, it was to denounce the proposal. After nearly a month, the commission went back to the nation's capital disappointed. Pratt angrily told the *Bismarck Tribune*, in an article published on September 21, that the government ought to simply enact the Sioux Act without Sioux approval.

With that statement, it was clear that something must be done. The commissioners had come to Standing Rock, and now it was time to return the favor. It was decided that sixty-one Lakota from several Dakota Territory agencies would go east.

THE numerous delegations of tribal leaders who visited Washington, D.C., in the late nineteenth century are among the most enduring images of Indians from that period. This is both because such conferences were long on symbolism for both sides, and because they presented excellent and well-utilized photo opportunities. In his book *Diplomats in Buckskins: A History of Indian Delegations in Washington City*, Herman J. Viola points out that "Delegations became an important component of Indian-white relations during the colonial wars of empire in the late seventeenth century," and he goes on to say that this became even more the case after the United States achieved its independence. In the last quarter of the nineteenth century, it became almost routine.

Even as they were long on symbolism, though, they were short on substance. Nevertheless, they were meaningful in the way that many of today's showy diplomatic exchanges and "summit conferences" are useful.

They gave the parties a chance to meet face to face. From among the Lakota, Red Cloud and Spotted Tail each went to the nation's capital in 1870 to meet Ulysses S. Grant at the White House. They were only two of many. Crazy Horse had wanted to go east to meet Rutherford B. Hayes, but a bullet denied him that opportunity.

For us, the press attention devoted to Sitting Bull's only "official" visit to the capital in October 1888 gives us an interesting opportunity for a close-up look at a week in his life.

Sitting Bull had made his first trip to Washington in 1885 with Buffalo Bill's Wild West. He may or may not have met President Grover Cleveland during the tour's engagement in Washington, but if he did, it would have been in the capacity of an entertainer, rather than as a delegate with official standing. His 1888 visit would be on official business, as part of a group, of which the *Washington Post* said "rarely has so notable a delegation of Indians appeared in Washington."

The Indians had come, not for symbolism, but for substance. They had serious business to discuss. It was not see and be seen for the Lakota this week, it was see and be heard. As the *Washington Post* reported on October 13, the Indians had come east to "confer with the President and the Secretary of the Interior in regard to the disposition of part of their reservation. They now hold possession of about 22 million acres of land in southwest Dakota, the greater part of which they have no use for."

No use for? The latter phrase is certainly worthy of a raised eyebrow in hindsight.

"The Government, therefore, has taken steps to dispose of 11 million acres, or half the tract, to settlers at 50 cents per acre," the *Washington Post* report continued. "This proposition was submitted to the Sioux nation some time ago [in July and August] by the Commissioners of the Government, but the leaders of the [Sioux] Nation are desirous of getting more for their land, and the chiefs come to Washington principally for that purpose."

Many of the Lakota had come to Washington shrewdly planning not to oppose the Sioux Act, but to amend it. At issue was both whether it should be sold, and, if so, for what price.

Just as with any group of political leaders, the sixty-one Lakota leaders had not all come to Washington with a single point of view. Among them were factions. Men such as American Horse represented the Lakota least likely to compromise with the U.S. government, while men such as John Grass were at the opposite end of the spectrum. Sitting Bull remained in the middle, wary of accepting the wasichu offer, but equally cautious not to reject it out of hand.

Sitting Bull's old friend and warrior comrade, Gall, who had typically aligned himself with Grass on such issues, was also among the Lakota who visited Washington in October 1888. So too was Gray Eagle, Sitting Bull's brother-in-law, and Mad Bear, also from Standing Rock. The stage was set for a showdown.

The Lakota visit took place when there were also showdowns within the wasichu world. In October 1888, Washington and the rest of the nation were in the final stretch of the presidential campaign that pitted incumbent Democrat Cleveland in a contentious and scandal-plagued campaign against Republican challenger Benjamin Harrison. Then too, there was the 1888 World Series.

Washington was abuzz with talk of the race between the Washington Senators and the Detroit Wolverines for seventh place in the National League. Neither team was a contender for the World Series, but the local fans didn't mind. Indeed, on October 12, just a few hours before Sitting Bull and the others were arriving in Washington, the Senators—with pitching by Hank O'Day, and the legendary Connie Mack as catcher—were in the process of beating the Detroit Wolverines five to two. The series, however, would see the New York Giants, who had just clinched their first National League pennant, matched against the St. Louis Browns of the American Association.

It strikes one as interesting to note that the Lakota, who represented something so primeval to the wasichu, were visiting Washington at the beginning of the World Series, something that wasichu regard as an institution of a much later age. Indeed, the *Washington Post* drew its readers' attention to the fact that "None of the Indians speak English and several of them have not long abandoned their tribal relations and nomadic life."

Sitting Bull, John Grass, and the others disembarked from their train at the Baltimore & Potomac station in Washington at 11:40 Friday evening—two hours late. Riding in two special coaches, they had been traveling since Monday. Wearing blue badges identifying their respective agencies, they were dressed most in what the press would quaintly refer to as "American attire," except for their beaded moccasins.

Media attention seemed to focus on the leaders who more favorably disposed to accepting the government's proposed sale. As John Grass was described as "the most sensible of all the Siouxs," it was said that Yellow Hair had "not led much of a wild life."

To their credit, the Washington journalists did not refer to Sitting Bull as the "murderer of Custer," but rather as "the great medicine man who planned the attack." Of course, it was Custer, not the Lakota, who planned and executed the attack. However, the reference to Custer indicates how closely the Lakota, especially Sitting Bull and Gall, were still associated with the Little Bighorn, and how large that battle still loomed in the wasichu consciousness. It was almost obligatory to mention the Little Bighorn when discussing anything having to do with the "Sioux." The line seems to have been thrown in, perhaps by the copy editor, to give readers some familiar context.

The things actually observed by the reporters, rather than their imaginary ramblings on mythic events, are of more use when looking back at their coverage of the Lakota arrival in Washington.

"The finest looking specimen in the entire lot physically is Chief John Grass," the *Washington Post* reported. "He has a massive frame and a large intellectual head. He is said to be the greatest statesman in the [Sioux] Nation and is regarded by the other chiefs as something of a leader. . . . Gall is a fine looking specimen of Indian manhood, but Sitting Bull shows signs of approaching old age and a decline of physical power."

Before we take exception to what reads as a condescending description of Sitting Bull, we should consider that he was a decade or so older than either Gall or Grass, and he had just spent the better part of a week on a train. Of course they all had been on the train, but Grass had been living comfortably at Standing Rock for decades while Sitting Bull was enduring hardship in Canada and captivity at Fort Randall. How would any of us look after a week of sitting in a coach seat?

Accompanying the sixty-one leaders were the Indian Agents representing the major agencies within the Great Sioux Reservation, each of which the government hoped to convert into smaller reservations. In addition to James McLaughlin, representing Standing Rock, they included Major B. F. Spencer of the Rosebud, Major Hugh D. Gallagher of Pine Ridge, Major Charles McChesney of Cheyenne River, and William W. Anderson of the Crow Creek and Lower Brule Agencies.

As they all arrived at the station, they were met and escorted to the Belvedere House Hotel by Indian Commissioners Wright, Pratt, and Cleveland. The bespectacled Reverend Cleveland held an impromptu press conference in which he outlined the government plan for the Lakota. "If this land is disposed of as is proposed, the Sioux Nation will have about 11 million acres remaining, or about 500 acres for every man, woman and child in their number," Cleveland explained. "Even this will be more than they can ever use." Specifically, to use Cleveland's own population estimate of 23,000, it would have come to 478 acres each.

The question arose, "How do they live at present?"

"A part of them are becoming civilized;" the reverend continued. "[They] have houses, cultivate patches of ground, wear citizen's clothes, and send their children to school, while another part equally as large, if not larger, still stick to their wild life, about which there seems to be much fascination."

Cleveland showed his disdain, shared by most well-intentioned men of his profession during the late nineteenth century, for the "wild life," and the failure of the Indians to fully assimilate despite the best efforts of missionaries like he had been. At the same time, we can find it amusing to hear him equally disgusted with the "fascination" that the wasichu media—and pulp-fiction-consuming public—had for the Indians who still practiced the "wild life."

One is tempted to cast him among those self-righteous ladies and gentlemen whom Nate Salsbury would characterize as "worthy cranks." Of course, we are reminded once gain that in the late nineteenth century, the "worthy cranks" sincerely believed that assimilation would lead to a better life for the people themselves.

On Saturday, October 13, the sixty-one Lakota leaders and their escorting agents rose early at the Belvedere House, had breakfast, and made their way to the Interior Department, the parent department of the Office of Indian Affairs. Here they had a 10 o'clock meeting with Secretary of the Interior William F. Vilas. Previously Cleveland's Postmaster General, he had taken over the top job at Interior from Lucius Q. C. Lamar seven months earlier. John Oberly, the Commissioner of Indian Affairs, was there and so was Reverend Cleveland.

"My friends, you have traveled a long way to visit Washington, and I am glad to see you come in white man's dress," Vilas said cordially, greeting the assembled Lakota leadership after an opening prayer in Lakota from Reverend Cleveland. He took their attire as evidence of the assimilation for which the wasichu government yearned. "I hope that you will have a pleasant visit in Washington, and I hope that your coming here will prove a good thing for you and your people left at home on the reservation. The Congress which makes the laws which govern the whole country, from the ocean on the East to the ocean on the West, and you in your long journey have not traversed half the way—Congress which makes the laws for this country, has made this law."

At this point, having tried to impress the Lakota with the geographic scale of the United States, he picked up a copy of the act passed by Congress which called for the sale of half the remaining Great Sioux Reservation. "Congress saw that the time had come," Vilas continued, "for the Sioux Indians to take sure steps toward civilization, and that the waste and unused lands of the reservation ought to be settled upon and made homes of."

One wonders if the leadership of the Department of the Interior truly believed that the sale of half their remaining land would result in their becoming more civilized—or whether it was merely a bold-faced con job. Apparently, many of the Lakota present took Vilas as being sincere. White Ghost, from the Crow Creek Agency, said that he was glad to see that "we all have a good heart." Swift Bird, from the Cheyenne River Agency, observed pointedly that "God has made our skins red [and yours white] but we are all friends and equal before God."

Sitting Bull is reported to have said nothing at the initial session at the Interior Department, but the following day, he had a lot to say when the Indians went away to discuss it among themselves. A meeting between various Lakota factions was held in a large room above the cigar store at 237 Pennsylvania Avenue on Sunday evening. A number of onlookers gathered across the street by the Botanical Gardens to watch the conference through the windows.

A reporter who was present wrote for the following day's *Washington Post* that "Sitting Bull made the opening speech, and every word of it was closely listened to by the hearers. He spoke nearly two hours. His style is, even to a person who cannot understand him, very impressive, and his gestures, though lavish, are graceful. He wags his head as he talks in a solemn way, and his remarks often elicited approving grunts from his companions. . . . Sitting Bull favors accepting the terms of the Government with an

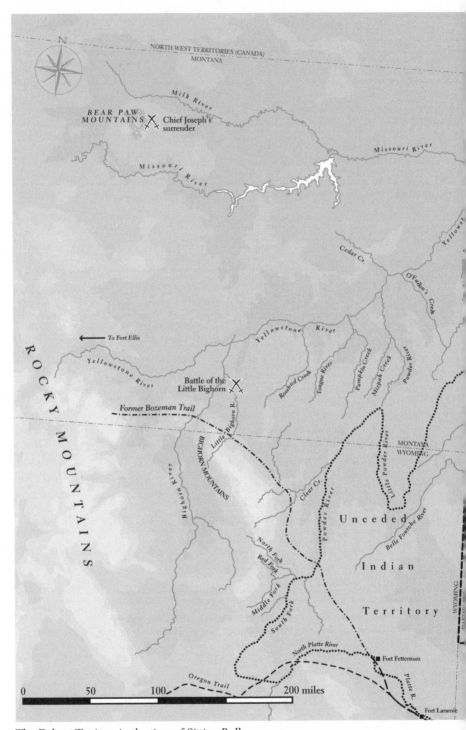

The Dakota Territory in the time of Sitting Bull.

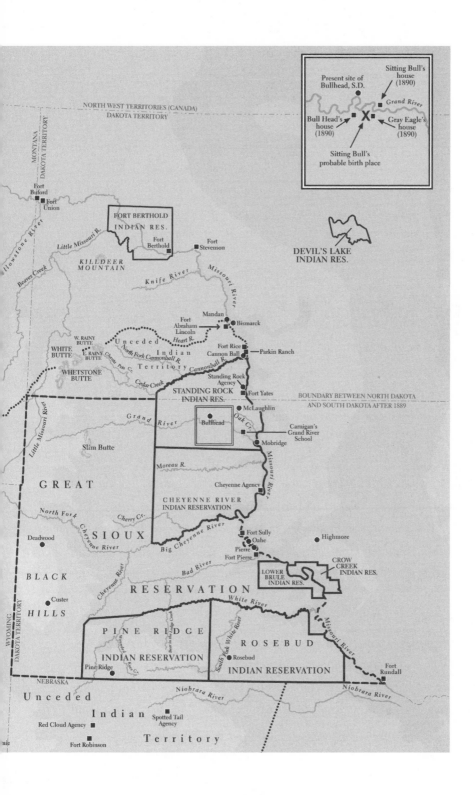

amendment so as to increase the price of the land relinquished to the price paid by the settlers."

As it turned out, one of those "approving grunts" was that of John Grass. Sitting Bull had managed to convince "the most sensible of all the Siouxs" to hold out for more money rather than to accept the wasichu offer of fifty cents an acre. Sitting Bull was intuitive enough to know that the wasichu could only be beaten by bargaining, not by intransigence. Sitting Bull would not have counseled negotiating a price for the priceless Black Hills, but the Black Hills had already been expropriated by the wasichu.

However, at the same time that Sitting Bull was discussing acceptance of the government sale, another group representing people from Pine Ridge and Rosebud was meeting at a boarding house at 224 Third Street to discuss holding out for no sale at all. These men, including American Horse and Swift Bear, decided that "the terms of the bill making the relinquishment of the land had never been fully explained to the people directly," and that the deal should be rejected.

Meanwhile, as Sitting Bull, John Grass, and American Horse debated the substance of their reason for being in Washington, Gall accepted a dinner invitation. If it were possible to travel back in time to that evening in Washington, one would be hard pressed to decide whether to attend Sitting Bull's oration on Pennsylvania Avenue, or to be a fly on the wall at Peterson's Restaurant on 15th Street. Here, Gall dined with Captain Edward S. Godfrey, who as a lieutenant had been part of Reno's command at the Little Bighorn. James McLaughlin and Major John McElroy were also at the table.

One longs to know what was said, and what was discussed between two men who had been on opposing sides at the most remembered of the battles of the Indian Wars. Unfortunately, the *Washington Post* account of this historic exchange only recalls Gall's eating habits. "The big Sioux mogul took to oysters in the shell like a Norfolk oysterman," observed the *Post*.

"He did eat with his knife, but did it as successfully as knife-eaters generally do. He ate slowly, deliberately and enjoyed every mouthful. He worked a palm-leaf fan every once in a while, as he was not accustomed to the close atmosphere of the dining-room. In facial expressions he is not unlike [Methodist] Bishop [John Philip] Newman, and physically he is a remarkably fine specimen of a man. While he is known as an educated man, he does not speak English."

On Monday morning, as the Lakota leaders returned to the Interior Department, Sitting Bull was in a conciliatory mood, having convinced John Grass, "the greatest statesman in the [Sioux] Nation," to ask for more money. "My friends, I do not wish to make a long speech," Sitting Bull smiled cynically. "I have but few words to say. I call you my friends because I am one of your people. I belong to the Government of the United States. As we have our own [divergent] views of this new law we wish to speak to you as man to man. I hope everything will be done in a quiet manner. This is all I have to say."

With this, John Grass, the man whom some wasichu called the "premier" of the "Sioux Nation," took the floor and drove a harder bargain than he might have without Sitting Bull's urging the evening before. He pointed out that part of the land not being sold was dusty and worthless. He then argued that instead of the 160 acres being assigned to each head of household, they should get twice that under the theory that the old men granted 160 acres would soon be dead and the allotment should be for their survivors, and therefore at least 320 acres.

"Think of our fathers," he said, waving his hand. "They used to own all these lands which the white man now lives upon. They were ours once, but we have been driven away from them. We are a poor and ignorant people, and you are the cause of our being poor. Looking back, I say to you that whatever we ask should have due consideration. Put the key that opens our reservation in your pocket for a while. Do not be in a hurry; wait until these matters are well considered. Ascertain first whether, after our lands [the 11 million acres to be sold] are gone, we will have enough left to us."

The argument was vintage Sitting Bull, so we are left to believe that he had given Grass the argument to use. Grass then wrapped up his remarks by demanding that the government increase its offer from fifty cents per acre to $1.25.

Mad Bear, who rose after John Grass concluded his remarks, underscored the Lakota interest in getting top dollar if they were to sell, and he reminded Vilas and the Indian Commissioners of the federal government's failure to honor the 1868 Fort Laramie Treaty. "Does a man who sells a horse for money to be paid in the future sell another horse to the same man if he refuses to pay for the first?"

White Ghost added his voice to the reminders of federal government misconduct with regard to the 1868 Treaty and was among those who said that this was enough to advocate rejecting the sale out of hand.

When the speeches concluded at 2:30 Monday afternoon, Vilas told the leaders that he would convey their remarks to Grover Cleveland and return with his reply at 10 on Wednesday morning. With that, the meeting was adjourned.

The following day, October 16, the same day that the World Series opened in New York, the Lakota leaders were entertained by a tour of Washington—and the press was entertained by following them around. This excursion took them to the Smithsonian, where they were especially excited by portraits of Plains Indians done of George Catlin in the 1830s. Some of them thought they recognized the people in the pictures, and asked to take the paintings. This request was politely denied.

At the National Zoo, the Lakota remarked that they felt sorry for the caged animals, especially the buffalo. They did, however, greatly enjoy watching the monkeys, which, of course, they had never seen. Gray Eagle was so taken with the monkeys that he offered to buy one. This request, like the earlier solicitation of a Catlin painting, was respectfully refused.

The Sioux leaders visiting Washington, D.C., in 1888 were photographed on the steps of the Capitol on October 15 by C. M. Bell. Sitting Bull is seen standing slightly apart from the group in the third row on the left. The three men on the far right of the same row are Gall, Louis Primeau, and Standing Rock Agent James McLaughlin. (*Library of Congress*)

All Washington visits by Indian delegations included the obligatory photo op, and for this one, it came that afternoon as they visited the Capitol building. Along with their agents, they arrayed themselves on the steps, facing eastward into the lens of photographer C. M. Bell. One is left to wonder whether it was intentional that Sitting Bull positioned himself slightly apart from the group at the opposite end of his row from James McLaughlin and Standing Rock interpreter Louis Primeau.

That evening, as they all returned to the Belvedere House they were the center of attention as they relaxed in the lobby. Once again, Sitting Bull placed himself apart from the crowd, holding court in the parlor above the rear of the lobby. The *Washington Post* reporter who was covering the gathering noted that "the ladies of the hotel seemed very much taken with the Indian warrior. They shook hands with him and gazed fondly into his classic face, while he in turn, told a lady that she looked like Mrs. Sitting Bull, only her hair wasn't red, and he asked for a lock of her hair." The lady reportedly laughed.

It is here that the newspaper description of the encounter ends. It was not reported whether any of the ladies showed similar interest in John Grass. Indeed, by the end of the week, the media seemed to have forgotten all about such "fine specimens" as Grass. All eyes were on Sitting Bull.

Wednesday, October 17, found the Lakota delegation back at the Interior Department meeting with Secretary Vilas. While the Indians had been viewing the monkeys and participating in the photo op, Vilas had been conferring with Grover Cleveland. "My friends, I have been very much pleased by the opportunity to see you and talk with you about this business," Vilas said, calling them friends, as Sitting Bull had earlier called the Interior Department men friends. "I think better of you for having seen you and talked with you. You have talked like sensible men, and I have laid before the President all you have said and just what your wishes are. I have consulted fully with the President about it, and I have brought you his answer. This Government wants your real interests preserved and taken care of. It wants you to have in this business what is best for you. The President knows that you are men and he hears the appeal which you make to him as a man. Bad men occasionally do wrong to the Indians; bad men are sometimes in the Indian service, but bad men do not represent the Government."

Vilas then went on to say that Cleveland would ask Congress in December to amend the bill so that the Indians would receive a dollar an acre for any land sold to settlers within three years, and seventy-five cents for the following two years. Cleveland had also proposed to double the million-dollar cash payment previously offered.

Having listened to the government counteroffer, the Lakota returned to the Belvedere, where they would discuss and debate it until nearly 9 o'clock Friday night. Sitting Bull now moved to lead the opposition the plan, and all but a reported fourteen or fifteen of the others aligned themselves with him. In their proposal to the counteroffer, the Lakota dug in their heels at the $1.25 per acre figure and insisted on an immediate cash payment rather than having the money paid out in dribs and drabs over five or more years. They maintained that if the government wanted their land, they should simply buy it outright for $13.75 million rather than taking it and paying the Lakota for it as it was resold.

As the *Washington Post* reported on October 20, "the Indians have decided that further parlaying is useless, and unless it be the Secretary's [Vilas's] desire that a further council be held, they will start for home tonight or tomorrow."

Vilas replied that he couldn't entertain their offer, and at 3 o'clock that afternoon, they paid a courtesy call on Cleveland at the White House. As the *Washington Post* reported the following day, "there was no speechmaking, the President simply shook the hand of each [Lakota leader] as he passed."

An hour and a half after calling on the president—as the Giants scored five runs in the bottom of the eighth inning to take a 6–4 win and assure their victory in the World Series—the Lakota boarded a Chesapeake & Ohio passenger train bound for Cincinnati and points west.

As for the presidential election, it was decided a couple of weeks after the Lakota left Washington. Cleveland received 5.5 million votes to Benjamin Harrison's 5.4 million. However, the Electoral College would cast 233 votes for Harrison and 168 for Cleveland, so the grandson of William Henry Harrison—the first president to succumb to the alleged zero-year curse—became the twenty-third President of the United States.

With Harrison in office as of March 1889, William Vilas was replaced as Secretary of the Interior by John Willock Noble, who was destined to preside over the last, and arguably darkest, hours of the Indian Bureau's involvement in the bloody conflict between the wasichu and the Plains Indians. Cleveland, the only president whom Sitting Bull met face to face, would win in a rematch with Harrison in 1892 to become the first president to serve two nonconsecutive terms.

THE 1888 effort by the U.S. government to dismember the Great Sioux Reservation would not be the last. With 1889, new winds were blowing, and the walls continued to close in on the Lakota. The wasichu population within Dakota Territory had continued to mushroom. In 1870, the population was 14,181, and in 1880 it stood at 135,177. By 1889, more than half a million wasichu lived there. These wasichu were calling loudly for statehood. Finally, in November 1889, Dakota Territory itself was sliced in half, with North Dakota being admitted as the thirty-ninth state, and South Dakota as the fortieth. Also during 1889, both Montana Territory and Washington Territory became states.

In order to achieve statehood for the Dakotas, the issue of the Great Sioux Reservation demanded resolution, and Congress passed an amended version of the Sioux Act. This 1889 incarnation carried the provisions that Secretary Vilas had put in his last counteroffer in October 1880, although the dollar-an-acre offer was upped to $1.25 for land sold in the first three years and seventy-five cents for the next two. Also included was the 320-acre allotment requested by John Grass—probably acting in concert with or on the orders of Sitting Bull. Amazingly, Congress accepted important parts of what had been put forward by the Lakota during the Washington conference.

In July 1889, as had been the case in 1883 and 1888, the U.S. government sent a commission to the Great Sioux Reservation to try to convince its people to accept its dissolution. Heading the commission for this round was General George Crook, the old soldier whose 1876 military campaign against these same men had gone so poorly. In the meantime, Crook had achieved somewhat more positive notoriety during his somewhat more successful campaign against Geronimo and the Apache in the Southwest.

Crook was now based in Chicago as the commander of the U.S. Army's Division of the Missouri, the region that contained the soon-to-be-divided Dakota Territory. In his later years, Crook had become an advocate for Indian rights. Although he subscribed to the notion of assimilation, he had been an outspoken critic of abuses by the Indian Bureau throughout his career. Like many well-meaning wasichu, Crook saw the Sioux Act as the best thing for the future of the Lakota, and he told them so.

This time, unlike in 1888, McLaughlin was thoroughly in favor of the scheme. He worked hard to convince as many people as possible to back the treaty. He went to men such as Gall, John Grass, and many others, telling them that they had gotten most of what they had asked for in Washington and they should agree to the new version of the Sioux Act. The agents at the other agencies did the same with the people under their jurisdiction.

Sitting Bull, though, thoroughly opposed the treaty. He had stated his position in Washington and that was what he believed. He was not inclined to further compromise.

Nobody was sure how the vote would go. In 1883 and 1888, the Lakota had rejected the proposal out of hand, but this time it went down to the wire. When the votes were finally tallied during the first week of August, 56 percent of the approximately 10,000 Indians casting ballots agreed to the Sioux Act of 1889. However, 44 percent had been in opposition, and the vote had left the people divided, often bitterly, along factional lines. To make matters worse, the Indian Bureau unilaterally cut the ration allotment for the agencies during the winter of 1889–1890.

For George Crook, it was the final victory in his career-long campaign against the Indians. He died unexpectedly on March 21, 1890, in Chicago. Red Cloud's epitaph for Crook was "He never lied to us." Considering most of the relations between the U.S. Army and the Lakota over the previous decades, that was a compliment.

There would be a postscript to the issue of the Black Hills, which had been unilaterally amputated from the Great Sioux Reservation a decade before it was finally subdivided. In 1923, the Sioux Nation filed suit in the United States Court of Claims. The suit did not demand monetary compensation, but that the Black Hills be returned to Lakota ownership. The suit was dismissed in 1942, but in 1977, the U.S. government offered $17.5 million for the Black Hills, which was rejected. The parties went back to court, and in 1980, the U.S. Supreme Court ruled that the Black Hills had been seized illegally and ordered a payment of almost $106 million. The Lakota refused the settlement, insisting that the Black Hills were "not for sale." Still unpaid, but still deposited in an interest-bearing account, the Black Hills settlement totaled in excess of three-quarters of a billion dollars in late 2007.

As the Great Sioux Reservation was officially and finally consigned to history, with the sum of its parts in no way equaling the whole, Sitting Bull quietly, but bitterly, accepted the new reality. He retired to his wasichu-style cabin north of the Grand River, determined to keep a low profile. His intention was to avoid politics, but his celebrity, especially among the wasichu, meant that remaining untouched by the limelight was not possible.

During the summer of 1889, even as Sitting Bull and the others were dickering and bickering over the Crook Commission, a wasichu woman arrived at Standing Rock looking for Sitting Bull. One Bull and White Bull saw her, and based on what they told Stanley Vestal, he refers to her as appearing at the agency like a "strange apparition."

When Sitting Bull went east, crowds had gathered, fascinated with this man and what he represented. The ladies, we recall, "shook hands with him and gazed fondly into his classic face." When Sitting Bull went west, he was visited occasionally by fascinated wasichu who sought him out at Standing Rock. Normally, McLaughlin was able to screen his callers, but a few got through. One such person who turned up on his doorstep was the woman who called herself Catherine Weldon. If Nate Salsbury had been there, he might have called her a "worthy crank."

Like the men whom Salsbury had seen accost Sitting Bull in Philadelphia that day in 1885 when he coined that colorful term, she was noted as having been a member of the National Indian Defense Association. As the stories go, she had come west from her home in Brooklyn, New York, specifically to meet Sitting Bull, having been inspired by the considerable publicity surrounding the Sioux Act and the perceived injustices that it wrought.

What distinguished her from most of the "worthy cranks" of the National Indian Defense Association was that she was willing to put her beliefs on the line and actually travel out to Standing Rock—not an easy thing for the average Victorian lady from Brooklyn. "She was a lady, well dressed, and not bad looking, indeed overdressed, with many showy rings and brooches, and fashionable clothes," Vestal says in his poetic description of her. "Yet this was but the surface of her novelty. For in her there flickered, as steadily as the winds of [East Coast] civilization would permit, a passionate, if somewhat incoherent, flame of enthusiasm for the good life."

Catherine Weldon was also an artist. As Vestal puts it, "Her talent was a curse, fit to drive her to absurdities in that world to which it had, and could have, no authentic relation."

McLaughlin didn't know what to make of this woman—cursed with an "artistic" temperament—who kept showing up at Standing Rock. She came in response to her perception of the injustice of the dissolution of the Great Sioux Reservation, but she stayed in response to her fascination with Sitting Bull personally. Apparently she took to him as a fan for a movie star, captivated by his considerable charisma.

And, apparently, so was he by her. By all accounts, Sitting Bull was intrigued by this bright and precocious lady who was not afraid to speak her mind and to walk the walk rather than merely talking the talk. Sitting Bull recognized this and gave her the Lakota name Woman Walking Ahead.

Mrs. Weldon has always been described as a thirty-something widow of considerable financial means, who appears in Sitting Bull's story as a colorful footnote to accounts and little more. It was not for more than a century that anyone did any detective work to find out who Catherine Weldon really was. In the 1990s, University of Michigan Professor Eileen Pollack picked up a very cold and difficult trail and published the first true biography of her, *Woman Walking Ahead*, in 2002.

Digging through such primary sources as the musty public records in New York City, Pollack discovered that Catherine Weldon was indeed a widow from Brooklyn, but not a widow of considerable financial means— she just seemed that way because she dressed as East Coast ladies dressed. She also carried a case of art supplies, something that was a bit out of the ordinary. To those who observed her in the Dakotas, all this made her seem rich. Those who described her later came to the same conclusion. Nobody questioned the assertion until Pollack discovered differently.

Nor was Catherine Weldon in her thirties. She was born Caroline Schlotter in Switzerland in 1838, and emigrated to the United States in 1871. Her stepfather was a doctor, and Pollack supposes that she probably grew up in comfortable, middle-class surroundings and that she attended college. She married a carpenter named Richard Weldon later in the decade, and their son, Christopher, known as Christie, was born in 1878. For some reason, she began using the name Catherine, although she returned to the name Caroline much later in life.

Though there have been some accounts to the contrary, Pollack tells us that at Standing Rock, she was befriended by a pair of part-Lakota half-sisters, Alma Parkin and Mary Louisa (better known as Louise) Van Solen, the daughters of Eagle Woman All Look At. Both girls had grown up at Standing Rock, and had taught school there. Alma's husband, Henry Parkin, owned a ranch near the Cannonball River, as well as a store and a hotel, where Catherine Weldon probably stayed for part of the time she was at Standing Rock. Louise's husband, George Van Solen, was a sawmill engineer at Fort Yates.

Sitting Bull and Four Robes at Fort Randall in 1882 with Sally Battles, the niece of then post commander, Colonel George Andrews. Sally is said to have befriended Sitting Bull's daughter Standing Holy. The wasichu child on the left is identified only as "Little Bell," while the two Lakota youngsters are Arrows Left in Him and Run Away From. The baby in Four Robes's cradle board is not identified, but the Fort Randall census data indicates that a daughter was born while Sitting Bull was at the post. Alternatively, it might be Sitting Eagle, born in 1880, who died at age four. The officer on horseback is Captain Charles Bentzoni, who commanded Company B of the 25th Infantry Regiment at Fort Randall. This is one of several photos taken of Sitting Bull at Fort Randall by the Bailey, Dix & Mead studio. (*Library of Congress*)

Gradually, Mrs. Weldon became Sitting Bull's champion, his patron, and his private secretary. She encouraged his opposition to the Crook Commission, and she incurred the wrath of McLaughlin as she wrote letters on Sitting Bull's behalf to the government. Being an artist, she painted several portraits of Sitting Bull, signing them "C.S. Weldon." It was not known until the research done by Pollack that the middle initial stood for her Swiss surname, Schlotter.

Weldon's being a friend of Sitting Bull naturally incurred McLaughlin's enmity. This, combined with the fact that her son Christie was in boarding school back east, led Catherine Weldon to decide not to winter at Standing Rock. However, she would return again in the spring of 1890.

WHAT Catherine Weldon witnessed at Standing Rock during 1889 was a culture in the final stages of collapse. Everything about Lakota culture was going through an enormous paradigm shift. The closing of the frontier in the American West was accompanied by the closing forever in a chapter in the history of the indigenous people that had lasted for centuries. Nowhere were the ramifications of this closing chapter more pronounced than on the Plains. In other regions, such as the Southwest, where agriculture had been adopted by most tribes prior to the arrival of Europeans and Euro-Americans, the change was less dramatic. On the Plains, where all aspects of life and culture had centered on a nomadic people following the great herds of buffalo, the change was profound. The buffalo were gone. The old ways were gone. If the old ways had been replaced by new ways, that would have been one thing, but they had not been.

The grand scheme had been to bring the Indian in from the "wild" and ensure his future posterity by teaching him the ways of wasichu civilization. The hunter could prosper as a farmer. It looked good on paper in Washington, but the grand scheme had failed, as the crops had failed. The western Plains of the Dakotas were not the rolling hills of Virginia or New England or Wisconsin. This was not the first time that the meager Lakota farms had disappointed the Lakota farmers, but this was the year that the Indian Bureau had decided to cut the rations that it would distribute. The reason was that reducing the rations would provide the Lakota with the incentive they needed to commit themselves more energetically to their farms. However, all the incentive in the world won't encourage crops to grow in land not suited for crops, nor during droughts such as the Dakotas were experiencing that year. Hungry, starving people sat forlornly in a truncated reservation, staring at withered cornstalks with nothing left but despair. When the snows came, things only got worse.

The winter of 1889–1890 would be a difficult one, filled with pestilence of Biblical proportions. On top of the crop failures came hunger. Next came plagues that could have been copied from the pages of the Book of Exodus. There were measles and whooping cough, and then a serious flu epidemic swept through the Dakota agencies. Imagine lying hungry and immobilized by flu symptoms as a blizzard blows its icy blast between the boards of an uninsulated cabin with hurricane force winds. Such was the winter of 1889–1890 in what had been the Great Sioux Reservation. In the spring, there would be no buffalo to hunt, only the desperate hope that the crops would not fail again in 1890.

The economic collapse was followed by a cultural collapse. As Plenty Coups had said, after the buffalo were gone, nothing happened. All the belief systems that had been ingrained into the culture of the Plains Indians for centuries just imploded during the winter of 1889–1890. When an ancient, well-ordered system of cultural and religious beliefs collapses, a void is created. Into this void can flow all sorts of mischief that preys upon despair.

Throughout history, countless prophets have appeared at such times with promises of a return to happier times, before the traditional ways were threatened by disaster wrought by alien doctrines imposed by outsiders. Such voids and such doctrines can be seen throughout history, and often they lead to religious warfare. The rise of Islamic fundamentalism in the twenty-first century can be seen as such a circumstance. In the context of nineteenth-century American cultural conflicts, Tenskwatawa, the Shawnee Prophet who had a large following in the early nineteenth century, was certainly such a shaman. In the 1880s, similar prophets, from Nakaidoklini of the Apache to Sword Bearer of the Crow, came and went, usually exiting violently after stirring their devotees to religious hysteria. They arrived on their respective scenes after all seemed lost, presenting themselves as the last hope to lead people back to the purity of the old ways.

The most important and influential of such prophets at the end of the nineteenth century was Wovoka (also known as Jack Wilson) a thirty-four-year-old Paiute shaman. Though he was based in Nevada, his message would have its most profound resonance on the Lakota reservations of South Dakota. Wovoka created a messianic dogma that borrowed elements from both native creeds and Christianity. He spoke of an Indian version of the fundamentalist Christian millennium concept. There would be a new life that would be happy and peaceful. A person would live forever. Ghosts would be people again. In the company of previously departed friends and relatives, people would follow the bygone way of life without any material wants. Wovoka preached that a new messiah would rid the world of the wasichu and the buffalo would return in immense numbers.

The essential ritual of Wovoka's teaching was a dance that came to be called the Ghost Dance. By singing and dancing, a Ghost Dance adherent could put himself or herself into a trance so as to glimpse ancestors living in the wonderful world beyond. To his credit, Wovoka cautioned that in order to reach this special place one had to live peacefully and nonviolently.

The enormous and widespread popularity of the Ghost Dance came as a complete surprise to the wasichu. It shouldn't have. The Indians on the Plains were ready to accept anything that promised a change for the better. As Bob Dylan wrote, when you got nothing, you got nothing to lose. In 1890, the same year that the Ghost Dance appeared, the Census Bureau had formally declared the end of the frontier, based on United States population density and land allocation. The Indians had been marginalized and placed on reservations. An era was declared to have ended, but then suddenly it had not. Once again, the wasichu were fearful.

The enormous and widespread popularity of the Ghost Dance probably came as a complete surprise to Wovoka himself. Short Bull from the

Ghost dancers photographed at the Pine Ridge Reservation in 1890. (*National Archives*)

Rosebud Reservation and Kicking Bear from the Cheyenne River Reservation went from South Dakota to Nevada to visit Wovoka and to learn what they could. They came back to South Dakota as converts in March 1890.

As often happens with religions, Wovoka's Ghost Dance was hijacked by an element of Lakota extremists who decided that a short cut to paradise would be to eliminate all of the Euro-Americans. By eliminating them from the traditional Lakota lands, a paradise on Earth might be created on the Northern Plains. Short Bull and Kicking Bear became the leading proponents among the Lakota of the extreme version of the Ghost Dance religion. They told the people that the Ghost Shirt, the essential vestment of the Ghost Dance, would make them bulletproof.

About the same time that these men came back from Nevada, George Crook died in office, General Nelson Miles assumed command of the Division of the Missouri, and Catherine Weldon had returned, with her son, to Standing Rock. All of these turns would play into events to come.

The Ghost Dance was not as popular at Standing Rock as it was at Pine Ridge, Cheyenne River, Rosebud, and some of the other reservations. While important leaders, such as the typically conciliatory Big Foot (formerly known as Spotted Elk) of the Minneconjou, embraced the Ghost Dance doctrine, Sitting Bull kept it at arm's length. At Cheyenne River, Big Foot, who had stood by Red Cloud when the accepted the 1868 Fort Laramie Treaty, and who had long since turned to farming, saw the decline in the standard of living on the reservations, and decided there must be another way. Sitting Bull was skeptical, not believing that the dead would rise again. He did not participate in the Ghost Dance, but neither did he denounce the new religion.

While Sitting Bull had shown little interest in the Ghost Dance doctrine, he had manifested great interest in the return of Mrs. Weldon. She had communicated with Sitting Bull—in letters generally intercepted and read by James McLaughlin—and now she had, as promised, returned. She resumed her role as Sitting Bull's advocate and private secretary, and began discussing the idea of starting a school at Standing Rock to teach domestic crafts, such as sewing, to Lakota girls. This year, unlike 1889, she brought her son Christie and announced that she planned to live at Standing Rock full-time. This was unusual, but not unprecedented. Other unmarried women, missionaries, and teachers such as Elaine Goodale and Mary Collins lived among the Lakota.

However, when Weldon moved into one of Sitting Bull's cabins at Grand River, eyebrows were raised. The rumors among the wasichu whispered that she was—or soon would become—Sitting Bull's next wife. It was still generally perceived, because of her well-scrubbed youthful appearance, that Catherine Weldon was a thirty-something tart. However, she was, by her biographer's reckoning, fifty-two. This made her older than either Four Robes or Seen by the Nation, who were in their early forties. The July 2 issue of the *Sioux City Journal* even carried the report of the intended nuptials of Sitting Bull and Mrs. Weldon. Most wasichu looked

Sitting Bull with Seen by the Nation and Four Robes at Fort Randall. (*National Archives*)

down on the practice of polygamy by the Lakota, but the thought of a wasichu becoming a Hunkpapa plural wife was considered especially scandalous.

As the newspapers picked up on the news of their relationship, they began using the provocative phrase "Sitting Bull's White Squaw," to describe her. We hasten to add that the term "squaw," once widely used, is no longer considered an acceptable term. It was originally derived from the Algonquian word denoting "young woman," and was used almost universally by wasichu Americans from the eighteenth century through most of the twentieth century to describe an "Indian wife." It was never considered to be a negative term until the 1970s, when it was suggested that it was also possibly a derogatory French corruption of Iroquoian word for a part of female anatomy. As a result of this, the term "squaw" is no longer in common use as a synonym for wife, and we have avoided using it except for this explanation. Since the negative connotation was widely reported in the 1990s, many states, including Idaho and Montana, have taken steps to rename places, especially mountains, that have the word as part of their traditional names.

controlling his power and charisma. She understood that McLaughlin was irrational enough to use the Ghost Dance to justify malicious action against the object of her own obsession.

On August 7, in a letter now in the National Archives, she wrote to Thomas J. Morgan, the Commissioner of Indian Affairs, that Sitting Bull had invited her to Standing Rock to assist him in helping the Lakota "become civilized as soon as possible." The urgency in her tone sprang from her belief that the Ghost Dance, or the wasichu reaction to it, would lead to disaster for Sitting Bull and the Lakota. She felt that by seeing to it that they were "civilized as soon as possible," disaster could be averted.

Sitting Bull's laissez-faire attitude toward the Ghost Dance, of neither embracing nor denouncing it, probably troubled her a great deal, but he was a thoughtful man. Even at this stage, Sitting Bull was pragmatic. Just as he was unwilling to dash blindly into the waiting arms of the Ghost Dance, he did not blindly reject all aspects of wasichu "civilization." "I have advised my people thus," he had said within earshot of One Bull and White Bull. "When you find anything good in the white man's road, pick it up; but when you find something bad, or that turns out bad, drop it, leave it alone."

He probably said the same thing of the Ghost Dance doctrine. At Standing Rock, the Ghost Dancers gathered and made their camp at Grand River near his own cabin, but he did not, as they might have hoped, become their outspoken champion. In retrospect, how could he be that when his own champion, Woman Walking Ahead, was such an outspoken foe?

As summer turned to fall, it was a season for misunderstandings. Catherine Weldon's motives for speaking out so stridently against the Ghost Dance were misinterpreted by the Hunkpapa at Standing Rock. She was just like all the wasichu, they felt. Distrust of the Ghost Dance was equated with a distrust of the Lakota.

Many agents, especially the new man at Pine Ridge, Daniel Royer, were growing increasingly nervous. The Oglala at Pine Ridge had even started referring jokingly to the jittery Royer as "Young Man Afraid of His Indians," a play on the name of the prominent Oglala leader, Young Man Afraid of His Horses. We should hasten to add that his name was correctly translated to mean They Even Fear His Horses. By 1890, he was no longer a young man—he was about Sitting Bull's age—and he was never nearly as afraid of his horses as Royer was of the Lakota under his care.

McLaughlin should have known better. Unlike the wasichu living in South Dakota and hearing about the Ghost Dance on the rumor mill, he was on the reservation where he could actually see what was happening—which was a lot less at Standing Rock than at Pine Ridge or Rosebud.

One man who did know better was Dr. Valentine McGillycuddy, whose experience in the West as a U.S. Army surgeon dated back to the 1870s, and who had served for a time as the Indian Agent at the Pine Ridge Agency. He was also the man who had pronounced Crazy Horse dead at Fort Robinson in September 1877. He knew and understood the Lakota as well as any wasichu. In a famous statement, contained in the 1891 Annual Report of the Commissioner of Indian Affairs, McGillycuddy said, "I should let the dance continue. The coming of the troops has frightened the Indians. If the Seventh-Day Adventists prepare their ascension robes for the second coming of the savior, the United States Army is not put in motion to prevent them. Why should the Indians not have the same privilege? If the troops remain, trouble is sure to come."

Were he not a man obsessed, McLaughlin's decade of experience at Standing Rock and his ability to understand at least the rudiments of the Lakota language should have furnished him the understanding that the Ghost Dance was essentially a nonviolent exercise. It also should have been apparent that it would probably become a passing fad before it became a catalyst for a major Indian assault on wasichu civilization.

As McGillycuddy suggested, McLaughlin should have seen that the Ghost Dance religion was no more threatening than an enthusiastic Christian revival meeting—but as we know, people are often fearful of the inexplicable among cultures other than their own. At the very least, he, if not all the agents, should have realized that the Indians had neither the weapons nor the logistics to support a major war.

Were he not a man obsessed, McLaughlin would have understood all this, and deep down, he probably did. Woman Walking Ahead was right. She was ahead of the curve in seeing that his reaction to the Ghost Dance was merely a dark veil for his dark intentions to get Sitting Bull under control. McLaughlin probably knew better, but he either irrationally ignored what his experience and ability told him, or he deliberately used the Ghost Dance as the pretext for extreme action aimed at bringing Sitting Bull down once and for all.

On October 17, according to the Annual Report of the Commissioner of Indian Affairs, McLaughlin wrote to that commissioner, Thomas J. Morgan, calling the Ghost Dance a "pernicious system of religion," and adding that Sitting Bull was the "high priest and leading apostle of this latest Indian absurdity."

His own rambling memo, long on illogical name-calling, was itself an exercise in absurdity. However, Morgan was predisposed to believe the worst. He had heard the reports about the Ghost Dance, and he heard about the fears of an uprising. He had probably heard, and probably spoken, the word "warpath."

The Lakota were hearing the same thing. At the same time, they were hearing Sitting Bull's house guest harshly denouncing the Ghost Dance. It sounded as though she was denouncing the Lakota. Woman Walking Ahead was now walking out of step with the very people she had come to help.

The more she said, the more Catherine Weldon was distrusted. This had to have put Sitting Bull in an awkward position, for just as the wasichu regarded him as the most important "Indian chief" on the Plains, many among his own people distrusted this man who seemed to put his faith in the wrong people.

Finally, it was time for her to leave Standing Rock, and she departed, having seen her best intentions backfire. Sitting Bull drove her personally to catch the steamboat at Cannon Ball, North Dakota, about twenty-five miles north of Fort Yates. (It should be pointed out that name of the town of Cannon Ball is spelled as two words, while the nearby river is spelled Cannonball.) What a cultural shift this represented. Here was the erstwhile archvillain of the Little Bighorn, seated next to a New York socialite, driving a buckboard on a wasichu road to catch the steamer *Abner O'Neal*.

On October 22, Sitting Bull bade farewell to Catherine Weldon for the last time. Some accounts about this moment recall that as her son Christie boarded the vessel, he cut his foot on a rusty nail. Others state that he had punctured his foot earlier and at least part of his mother's reason for leaving Standing Rock was to seek medical attention for the infection downstream in Pierre.

Most accounts agree that it was a bad omen. The November 20 issue of the *Bismarck Tribune*, repeating a dispatch from the *Pierre Capital*, notes that Christie died a painful death aboard the ship the night before and that his mother "is nearly crazed with grief."

A lot of terrible things would happen in the Lakota country over the next few months. Rumors of Sitting Bull's impending arrest were already circulating around Fort Yates even before October 25, when he stopped off there on his way home from Cannon Ball to pick up rations. At that point, they were still rumors.

On October 29, just four days after Sitting Bull passed though Fort Yates, the Commissioner of Indian Affairs replied to James McLaughlin. If the agent said that Sitting Bull was the driving force behind the unrest, that far be it for him to question that assessment. Was not Sitting Bull the greatest "Indian chief" in America? That was the accepted wasichu preconception. If there was trouble, then it was only logical to assume that Sitting Bull was the kingpin. Morgan instructed McLaughlin to tell Sitting Bull that the Indian Bureau was greatly displeased, and that Sitting Bull would be held personally accountable for any trouble.

Morgan had instructed McLaughlin to convey this message to Sitting Bull, but it would be nearly three weeks before McLaughlin went down to Grand River to call on Sitting Bull face to face.

Meanwhile, there was trouble. Royer, the fidgety novice agent at Pine Ridge, panicked and sent a telegram to Commissioner Morgan, informing him that his agency was without protection and "at the mercy of these crazy dancers." This fateful telegram was like tipping the first in a line of dominoes.

The dominoes, still preserved in the National Archives, consist of a series of telegrams and memos dated between November 12 and 15. They began with Royer and worked their way up to Secretary of the Interior John Willock Noble who, in turn, involved President Harrison. Up the chain of command to the top via the Interior Department went the dominoes—then back down the chain of command by way of the War Department they fell. Harrison ordered Secretary of War Redfield Proctor to tell the U.S. Army to get involved, and the order worked its way back down to Major General Nelson Miles, who had just taken over as Commander of the Division of the Missouri.

Bear Coat was back. For the first time since Sitting Bull was in Canada, his principal antagonist in a blue coat would be the tenacious Miles.

Directly below Miles's Missouri Division in the chain of command were the U.S. Army's Department of Dakota and the Department of the Platte. Although both McLaughlin's Standing Rock Agency and Royer's Pine Ridge Agency were in the state of South Dakota, they were in separate military departments. Standing Rock was in the Dakota, Pine Ridge in the Platte. Brigadier General Thomas Ruger commanded the Department of Dakota from his headquarters in St. Paul.

In the chain of command beneath Ruger, in descending order, were Lieutenant Colonel William Drum, the U.S. Army commander at Fort Yates, and Captain Edmond Fechét, who commanded the 8th Cavalry Regiment at Fort Yates. James McLaughlin, as the Indian Agent for Standing Rock and the highest ranking representative of the Indian Bureau on site, was Drum's opposite number on the civilian side at Fort Yates. Though he is often referred to with the title of "Major," McLaughlin was a civilian.

The Indian Bureau traditionally had the lead responsibility for managing the reservations, and the U.S. Army remained in a secondary support role. However, the president's referral of the matter of the Ghost Dance troubles to the Secretary of War officially declared martial law, giving the Army the primary responsibility for the suppression of an Indian uprising, should such a thing actually materialize.

Brigadier General John Brooke, commander of the Department of the Platte, left his headquarters in Omaha to assume direct command at a forward operating headquarters at Pine Ridge itself. Beginning on November 20, under terms of the presidential directive, Brooke undertook a military occupation of both the Pine Ridge and Rosebud Agencies using elements of the 2nd and 9th Infantry Regiments, as well as the 9th Cavalry and Custer's old command, the 7th Cavalry. Ironically, before Brooke arrived to occupy the agencies, many of the more ardent and militant Lakota had left these agencies to hide out in the Badlands to the west.

As Brooke was moving his troops toward the southern agencies, the troops at Standing Rock had not yet been mobilized. Drum was concerned that the primarily Hunkpapa Lakota people at Standing Rock might also leave the reservation if his troopers were mobilized, but he preferred keeping a low profile for the time being. It would look bad to have Indians that were supposed to be under his control slip outside his control.

At the time, Drum's command consisted of two companies of the 12th Infantry and two companies of the 8th Cavalry under Fechét.

Meanwhile, McLaughlin loaded Standing Rock Agency interpreter Louis Primeau into his buckboard and went down to Grand River to call on his old nemesis. Finding Sitting Bull's settlement filled with Ghost Dancers, McLaughlin decided it would be best to go away and return with a bit of backup.

As noted earlier, part of the Indian Bureau's means of asserting control over the agencies was the creation of a paramilitary police force comprised entirely of members of the tribes associated with each agency. McLaughlin had long made extensive and effective use of the Standing Rock Indian Police. By shrewdly exploiting the factionalism within the tribe, McLaughlin was able to mold a cadre of officers who, though Lakota, were more loyal to him than to Lakota leaders such as Sitting Bull.

One such man was Lieutenant of Police Henry Tatankapah, also known as Bull Head, who was said to be a long-time rival of Sitting Bull. Though Bull Head was a veteran of the Rosebud and the Little Bighorn battles, and had ridden with the men who had ridden with Sitting Bull before that, he had switched sides and was completely devoted to McLaughlin.

With the uniformed Lieutenant Bull Head escorting them, McLaughlin and Primeau reached Sitting Bull's home early on the cold morning of November 18, interrupting him as he was walking back to his house from his sweat lodge.

They sat down with the itancan and had what diplomats would call a frank discussion. Sitting Bull summarized his perspective on the Ghost Dance with an extremely well-reasoned and constructive proposal. "White Hair, you do not like me personally. You do not understand this dance," Sitting Bull said to McLaughlin, according to the oral histories gathered by Stanley Vestal from those who were there. "But I am willing to be convinced. You and I will go together to the tribes from which this dance

came, and when we reach the last one, where it started, if they cannot produce the Messiah, and if we do not find all the nations of the dead coming this way, then I will return and tell the Sioux it is all a lie. That will
end the dance. If we find the Messiah, then you are to let the dance go
on."

In retrospect, such an offer to confront Wovoka face-to-face was
extraordinary. Sitting Bull's recommendation was the silver bullet that
could have defused the growing confrontation that had grown up around
the Ghost Dance, and which was fast rocketing out of control. Sitting
Bull's word that the Ghost Dance religion was a lie, a statement based on
his first-hand encounter with the prophet of the Ghost Dance, would
have meant a great deal. Sitting Bull's word still carried enormous weight
among the Lakota. Even if denounced by his detractors—of which Bull
Head was not alone—Sitting Bull would have been able to take much, if
not most, of the wind out of the sails of the Ghost Dance movement.
Even if diehard devotees remained, the "hysteria" that the wasichu feared
would have dissipated.

McLaughlin should have known to accept Sitting Bull's offer, but he
didn't. He dismissed Sitting Bull's silver bullet out of hand, telling him
that it was too late to do such a thing—besides, he told Sitting Bull, there
was not enough money in the Standing Rock travel budget to send him to
Nevada.

In fact, McLaughlin did not want Sitting Bull to visit Wovoka and
declare his gospel to be a lie. McLaughlin would not have minded seeing
Wovoka exposed as a charlatan, he just did not want Sitting Bull to be the
one who did it. If Sitting Bull had ended the Ghost Dance "hysteria"
through the influence that he had among the Lakota, then he would not
be the inconsequential has-been that McLaughlin repeatedly insisted he
was. The Ghost Dance was a big deal. The papers back East carried it as
front-page news. For Sitting Bull to have ended the feared "uprising" before
it started would have made him a national hero, ensuring him permanent

importance. Nothing could be farther from what McLaughlin wanted, so he was unwilling to have Sitting Bull even try. In so doing, McLaughlin was playing with fire.

Bear Coat Miles would eventually know of Sitting Bull's proposal because it was reported in the newspapers. Apparently, he agreed with McLaughlin that it would be too little, too late. If Miles had acted, would the course of history have been changed? As McLaughlin was departing Grand River on that cold afternoon, Miles still considered Standing Rock a sideshow in the upcoming confrontation.

McLaughlin obsessively set about convincing the world, if not himself, that Sitting Bull was truly the high priest of the Ghost Dance movement. He later told Herbert Welsh of the Indian Rights Association that "Sitting Bull's old followers, over whom he always exerted a baneful influence . . . fell easy victims to his subtlety, and believed blindly in the absurdities he preached of the Indian millennium. He promised them the return of their dead ancestors and restoration of their old Indian life, together with the removal of the white race; that the white man's gunpowder could not throw a bullet with sufficient force in future to injure true believers; and even if Indians should be killed while obeying this call of the Messiah, they would only be the sooner united with their dead relatives, who were now all upon the earth (having returned from the clouds), as the living and dead would be reunited in the flesh next spring. You will readily understand what a dangerous doctrine this was to get hold of a superstitious and semi-civilized people, and how the more cunning 'medicine men' could impose upon the credulity of the average uncivilized Indian." The goal of the Indian Rights Association was to civilize the Indians, and McLaughlin cast Sitting Bull is the single biggest obstacle to that goal.

Meanwhile, Miles was getting creative in his efforts to curb the Ghost Dance and to avoid confrontation. He, like everyone else in the chain of command east of South Dakota, was operating under the premise that Sitting Bull was the chief instigator and provocateur. Therefore, his idea had to do with convincing Sitting Bull to depart from this dangerous path. To accomplish this, Miles sent a telegram to a mutual friend.

BUFFALO BILL CODY was in New York City, having just arrived from a successful European tour with the Wild West. The wire from Miles reached him even before he left the ship, but not before he had seen the headlines in the New York papers that screamed of an impending Indian war in South Dakota.

In his message, Miles succinctly requested that Cody go west and take Sitting Bull under his wing to head off the impending disaster. Cody canceled his New York engagements, caught the first train, and reported to General Miles in his Chicago headquarters thirty-six hours later on November 24. As Cody later recounted in his autobiography, Miles told him that the Indians "were getting ready for war" in South Dakota and that Sitting Bull was "haranguing the Indians thereabout, spreading the Messiah talk and getting them to join him."

Miles asked Cody to go immediately to Standing Rock and gave him written orders to travel to Sitting Bull's camp and "deliver him" to the nearest U.S. Army post. "He knew that I was an old friend of the chief, and he believed that if anyone could induce the old fox to abandon his plans for a general war I could," Cody reflected. "If I could not dissuade him from the warpath the general was of the opinion that I might be able to delay him in taking it, so that troops could be sent into the country in time to prevent a horrible massacre of the defenseless white settlers, who were already in terror of their lives."

Such was the case as Cody said it was presented. He went on to say that he was sure that if he could reach Sitting Bull he would at least listen. Cody told Miles that "in the present inflamed state of the Indian mind it would be next to impossible to get to his camp alive," but that he was quite ready to take the risk. This was probably a stretch of the truth, but Cody may have deduced this from what he'd read in the papers.

As Cody explained, he had no standing as an army officer or as a government agent, so he would need "some sort of credentials, in order to secure the assistance I should need on my mission." With this, Miles took one of his visiting cards from a case and wrote on the back:

> To commanding officers of United States Troops:
>
> Furnish Colonel William F. Cody with any assistance or escort that he may ask for.
>
> Nelson A. Miles.

Buffalo Bill and his small entourage took the next train to Mandan, North Dakota, the Northern Pacific stop west of Bismarck. Here, with great difficulty (against the backdrop of the impending war), he finally hired a team and driver who were willing to take him the sixty-five miles to Standing Rock. Cody reached Fort Yates on November 28, where he sought out James McLaughlin, who he had met previously. The agent was surprised to hear what Buffalo Bill intended and expressed concern for his safety.

"The Sioux are threatening a great war," McLaughlin told Cody. "At this very moment we do not know when the Indians here at the Agency may rise. We can take care of our own situation, for we have four troops of cavalry here, but we cannot permit you to go to Sitting Bull's camp. Not only would you be killed before you got halfway there, but your presence in the country would precipitate hostilities for which we are not in the least prepared. I'm sorry, Cody, but it can't be done. . . . The only thing for you to do is to stay all night with us and then return to the railroad. Even that will be risky enough, even for you."

In turn, Cody presented his orders from Miles to McLaughlin and Lieutenant Colonel William Drum—who, for some reason, is referred to in Cody's memoirs as "Colonel Brown." It is possible that Cody felt a need to disguise Drum's identity, but it may also have been a transcription error, as Captain Edmond Fechét, an old acquaintance of Cody's who was also present, is mentioned in Cody's autobiography as "Captain Fatchett." In any case, the orders from Miles trumped the authority possessed by McLaughlin, Drum, and everyone at Fort Yates.

McLaughlin and Drum bristled with resentment that Miles had sent a high profile civilian onto *their* turf, to ostensibly do their job. McLaughlin and Drum did not always see eye to eye on the various matters that came up at Standing Rock, but on this one, they could agree.

Fechét apparently was quite impressed by the two men. In an article that he penned for *Cosmopolitan* magazine in 1896, he said glowingly that "Throughout the entire civil and military services, two men better fitted for the trying and delicate duty to come could not have been found."

McLaughlin and Drum fumed. There was an interloper loping in their midst, and they were especially annoyed that there was almost nothing they could do about it—*almost* nothing.

Having told McLaughlin and the officers that he planned to visit Sitting Bull the following day, Cody strolled about the post, casually chatting with a number of old friends who were among the officers. As he recalls, everyone spent a pleasant afternoon and evening talking over old times, and "the present situation."

Apparently, during his discussions with the officers on the evening regarding "the present situation," Cody spoke with no one who had been able to tell him the location of Sitting Bull's home. He recalls having spent valuable time the following morning looking for someone to give him directions. This seems strange, given the fact that McLaughlin and Primeau had been there a little over a week earlier. Had Cody asked McLaughlin? If not, why had McLaughlin not volunteered this information, knowing that Cody was planning to go there?

Meanwhile, as Cody wrote in his memoirs, "I also wanted a first-class interpreter, as I would have matters to discuss with Sitting Bull beyond his mastery of English or mine of Sioux to express. At last I found a man who agreed to go with me as guide for five hundred dollars, which I promised him without a protest." He does not name the man, but we can suppose that it may have been Louis Primeau, who certainly was a competent man for the job. If so, why had McLaughlin not suggested Primeau the day before, and why had Primeau not told Cody the location of Sitting Bull's home on the Grand River?

Cody declined Drum's offer of a cavalry escort for his visit, because he believed that "the presence of a number of armed men in the Indian country would be sure to start the trouble it was our purpose to avoid." Instead, he asked Drum to lend him a light spring-wagon and a team of mules. He needed this, rather than just a saddle horse, because he had bought a large number of gifts for Sitting Bull and his family at the post trader's store. "Wait an hour or two," Drum to Buffalo Bill. "I'll send the quartermaster to you."

If Cody had been carrying a watch, this is the point where we can imagine him taking it out to check it. Time was slipping away, and the early start that Cody almost certainly wanted to achieve, had slipped away.

As Cody would not learn until later, Drum was stalling for time. As he paced the dusty parade ground, McLaughlin and the Lieutenant Colonel were sending telegrams to General Miles, the Commissioner of Indian Affairs, the Secretary of the Interior, and possibly even to President Harrison, in a frantic effort to obtain the authority to stop Buffalo Bill. Their excuse, Cody later learned, was an expressed concern that "going to Sitting Bull's camp . . . would not only result in my death, but would precipitate the outbreak then brewing, and for which he was not at all prepared." This is confirmed by Captain A. R. Chapin, the assistant surgeon at Fort Yates, whom Vestal quotes as saying that the officers at the post were all asked to assist in the effort to keep Cody distracted while McLaughlin and Drum sent their telegrams.

When Cody returned to Drum's quarters to see how things were progressing with his request for a team and wagon, the officer "endeavored once more to put me off. But I would not be put off." Cody informed him that he had explicit orders from General Miles as to his mission, and "that if he interfered with me he was violating the orders of his commanding officer and running into very serious trouble."

Finally, Drum "reluctantly," in Cody's words, sent for the quartermaster, and ordered him to have a span of mules hitched to a light wagon. He could have done this two hours before. The wagon was driven to the post trader's store, where Buffalo Bill connected with his guide and interpreter, and loaded the presents he had bought. "With plenty of robes to keep out the intense cold, we started out on our journey, a little apprehensive, but fully determined to go through with it," Cody recalled. Captain Chapin recalls that he was on the road by 11 o'clock on the morning of November 29.

About five miles from Fort Yates, Cody met three men in a wagon driving toward the agency. They told him that Sitting Bull's camp had been moved, and that it was now further down the Grand River. "I knew that if the old man was really on the warpath he would be moving up the river, not down, so I felt considerably reassured," Cody observed, taking this information as a good sign. In fact, Sitting Bull had not moved. He lived in a wasichu-style frame house, where McLaughlin had visited him earlier in the month.

Cody had not gone more than another five miles when one of McLaughlin's Indian Police overtook him on horseback. As Cody recalled in his memoirs, the man carried a telegram from no less an authority than President Benjamin Harrison. At the urging of McLaughlin and Drum, the president rescinded Cody's orders from Miles to coax Sitting Bull in to Fort Yates, and ordered him to return to Chicago to report to Miles. "That ended my mission to Sitting Bull," Cody wrote sadly. "I still believe I could have got safely through the country, though there were plenty of chances that I would be killed or wounded in the attempt. I returned to the Post, turned back my presents at a loss to myself, and paid the interpreter fifty dollars for his day's work. He was very glad to have fifty and a whole skin, for he could not figure how the five hundred would be of much help to him if he had been stretched out on the Plains with an Indian bullet through him."

McLaughlin and Drum had also felt they had dodged a bullet. Cody, the high-profile "meddler," left Fort Yates on the last day of November, bound for the Northern Pacific train station at Mandan.

Sitting Bull was not told that Buffalo Bill Cody was nearby, but he probably found out about it soon after from people who had seen Cody around Fort Yates.

Had Cody completed the last twenty miles or so of his planned journey, he would have met Sitting Bull and he would have quickly ascertained that Sitting Bull was not, as the outside world believed, the driving force behind the Ghost Dance and the unrest that the wasichu were predicting and reading. Sitting Bull would have told him of the offer that he made to McLaughlin, the offer to go to Nevada and look Wovoka straight in the eye.

Had Cody not decided to buy the presents and wait for Drum to lend him a wagon—not knowing that Drum would purposely stall for time, he could have gotten a much earlier start on horseback, and he would have reached the Grand River well ahead of McLaughlin's policeman. He probably would have been talking with Sitting Bull even as the telegram from Harrison reached Fort Yates—and history would have been so very different.

Cody would have replied to Harrison and he would have sent a message to Miles. He would have told them the truth about the misconception regarding Sitting Bull's role in what was happening in South Dakota. He would have explained Sitting Bull's reasonable offer to go to Nevada, and he almost certainly would have offered to escort him there. As for the travel expenses, McLaughlin's lame excuse of a limited budget would have gone out the window. Cody could easily have picked up the tab for Sitting Bull's train ticket—and he would have.

Even if Harrison would have turned down such a request, Cody would have had recourse to the press. There were journalists hovering around him. The newspapers would have explained what Sitting Bull had said to Buffalo Bill. Even if the journalists had not traveled with Cody to Grand River, the story would have gotten out. In 1890, Buffalo Bill was the most famous American in the world. His word had credibility.

It is easy to see why McLaughlin was so desperate to stop Buffalo Bill. One can imagine the headlines as Buffalo Bill and Sitting Bull confront-ed Wovoka and stopped the feared uprising. The media attention would be double that which would have been lavished on Sitting Bull alone. Sitting Bull's status would be elevated so high in the eyes of the wasichu that all of McLaughlin's efforts to resign him to the dust bin of history as inconsequential would have been for naught.

Could it be that Drum and McLaughlin genuinely feared for Cody's life? This is unlikely. Certainly to have the most famous American in the world killed on their reservation would have been a profound embarrass-ment, but perhaps more than that, they had resented from the beginning that Miles had sent in a civilian to do their job.

Could it be that Cody's life actually *was* in danger? This is unlikely. McLaughlin himself had gone to Sitting Bull's home on the Grand River less than two weeks before. Sure, there were a lot of dancers milling around, but Sitting Bull knew Cody, and the two were friends—possibly even adopted brothers.

Beyond that, even as Cody was pacing the grounds waiting for a wagon, McLaughlin had on his desk a note from John Carignan, a teacher at Grand River who had been at "a council held at Iron Star's house" on November 27. In his letter, penned the same day and quoted by Stanley Vestal in his *New Sources of Indian History*, Carignan told the agent, "The Indians seem to be very peaceably inclined, and I do not apprehend any trouble. . . . The Indians have been told that soldiers are coming down here, and are badly frightened. If they were assured different, there would be no danger of their leaving. I have done all I could in telling them that the reports they have heard are all lies, and that no one would try to prevent them from dancing. I am positive that no trouble need be apprehended from Sitting Bull and his followers, unless they are forced to defend themselves."

Carignan added that he thought it "advisable to keep all strangers, other than employees who have business amongst the Indians away from here," but certainly a visit from Buffalo Bill would have been welcomed by Sitting Bull.

In closing his November 27 memo, Carignan did tell McLaughlin that "Sitting Bull has lost all confidence in the whites since Mrs. Weldon left him." This was not without reason, but what Carignan knew, but left unsaid, was that the wasichu were not the only people who the old itancan needed to fear.

Sitting Bull's admirer, Catherine Weldon, painted this portrait of him in 1889. Based on one of the 1885 Notman photographs, the painting was in Sitting Bull's home at the time of his death. One of the Indian Police who was present at his killing ripped the painting off the wall and slashed it with his rifle, causing the visible tear across the left side. Lieutenant Matthew Steele, one of the military officers who arrived shortly after Sitting Bull died, grabbed the painting as a souvenir and later gave Sitting Bull's widows two dollars for it. In 1953, Steele donated the painting to the State Historical Society of North Dakota. (*State Historical Society of North Dakota*)

6

FADE TO BLACK

I N THE EARLY WEEKS OF DECEMBER 1890, A MEADOWLARK spoke to
Sitting Bull. This is according to the words of the old men who had
been young men in December 1890. The meadowlarks had often spoken
to him, and he knew their language. The old men said that when the bird
spoke to Sitting Bull that winter, it was with a warning. The meadowlark
told him that his own people, not the wasichu, would kill him.

A few days after Buffalo Bill Cody departed, Sitting Bull was invited to
come to Pine Ridge, so he decided to ask Standing Rock Agent James
McLaughlin for permission to leave the reservation and go south. He
asked Andrew Fox, who knew English, to translate his words. Fox had
been the husband of his daughter, Walks Looking, who had died of an
unnamed disease in 1887 at the age of nineteen. The contents of this letter, now lost, were related to Stanley Vestal by Andrew Fox. He is said to
have been in his late twenties in 1890, which would have made him in his
early sixties when Vestal was doing his research.

According to Vestal's paraphrase, Sitting Bull began his letter by saying that all men, red and white, should pray to God for life and for a good road to travel, admonishing McLaughlin to say nothing against the Lakota religion because both the Lakota and the wasichu prayed to the same God. He told McLaughlin pointedly that he knew the agent described him to the press as a fool, and that McLaughlin had characterized Sitting Bull as the obstacle to all the Indians at Standing Rock becoming civilized. Sitting Bull said that he would overlook McLaughlin's saying that he was foolish to pray to God. He closed by telling the agent that he felt obliged to go to Pine Ridge Agency and investigate the Ghost Dance religion. Sitting Bull handed the letter to Bull Ghost, who took it to Fort Yates.

McLaughlin received the missive late on December 12. Meanwhile, that same day, Lieutenant Colonel Drum received orders from General Thomas Ruger, commander of the Department of Dakota, headquartered in St. Paul. Ruger had received his own orders two days before from General Miles. Everyone within the U.S. Army's chain of command still believed that an Indian uprising was imminent and that the best way to quell this potential disaster was to bring this man they regarded as its principal instigator under control. They reasoned that Sitting Bull was a very dangerous man. Indeed, Cody had been called back under the misconception that Sitting Bull was so dangerous as to be a threat even to his old friend.

The orders passed down through the chain of command and, as referenced in the *Annual Report of the Commissioner of Indian Affairs* for 1891, were essentially the same as Miles had given to Cody—to "secure the person of Sitting Bull." If it was too dangerous for Cody to do this diplomatically, then Miles would give Drum the option to use force.

Faced with the letter, and Bull Ghost's request for papers permitting Sitting Bull to travel to Pine Ridge, McLaughlin did as he and Drum had with Cody, he stalled. Bull Ghost left Fort Yates empty-handed, but the news was already circulating that Drum had been ordered to use force to "secure the person of Sitting Bull."

Just as McLaughlin used his Indian Police to spy on Sitting Bull's people at Grand River, Sitting Bull got information about what McLaughlin
was doing from sympathizers within the Indian Police. Each of the policemen had relatives with whom they shared confidences, and news traveled
fast. Iron Thunder, one of the Indian Police, told his brother, One Elk,
that he'd heard that Sitting Bull was to be arrested. One Elk lived at Grand
River, and Iron Thunder told him to stay away from Sitting Bull on
December 15. In turn, One Elk ran into Jumping Bull, Sitting Bull's
adopted Assiniboine brother.

In fact, the December 15 date had not yet been established for "securing" Sitting Bull. According to accounts by the wasichu at Fort Yates,
including that written by Captain Fechét, McLaughlin and Drum had
originally decided to "secure the person of Sitting Bull" on December 20,
which was the day that the people were scheduled to come up from Grand
River to collect their government rations. Sitting Bull usually—albeit not
always—came personally.

As McLaughlin recalled in a letter written about a month later, Drum
had "sent for me [on December 12], and held a consultation as to the best
means to effect the desired arrest. It was contrary to my judgment to
attempt the arrest at any time other than upon one of the bi-weekly ration
days when there would be but a few Indians in Sitting Bull's neighbor-
hood, thus lessening the chances of opposition or excitement of his followers. The Post Commander saw the wisdom of my reasoning, and consent-
ed to defer the arrest until Saturday morning, December 20th, with the
distinct understanding, however, that the Indian Police keep Sitting Bull
and his followers under strict surveillance to prevent their leaving the
reservation, and report promptly any suspicious movements among them."

However, the next day, December 13, Indian Police spies down at
Grand River informed Lieutenant Bull Head that Sitting Bull was planning to leave Standing Rock on December 15, whether McLaughlin gave
him the papers or not.

Bull Head, who did not write English, went to the Grand River School, where John Carignan wrote out a description of what was going on in Sitting Bull's camp. Shortly after midnight, Bull Head handed this to David Hawk Man, one of the Indian Police under his command, and told him to take it to Fort Yates. Bull Head then stood by at Grand River to await McLaughlin's orders.

When McLaughlin received the Bull Head message on the afternoon of December 14, he jumped to the same conclusion as George Armstrong Custer had made on the morning of June 25, 1876. Something had to be done before the Indians got away.

On December 14, faced with the intelligence report of Sitting Bull's impending departure for Pine Ridge, McLaughlin and Drum mulled their options. Obviously, if Sitting Bull was packing to leave the Standing Rock Reservation, they could not wait until December 20 to secure his person. Under President Harrison's directive of exactly one month prior, Drum had the lead authority to intercede and take Sitting Bull by force. However, McLaughlin convinced the military officer to permit the actual arrest to be conducted by McLaughlin's Indian Police force.

Drum agreed to McLaughlin's proposal and ordered Captain Fechét to ride down to Grand River with the 8th Cavalry only to provide backup. At 4:30 p.m., McLaughlin sat down and scrawled out his orders. He addressed it to Bull Head, but as an afterthought, he also penciled in the name of Bull Head's deputy, Sergeant Shave Head, also known as Charles Kashlah. The "Sitting Bull arrest warrant" read:

> From report brought by scout "Hawk Man" I believe that the time has arrived for the arrest of Sitting Bull and that can be made by the Indian Police without much risk. I therefore want you to make the arrest before daylight tomorrow morning [December 15] and try to get back to the Sitting Bull road crossing of Oak Creek by daylight

Indian Agent James McLaughlin penned the infamous arrest warrant for Sitting Bull on December 14, 1890. He addressed it to Bull Head, adding Shave Head's name as an afterthought. His ominous footnote reads: "You must not let him escape under any circumstances." (*National Archives*)

tomorrow morning or as soon after as possible. The Cavalry will leave here tonight and will reach the Sitting Bull crossing of Oak Creek before daylight tomorrow (Monday) morning, where they will remain until they hear from you.

Louis Primeau will go with the Cavalry command as guide and I want you to send a message to the Cavalry command as soon as you can after you arrest him so that they may be able to know how to act in aiding you or preventing any attempt at his rescue.

I have ordered all the police at Oak Creek to proceed to Carignan's school and await your orders. This gives you a force of 42 policemen for the arrest.

Very respectfully

James McLaughlin

U.S. Indian Agent

P.S. You must not let him escape under any circumstances.

McLaughlin's nervous postscript was filled with momentous portent. In retrospect, it seems to give Bull Head a great deal of latitude in dealing with the situations that might arise during the arrest.

McLaughlin handed the arrest warrant to Sergeant Marcelus Chankpidutah, known as Red Tomahawk, who took it to Bull Head at his home on the south side of the Grand River around 10 p.m. Coincidentally, Bull Head's house was located upstream on the Grand River from Sitting Bull's present settlement, near the place where tradition now says Sitting Bull was born six decades earlier.

Meanwhile, at 6 p.m. that evening, Captain Fechét was given his orders to move out. "We were enjoying the usual after dinner cigars beside our comfortable firesides," Fechét recalled.

> Officers' [bugle] call rang out loud and shrill on the clear, frosty air. In a few minutes all of the officers of the post were assembled in Colonel Drum's office. He informed us briefly that the attempt to arrest Sitting Bull would be made that night; then turning, he said that charge of the troops going out would be given to me, that my orders would be made out in a short time, and that my command would move at midnight. . . . Everything had been put in shape for a sharp and quick movement of the cavalry squadron, the troopers and horses designated for duty (fifty from each troop), gun detachments for the Gatling and Hotchkiss guns told off and drilled, one day's supply of rations and grain, buffalo overcoats and horse-covers, extra ammunition—all packed ready to be loaded. The transportation selected was one spring escort wagon drawn by four horses, and one red-cross ambulance.

The wagon was loaded and a hot supper was served to the men at 11 p.m. Fechét went to Colonel Drum's house for final instructions and found that he was with McLaughlin, who told him Bull Head's message said that Sitting Bull was evidently making preparations to leave the reservation, as "he had fitted his horses for a long and hard ride."

Bull Head, left. (*Denver Public Library*) Red Tomahawk, right. (*National Archives*)

Fechét was told verbally to rendezvous with Bull Head and his men at Oak Creek and to take custody of Sitting Bull. In fact, the transfer of custody was not explicitly spelled out in McLaughlin's written orders to Bull Head. Fechét told Drum and McLaughlin that he was concerned that his command was being ordered to wait at Oak Creek.

"This seemed faulty to me," Fechét later reflected. "Oak Creek was 18 miles from Grand River, and my force would not be within supporting distance of the police if there should be a fight. Moreover, if he [Sitting Bull] should succeed in escaping from the police, it was the intention to pursue him to the utmost, and in the race for the Bad Lands, which would ensue, he would have a start of at least 30 miles."

Fechét raised this point with Drum and the agent, and after some discussion, it was decided that Fechét should go up to twelve miles beyond Oak Creek toward Grand River. Drum's final words to Fechét were: "Captain, after you leave here use your own discretion. You know the object of the movement; do your best to make it a success."

The 8th Cavalry squadron moved out promptly at midnight, with two Indian scouts, Smell the Bear and Iron Dog, and with Louis Primeau as guide and interpreter. The U.S. Army continent included forty-eight men from Troop F under lieutenants S. L. H. Slocum and Matthew Steele, and fifty-one men from Troop G under Fechét and Lieutenant E. H. Crowder. Lieutenant E. C. Brooks was the artillery officer and Captain A. R. Chapin served as medical officer.

Moving through the cold drizzle, at what Fechét described as a "brisk trot," the command reached Oak Creek at 4:30 a.m. on December 15.

"I was greatly surprised and concerned to find that the scout whom Bull Head had been directed to send to meet me at that point, had not arrived," Fechét complained. In fact, Bull Head had been told that Fechét would wait at Oak Creek, and that he should be at Oak Creek by daylight. There was no explicit reason why Fechét should have been concerned by not finding an Indian Policeman there. It was still well before dawn.

"I realized that there was but one thing to be done," Fechét decided. "To push my command to Grand River as rapidly as possible, and act according to the situation found. The gallop was the gait from this time on. I was pushing the animals, but still not too fast to impair pursuit beyond Grand River, should I find that Sitting Bull had escaped."

By 4:30 a.m., Bull Head had already been to Carignan's house and had assembled his entire command. Accounts vary as to how many he had, but it was about thirty-nine (a number that McLaughlin later cited), including himself, or perhaps slightly more. Among them were two men named Hawk Man, including David Hawk Man, Bull Head's courier. Also present in Bull Head's command was an impetuous young loner, appropriately named Lone Man. About half were police auxiliaries who were not in uniform. They wore white armbands so that they could be distinguished in the dark if there was a fight. Bull Head's uniformed contingent included Sergeant Shave Head, Sergeant Red Tomahawk, and two other sergeants. The uniformed police were referred to by the Lakota as "metal breasts" because of their shiny brass police badges.

As Fechét was making his decision not to wait at Oak Creek, Bull Head had reached the cabin of Gray Eagle, the brother of Sitting Bull's wives.

Here the Indian Police spent considerable time. Gray Eagle, who was now also known by his Christian name Gabriel, was a judge in the Standing Rock Court of Indian Offenses, and a supporter of McLaughlin's efforts to "civilize" the Hunkpapa Lakota. Gray Eagle had agreed to accompany the Indian Police to Sitting Bull's home, where he would convince Sitting Bull to surrender. As with many of his fellow tribal members, Gray Eagle had his change of heart—and change of allegiance—during the summer of 1889, at the time of the Crook Commission visit. Others who had experi-

Gray Eagle. (*Library of Congress*)

enced a similar change of direction, and who would accompany Bull Head this night, included Otter Robe, Spotted Thunder, and Young Eagle.

As Fechét headed toward Sitting Bull's settlement, guided by Primeau, the Indian Police, accompanied by Gray Eagle, were fording the partially frozen Grand River in the dark, a difficult and precarious task with a frozen rain falling out of the low clouds.

As usual, the Ghost Dancers had danced at Sitting Bull's settlement the night before. According to the stories, some of them had visions of deceased ancestors, but others did not. Sitting Bull and his family went to bed in the two cabins they occupied at the settlement. Sitting Bull and Seen by the Nation were in the larger house, along with Crow Foot, Sitting Bull's favored son, and a few others, including Red Whirlwind, One Bull's pregnant wife. One Bull himself was away. He had been hauling freight on the road north of Fort Yates, but he was due back early on December 15.

Those in Sitting Bull's cabin were awakened at around 5:50 a.m. on December 15 by the sounds of horses and the barking of dogs. It was still dark outside and must have felt like the middle of the night. Sitting Bull sat up as someone slammed open the front door using a rifle butt.

Some people burst into the room, but it was impossible to tell who or how many. There was the sound, the flash, and the smell of a match being struck, and Sitting Bull felt himself being grabbed and pulled to his feet by two of the men. These men who grabbed the naked Sitting Bull from the mat on which he was sleeping were Eagle Man and Weasel Bear. This is according to Stanley Vestal, who interviewed people who were at the Grand River that morning—including One Bull, whose wife was in the room. They also found a rifle, pistol, and knife among Sitting Bull's blankets.

As someone lit the kerosene lantern that was hanging on the wall, Sitting Bull probably recognized Bull Head and Shave Head, who told him that they had come here to seize him. At this point, that fact had to have been rather apparent. Red Tomahawk, who was also there, reportedly told Sitting Bull that if he tried to fight, he would be killed.

With his arms held by two men less than half his age, Sitting Bull was in no position to put up a struggle. Indeed, nobody in the room raised a weapon against the intruders. Seen by the Nation, however, lashed at the men with her tongue, demanding to know what these "jealous people" were doing there.

They explained that they were taking her husband away and that he needed to get dressed. She said that his clothes were in the other house and she left to go get them. When she was outside, she told someone to go saddle Sitting Bull's gray horse. By this, she meant the show horse that had been given to her husband five years earlier by Buffalo Bill. White Bird, one of Bull Head's men, went with another man to the corral to find and saddle the horse.

The Indian Police raid on Sitting Bull's settlement had been executed with military precision. They achieved the goal of surprise, and they had accomplished the objective of securing the person of the man himself within minutes. However, things quickly began to unravel. By the time that Seen by the Nation left to go for her husband's clothes, the camp was awake and people had begun to gather around Sitting Bull's house. When they saw that the building was surrounded by the metal breasts, with their badges and blue uniforms, it took no stretch of the imagination to know exactly what was going on.

Not waiting for Seen by the Nation to return, the metal breasts in the cabin found what they presumed to be some of Sitting Bull's clothes, and started the awkward and humiliating task of dressing him. He told them to let him go, that he could dress himself, but they ignored him. When the clothes had been pulled on, they dragged him toward the doorway. They had his arms, but he put his feet out to try to grab the door frame. This worked for a moment, but Eagle Man kicked his feet and they were able to manhandle him out into the cold, waning night.

By now, the Indian Police faced a growing crowd of angry people. Among them were Brave Thunder, Crawler, Spotted Horn Bull, and Strikes the Kettle, as well as Catch the Bear, who is said to have been Sitting Bull's principal bodyguard. As this crowd closed in, the Indian Police kicked and jostled Sitting Bull, to try to push him through the crowd.

He was not walking; they were half dragging, half carrying him. At least two men, possibly Eagle Man and Weasel Bear, still had his arms, and Red Tomahawk had him around the waist. Both Shave Head and Bull Head were also nearby, and may also have had their hands on Sitting Bull. Most of the Indian Police, including Red Tomahawk and Bull Head, had their guns drawn.

It is generally recalled that Sitting Bull was not struggling at this point, probably because he knew it would be futile, although some have suggested that Sitting Bull might have been going with these men willingly.

The crowd was much less willing. They were growing more angry by the moment, and there were yells and screams. Some shouted for the

the Bear, struck Sitting Bull in the back between his left tenth and eleventh ribs.

It is recalled that Sitting Bull staggered slightly, but almost immediately, Red Tomahawk shot him in the head. If Bull Head's bullet had not inflicted a mortal injury, Red Tomahawk's certainly did. Sitting Bull's dead weight collapsed on the frozen ground about ten to fifteen yards from his cabin.

Red Whirlwind, who was present during this phase of the confrontation, recalled that Bull Head, not Catch the Bear, had fired the first shot, but most other accounts say it was Catch the Bear.

At the sound of the shots, Sitting Bull's horse calmly raised his front hoof, as he had been trained to do at the sound of a gunshot.

The already jittery Indian Police, who had never seen such a thing, were terrified. It was as though Sitting Bull's ghost had suddenly transmigrated to his performing horse.

As could have been expected, the opening volley in front of Sitting Bull's cabin ignited a huge gunfight. Bullets flew and men fell. Catch the Bear was killed by the metal breast named Lone Man. Strikes the Kettle shot Shave Head, and in turn, was wounded himself. Jumping Bull, who was unarmed, was among those who were killed, and so was his twenty-four-year-old son, Chase Them Wounded.

Sitting Bull's son Crow Foot took refuge in the cabin.

With Bull Head and Shave Head injured, Red Tomahawk took charge of the metal breasts and led them also to retreat back into Sitting Bull's house to take cover. Here they scrambled, dragging their wounded. Both Bull Head—who had been shot more than once by now—and Shave Head were hit badly and bleeding profusely. With bullets flying, it was a grisly mess inside the house.

When the metal breasts discovered Crow Foot hiding there, he begged for mercy. Bull Head was asked what they should do with the boy. Some sources say that he ordered them to kill him, while others tell that Bull Head said he didn't care what they did. Bull Head was in great pain from his wounds, but he reminded them that Crow Foot was Sitting Bull's son and Sitting Bull had caused all this trouble. Lone Man impulsively slammed the teenager in the head with the butt of his rifle and the others finished him off with bullets.

At about this time, Captain Edmond Fechét and his 8th Cavalry contingent were making their way from Oak Creek, guided by Louis Primeau, who knew the way. Just as the first gray light of dawn was tinting the sky, they were met by a mounted rider. It was the second of the two metal breasts named Hawk Man, not David Hawk Man. He was riding Sitting Bull's gray show horse.

Fechét recalled him reporting "that all the other police had been killed." This was untrue, but Hawk Man had ridden away at the height of the gun battle and it may have seemed as though this was about to happen. Fechét forwarded the information to Colonel Drum by courier and ordered his men to prepare for action by removing and stowing their overcoats and fur gloves. While they were doing this, he rode along the line, "taking a good look at each man. Their bearing was such as to inspire me with the fullest confidence that they would do their duty."

The troopers moved forward, traveling as fast as possible given that Fechét wanted to make sure he had the artillery was still with them when they reached the scene of the battle. Soon, they met another metal breast, who said that "Sitting Bull's people had a number of the police penned up in his house; that they were nearly out of ammunition, and could not hold out much longer."

By this time Fechét and his men could hear some firing, and in a few minutes they were in position on the hills overlooking the scene. He recalled that the firing was coming from "three different and widely separated points: from the house, from a clump of timber beyond the house, and from a party, apparently 40 or 50, on our right front. . . . At first there was nothing to indicate the position of the police. Our approach had apparently not been noticed by either party, so intent were they upon the business on hand."

It had been prearranged that the troops and Indian Police would signal one another by waving white flags. The soldiers did this, but when the gesture went unanswered, Fechét ordered that a round from the Hotchkiss gun be dropped "between the house and the clump of timber just beyond." The idea was to alert the police to the fact that the cavalry had arrived. This worked, and the metal breasts inside the house signaled back.

Now knowing where the men in blue were, Fechét moved in. As he later described it,

> Slocum and Steele, with their men dismounted, advanced directly
> on the house; Crowder with G Troop was ordered to move along the
> crest and protect the right flank of the dismounted line, [artillery-
> man] Brooks threw a few shells into the timber, also against the party
> which had been on our right front, but was now moving rapidly into
> the valley. As Slocum's line approached the house, the police came
> out and joined it. The line was pushed into the timber, dislodging
> the few hostiles who remained, I now caused the dismounted line to
> fall back to the vicinity of the house, pickets being left at the farthest
> point gained by the advance, All the hostiles having disappeared,
> Crowder was recalled, I had moved with the dismounted line, and in
> passing the house had noticed Sitting Bull's body lying on the
> ground.

Fechét went on to describe the scene of the fight. "I saw the evidences of a most desperate encounter," he wrote. "In front of the house, and within a radius of fifty yards, were the bodies of eight dead Indians including that of Sitting Bull, and two dead horses. In the house were four dead policemen and three wounded, two mortally. To add to the horror of the scene, the [two widows] of Sitting Bull, who were in a small house nearby, kept up a great wailing."

Both Sitting Bull and Jumping Bull had died and so had their sons. Catch the Bear was dead, and so too were Blackbird and Spotted Horn Bull. Brave Thunder and Bull Ghost were wounded, as was Strikes the Kettle, who was taken into custody and sent to Fort Sully. The metal breasts Afraid of Soldiers, John Armstrong (aka Strong Arm), and Little Eagle lay on the ground near where Sitting Bull had died. So too did David Hawk Man, who had delivered Bull Head's message to McLaughlin at Fort Yates the day before. The two whom Fechét had described as mortally wounded were Bull Head and Shave Head.

There would later be rumors that the Indian Police had been drinking, or were drunk, at the time of Sitting Bull's arrest. However, Fechét makes no mention of having observed this after he arrived, and there seems to be no credible evidence of this. It is highly improbable that Gray Eagle would have gone with them from his cabin if they were drunk or if they smelled of liquor. Certainly the apocryphal yarn that McLaughlin sent a barrel of whisky to Bull Head on the afternoon of December 14 can be ruled out as impossible.

As Fechét began interviewing witnesses to ascertain the circumstances of Sitting Bull's death, the Army cooks prepared breakfast for the troops. It must have been a bizarre scene. Here was the man who was arguably the most famous Indian in America, lying dead where he fell, and the Army officers were standing in line for coffee. "Going to the cookfire for a cup of coffee, which I had just raised to my lips, I was startled by the exclamations of the police," Fechét later wrote. "On looking up the road to where they pointed saw one of the Ghost Dancers in full war array, including the Ghost Shirt, on his horse, not to exceed 80 yards away. In a flash the police opened fire on him; at this he turned his horse and in an instant was out of sight in the willows. Coming in view again some four hundred yards farther on, another volley was sent after him. Still further on he passed between two of my picket posts, both of which fired on him. From all this fire he escaped unharmed."

Private A. L. Bloomer, whom Fechét tasked with looking after Sitting Bull's body, told Stanley Vestal many years later that "after it was all over and I was ordered to move the body away from a large pool of blood, I took hold of his arm and tried to drag him away so his body would not freeze to the ground. . . . He was lying on his back, with his head toward his cabin."

Fechét took Sitting Bull's widows, Four Robes and Seen by the Nation, into custody briefly, but decided to release them before the troopers pulled out. They were later taken to Fort Yates, but again released. The troops searched—some recall it as ransacked, which may be closer to the truth—both of Sitting Bull's houses. They discovered Crow Foot's bullet-riddled corpse in the one, and in the smaller of houses, they found some young boys hiding under a mound of blankets. One of these boys was Sitting Bull's deaf-mute son, who a dozen years later traveled to Europe with Buffalo Bill's Wild West under the name John Sitting Bull.

Also in this house, Lieutenant—later Colonel—Matthew Steele found Catherine Weldon's portrait of Sitting Bull hanging on one wall. As he watched, one of the Indian Police, whose brother had been killed that morning, slammed the painting with his rifle butt. Steele intervened to stop further damage, and later paid Sitting Bull's widows two dollars for the painting. It remained in the Steele family until 1953, when it was donated to the State Historical Society of North Dakota.

The 8th Cavalry left the Grand River settlement at about 1 p.m. on the afternoon of December 15. The injured, including Alexander Middle, as well as Bull Head and Shave Head, were placed in the ambulance. The troops loaded the bodies of the dead Indian Police into a wagon commandeered from the Grand River Hunkpapa, and left all of the other Indian deceased behind—except for the remains of Sitting

Bull. The Indian Police reportedly resented their dead being put into the same wagon with Sitting Bull, but it was decided to put him on the bottom, beneath the others.

The other dead were placed in Sitting Bull's cabin temporarily. Some time later, a Congregational minister, Reverend T. L. Riggs, presided over a Christian funeral, and they were all placed in a common unmarked grave.

Most of the people living at the settlement had fled, but Fechét told those who remained that the fight was over, and the U.S. Army would not return to bother them. This was correct, although at that time, this course of action—or nonaction—had not yet been officially decided.

One Bull had returned during the night and was sleeping in his own house when he was awakened by the shooting. Knowing that his pregnant wife was at Sitting Bull's home, he made a mad dash for the scene, arriving as the shooting was winding down. Red Whirlwind had managed to slip away from the firefight and One Bull was able to get her to safety. He didn't go to Sitting Bull's house until after the troops had gone.

Subsequent speculation has surmised that One Bull had been sent on his errand up north of Fort Yates that night because McLaughlin deliberately wanted him out of the way. This seems improbable because there was no compelling reason to have One Bull—of all people—out of the way. Furthermore, such a ruse would have taken time, and the arrest warrant had been written only twelve hours before the arrest—long after One Bull had gone north. Indeed, he was home from the errand before the arrest was attempted.

The 8th Cavalry column reached Oak Creek at about 5:00 p.m., where they met a courier with a message from Lieutenant Colonel Drum saying that he was bringing the 12th Infantry to support Fechét in any action that might be taken against the Hunkpapa. The two columns met around midnight, camped, ate, and spent the night on the cold, open Plains.

In consulting with Fechét, Drum decided that further offensive action against the Grand River settlements would cause further unrest. It was feared that it might also encourage the Standing Rock Hunkpapa to join the Oglala from Pine Ridge in the Badlands, which would be counterproductive. In order not to further enflame the situation at Standing Rock, they decided that all the troops should return to Fort Yates. As it turned out, this was a wise course. Of the Lakota who had left Standing Rock when they heard about Sitting Bull's death, the majority returned a short time later.

SITTING BULL'S body arrived at Fort Yates at 4:30 p.m. on December 16, 1890, exactly forty-eight hours after McLaughlin had penned his arrest warrant. The agent had not used the notorious Old West phrase "dead or alive," but he had told Bull Head and Shave Head to "not let him escape under any circumstances." They had not, nor had they escaped injury themselves. Both survived the rugged trip back to Fort Yates, but Shave Head died the next day. Bull Head, who was in and out of a coma, survived until December 18, when he finally succumbed to his wounds. By that time, Sitting Bull had been buried.

McLaughlin made an initial report of Sitting Bull's death to Commissioner of Indian Affairs Thomas Morgan in a telegram that reached Washington, D.C., on December 15, even before Sitting Bull's body reached Standing Rock. He followed up with a seven-page written memorandum the following day.

In this letter, McLaughlin told Morgan that Sitting Bull "at first seemed inclined to offer no resistance and they allowed him to dress, during which time he changed his mind and they took him forcibly from the house." This seems at variance with the accounts that say he was forcibly dressed, and that he changed his mind while still inside, rather than when he was some distance from the building, but it is easy to see how McLaughlin's interpretation of events could have been arrived at after interviewing exhausted witnesses following their long journey back from Grand River.

McLaughlin's December 16 report said that Catch the Bear shot first, which is probably correct, and that Bull Head and Red Tomahawk both shot Sitting Bull, which is true by all accounts. In his report, he noted that the wounded Bull Head "may recover," but he did not.

McLaughlin also began what would be years of lobbying for pensions for the Indian Police who had taken part in the historic debacle. He asked Morgan that "the Interior Department cooperate with the War Department in obtaining Congressional action which will secure to these brave survivors and to the families of the dead a full and generous reward." To the Indian Police, he added the names of the Hunkpapa who had aided the Indian Police that day, including Gray Eagle, as well as Otter Robe, Spotted Thunder, and Young Eagle.

McLaughlin assured Morgan that most of the Indians at Standing Rock remained loyal to the United States government and predicted that Sitting Bull's death would "end the Ghost Craze."

In closing, the agent said that while he regretted the loss of the Indian Police, whom he called "noble and brave," (underlining these words), and said he felt that "the great good accomplished by the ending of Sitting Bull's career whose influence has been of such a retarding nature, and the determination the police manifested in maintaining the will of the government, is most gratifying."

Initially, Sitting Bull's body was turned over to the post surgeon, Dr. Horace M. Deeble, who assessed his injuries to determine cause of death. Either shot, Deeble decided, would have been fatal. Like Custer, Sitting Bull died with two bullet wounds, one of them in the head. Like Crazy Horse he died at night near the doorway of a wood-frame building, shot while in custody by nervous Lakota loyal to the wasichu. As with Crazy Horse, it was a clumsy, violent death that should not have happened.

Years later, Stanley Vestal spoke with John F. Waggoner, the soldier at the Fort Yates carpenter shop who built Sitting Bull's coffin, a pine box measuring two by two feet, and seventy-six inches long. Waggoner had known Sitting Bull in life and was predisposed to like him. Many soldiers were not. He recalled that as he was building the box, many of the troops came in, each wanting to drive a nail into the coffin of Sitting Bull. Waggoner explained to Vestal that the body was not prepared, but rather it was delivered to him still dressed in the clothes that had been forced on him at Grand River. He was, as the carpenter remembered, "wrapped in a blanket frozen stiff with blood."

Waggoner observed that his jaw had been broken post mortem. He also estimated that the body had been shot five times after the two potentially fatal wounds were inflicted. One can imagine that just as there were men who wanted to say that they had put a nail in Sitting Bull's coffin, there were those who wanted to say they had shot Sitting Bull. If they did, their words are now long forgotten, and Sitting Bull is not.

As often occurs, there is an alternative to Waggoner's account that he was the man who built Sitting Bull's coffin. This story, reported in the April 12, 1953, issue of the *Fargo Forum*, comes in the form of correspondence from the rival carpenter to, of all persons, the first man to rob Sitting Bull's grave. Frank B. Fiske, whose ghoulish escapade is recounted in the following chapter, received a letter from retired 1st Sergeant Edward Forte, formerly of Troop D, Seventh Cavalry, dated November 7, 1932.

Forte, who was a civilian carpenter at Fort Yates in 1890, wrote to Fiske from his home in Johnson City, Tennessee, stating that "the body of Sitting Bull was buried in the military grounds in a pine coffin made by me. I being the agency carpenter. I made the coffin, regardless of what anybody says about it. I not only made the coffin but I still have the Henry Disston hand-saw with which the work was done. I refer you to James Yellow Fat and George Pleets, who were apprentices in the carpenter shop at the time."

Whether it was Forte or Waggoner, we will probably never know. Perhaps they both worked on the project.

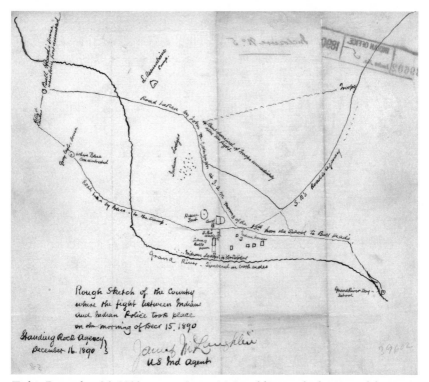

To his December 16, 1890, memo, James McLaughlin attached a map of the scene surrounding Sitting Bull's home where the fight and the deaths took place. Note the location of the Grand River, on whose shores Sitting Bull was born nearly six decades earlier. (*National Archives*)

The Indian Police were buried with full military honors in the Catholic graveyard at Standing Rock Agency, but the families did not want Sitting Bull there. The priest, Father Bernard Strassmeier, who had known Sitting Bull, was consulted regarding a public funeral, but he recalled that most people didn't want that. He was not a Catholic, nor a Christian of any kind, so a Catholic funeral was uncalled for.

Having been sewn into a makeshift canvas body bag and placed in the box built by Waggoner or Forte or perhaps both, Sitting Bull was buried at the Fort Yates cemetery without ceremony on December 17, 1890. Waggoner or Forte, or perhaps both, were there. So too was Lieutenant P.

G. Wood of the 12th Infantry, Wood's son Guy, a hospital steward named Saddler, and a teamster named Johnny Hughes who drove the wagon that carried the coffin. Lieutenant Matthew Steele, who had come home from Grand River with the Catherine Weldon portrait of Sitting Bull, would tell people in the early twentieth century that he too had been at the burial. Deeble and Chapin also later claimed to have been there. Agent McLaughlin said in his January 27, 1891, report that he reached the grave when it was "partly filled in with soil."

As described by Waggoner, Sitting Bull's funeral consisted of pouring "five gallons of chloride of lime" and "a suitable amount of muriatic acid" into the open casket before the lid was nailed down. Waggoner reported that the fumes from the quicklime were already billowing as the dirt was being shoveled in. "We laid the noble old Chief away without a hymn or a prayer or a sprinkle of earth," Waggoner told the interviewer many decades after that cold December day. "Quicklime was used instead. It made me angry. I had always admired the Chief for his courage and his generalship. He was a man!"

As invariably happens after the violent deaths of great men, rumors spring up quickly. Among the first was one that circulated in Bismarck within days of his demise. It whispered that Sitting Bull's coffin was empty, and that his body had been sold to a ghoulish collector. As the *Fargo Forum* later reported, the rumors included one to the effect that "his body had been taken into a dissecting room in the post hospital, that a plot was afoot to sell his bones for exhibition purposes and that a Bismarck merchant had offered $1,000 for his skin, probably intending to tan it and sell bits of it as souvenirs."

The rumors created a groundswell of effrontery among those, such as the members of organizations like the National Indian Defense Association, who were generally outraged by his death. Their complaints led to a probe by the Indian Bureau, which in turn led to a statement from Post Surgeon Deeble that the body of Sitting Bull "was in my custody until it was buried on the 17th. During that time it was not mutilated or disfig-ured in any manner. I saw the body sewed up in a canvas, put in a coffin and the lid screwed down and afterwards buried in the Northwest corner of the post cemetery in a grave about eight feet deep, in the presence of Capt. A. R. Chapin, assistant surgeon, U.S. Army, Lt. P. G. Wood, 12th Infantry, Post Quartermaster, and myself."

Also put on the defensive, McLaughlin issued a disclaimer of the muti-lation rumor, stating in his January 27 report that "I feel confident that he was neither dissected, nor scalped before burial and also quite confident that his grave has not been disturbed since."

Sitting Bull's body was probably in the grave. Men who had no reason to lie said it was. Aside from the additional gunshots fired into his body and the broken jaw, Sitting Bull's body was apparently not mutilated. Waggoner and those who were the last to see it recalled that it had not been scalped, although it was later reported that Agent James McLaughlin had saved a lock of Sitting Bull's hair. So too had Deeble, but that fact was not widely known until 2007.

Even before his ignoble interment, the news of Sitting Bull's death made headlines around the world. As might have been expected, there were vari-ations on the facts.

When he received the telegram sent by Agent McLaughlin on December 15, Thomas Morgan, the Commissioner of Indian Affairs, handed it to President Benjamin Harrison, and copies of it to the media. The telegram stated that "The Indian Police arrested Sitting Bull at his camp . . . this morning at daylight. His followers attempted a rescue and fighting commenced." This brief and reasonably accurate description would be embellished considerably. McLaughlin's telegram went on to correctly state the casualties, but this too, would be exaggerated in time.

President Harrison, having read McLaughlin's telegram, made comments that were also widely quoted. On December 16, the *New York Herald* told its readers that Harrison "had regarded Sitting Bull as the great disturbing element in his tribe, and now that he was out of the way he hoped that a settlement of the difficulties could be reached without further bloodshed."

The views of the Indian rights groups notwithstanding, most public opinion took its cue from the President and the mainstream press to breathe a sigh of relief. It was not so much relief that the "wicked" Sitting Bull was dead, but that his death would finally bring an end to the bloodshed on the Plains that had filled the papers for generations. Of course, these readers would be disabused of this rosy projection by the headlines that would appear two weeks later, datelined from Wounded Knee Creek.

The headline in the December 16 *San Francisco Chronicle* stated "Sitting Bull Dead: A Tragedy Which Is Likely to Prevent the Threatened Outbreak of Hostilities." Meanwhile, the rival *San Francisco Examiner*, recently under the proprietorship of young William Randolph Hearst, trumpeted "Sitting Bull Shot Dead: The Wily Old Chieftain Has Gone to the Happy Hunting Grounds." Citizen Hearst's coverage went on to describe Sitting Bull as "perhaps the most dangerous Indian still at liberty." The *Examiner* also informed its readers by the Bay that "Seven of the police lost their lives in the attempt to take the peace-disturber back to the [Standing Rock] Agency."

In a special report beneath its December 16 headline, the *San Francisco Chronicle*—and other papers as well—carried a story that recounted McLaughlin's meeting with Sitting Bull at Grand River a month earlier, in which Sitting Bull had offered to meet Wovoka face to face. The report said that McLaughlin told Sitting Bull that to try to stop the Ghost Dance at that point would have been "similar to the attempt to catch the wind that blew last year." The newspaper report went on to say that McLaughlin had then invited him to Fort Yates, but that Sitting Bull had declined.

In its capsule biography of Sitting Bull in that day's edition, the *San Francisco Examiner* reflected with unvarnished vitriol, "There have been few American Indians in all the history of Indian warfare who have excelled Sitting Bull in craftiness, in generalship and in the rude diplomacy which has characterized the race since Powhatan. His name will always be associated with the awful Custer massacre, and until the prairies are populated with cities and the Indians swept out of existence the memory of his influence and his legacy of hate will remain a menace to the timid." Hearst may or may not have penned this lurid prose himself.

On December 17, the *New York Times* carried what it described as "the actual details of the fight in which Sitting Bull was killed." As the paper reported, "While Bull Head and Shave Head were in the shack where the old chief was getting ready, two bucks enveloped in blankets entered the shack, and throwing off their blankets opened fire on the police. . . . Sitting Bull's wife had gone out and set up a howl, which seems to have been the signal for the assault [against the police]."

In St. Paul, Minnesota, a dispatch was carried in the *Pioneer Press*—and widely repeated by other papers—that told readers "when the Indian Police reached the camp, they found the Indians [loyal to Sitting Bull] ready to march. Their ponies were painted and many of the savages had stripped for war. The police made a dash into the camp and seized Sitting Bull. They were on their way back to Standing Rock when the son of the famous chief urged his comrades to recapture the old man. The women and children hid in the bushes and then with yells the hostiles charged upon the police, firing as they came. A hand-to-hand struggle ensued, during which Sitting Bull, who was not shackled, gave orders in a loud voice. . . . In the fierce fusillade Sitting Bull fell out of his saddle, pierced by a bullet."

In his January 12, 1891, letter to Herbert Welsh of the Indian Rights Association, even James McLaughlin said, "The newspaper reports regarding the arrest and death of Sitting Bull have nearly all been ridiculously absurd."

Before one jumps to quip, "the next casualty was the truth," we should bear in mind that erroneous first reports of tragedies such as this are still with us, even in the age of satellite uplinks, continuous cable new channels, and the notoriously unreliable blogosphere. Unfortunately, as we well know, inaccurate data in early reports has a way of embedding itself in the permanent record. As late as April 20, 1953, *Time* magazine reported that sixteen men were killed in the Grand River fight. Of course, the point of the piece was not the facts. In this same article *Time* used the dialect of what should have been left behind in an earlier generation of journalism when it crowed that the "western plains produced few nobler redskins than Chief Sitting Bull."

How the news was circulated in the early days after Sitting Bull's death is related by a short item that appeared in the *San Francisco Chronicle* of December 17 and elsewhere. Originating in Bismarck on December 16, the piece complains that "little word has been obtained from Standing Rock to-day or to-night as the iron-clad non-intercourse rule of the military holds a rein over the military telegraph. All the newspapers are cut off from any communication by wire with the agency."

Then, as now, government control of communications served only to fuel the rumor mill. Just as we might have today via e-mail or the Internet, there soon came the speculation that Sitting Bull's death was all for the best. A story carrying the Standing Rock dateline on December 16 that was printed in the *San Francisco Examiner*, among others, provided the prevailing view of Sitting Bull's death from the place where he would soon be buried: "That the Government authorities, civil as well as Military, from President Harrison and General Miles on down, preferred the death of the famous old savage to his capture whole-skinned, few persons here, Indian or white, have a doubt. . . . It had to be. . . . It was felt that Sitting Bull's presence anywhere behind iron bars would be a cause of endless troubles, while should he fall victim to the ready Winchester, the thousands of the Messiah-crazed ghost dancers would rudely realize that his medicine, which made them bullet-proof and yet could not save so great an oracle, must be worthless after all, and should be forsaken for paths of peace."

Also citing a December 16 dispatch from Standing Rock, the *New York Herald* of December 17 carried an ominous story that implied a "wanted dead or alive" attitude in the U.S. Army and the Indian Police: "It is stated today that there was a quiet understanding between the officers of the Indian and military departments that it would be impossible to bring Sitting Bull to Standing Rock alive, and that if brought in, nobody would know precisely what to do with him. He would, though under arrest, still be a source of great annoyance, and his followers would continue their dances and threats against neighboring settlers. There was, therefore, cruel as it may seem, a complete understanding from the Commanding Officer to the Indian Police that the slightest attempt to rescue the old medicine man should be a signal to send Sitting Bull to the happy hunting ground."

There is no evidence that either Harrison or Miles had articulated a "wanted dead or alive" order, although there seems to have been a general understanding that this is how they really felt. Certainly, the sigh of relief that one senses in Harrison's calling Sitting Bull a "great disturbing element" bears this out.

"It is learned that Sitting Bull's body, when brought in from Grand River, was taken to the military hospital to be dissected," wrote a *Chicago Tribune* correspondent quoted by W. Fletcher Johnson in his *The Life of Sitting Bull and History of the Indian War of 1890–'91.* This may be the source of that rumor, or perhaps, the Chicago correspondent was merely quoting the rumor. "The Indians at the agency, the police and friendly Indians, would have nothing to do with the remains. It is said the morning they were to be buried a couple of soldiers took the box supposed to contain the remains and dumped it in an isolated grave away from the graves of other Indians and a guard placed around it. It is an open secret that really the box did not contain the remains and that the guard was put on the grave as a blind. It is believed Sitting Hull's body is now in the dissecting-room, and that in time the skeleton will turn up either in the Government museum or some other place."

The influential author William Henry Harrison Murray recoiled in horror and called it "murder" in the pages of the *New York World*. Also known as "Adirondack Murray," he was the clergyman and author who wrote a series of books which were the catalyst for the "Outdoor Movement," a late nineteenth-century phenomenon in which Eastern city dwellers discovered the joys of nature and hiking in the outdoors. Naturally, people living on the Plains and in the West in general — especially on the reservations — had no need to "discover" the outdoors. Murray also called on the paper to rally its readers to erect a monument in Sitting Bull's honor.

"I read in a great journal that everybody is well satisfied with his death [indeed many great journals carried this perspective]. And I cried out against the saying as I had against the deed," wrote Murray in an op-ed piece in the *New York World*, responding to that sigh of relief that filled the headlines during the third week of December. "I read that they have buried his body like a dog's — without funeral rites, without tribal wail, with no solemn song or act. That is the deed of to-day. That is the best that this generation has to give to this noble historic character, this man who in his person ends the line of aboriginal sanctities older than the religion of Christian or Jew. Very well. So let it stand for the present. But there is a generation coming that shall reverse this judgment of ours. Our children shall build monuments to those whom we stoned, and the great aboriginals whom we killed will be counted by the future American as among the historic characters of the Continent."

On December 20, 1890, the *Minneapolis Tribune* carried a report from a correspondent in Pierre, South Dakota. A rancher named Tom Hetlund had arrived in Pierre that day, "and what he tells creates a decided sensation, as he is a reliable witness." The story was even carried among the items deemed "fit the print" in the following day's *New York Times*. "Night before last some Indians were returning from a little social gathering when a sight met their eyes that chilled them to the bone," Hetlund related. "One of their number directed attention to the top of a bluff, and there stood a figure in white perfectly motionless. Suddenly, one of them cried out in Sioux, `It's Sitting Bull.' The phantom suddenly commenced waving an arm, as if motioning them to follow, and with the speed of a bird glided from hilltop to hilltop, finally disappearing in the direction of the Bad Lands." The *New York Times* observed that "only one interpretation could be given this ghostly visitation. Sitting Bull is thus identified as the . . . long danced-for Messiah."

THAT sigh of relief we sense from President Harrison's initial comment was echoed throughout the mainstream press during the days after Sitting Bull's death. It was generally believed that, with Sitting Bull dead, the Ghost Dance "craze" had lost its leader. Of course, if the premise is not true, the conclusion is usually incorrect. Those in the field knew better. The opposite was true. If the dreaded uprising took place, it would do so without regard to Sitting Bull's death, or it would be brought on by it.

Even as Sitting Bull was being loaded into the purloined wagon on the Grand River, General Nelson Miles had donned his bear coat, left his headquarters in Chicago, and was headed west to personally take command of operations in South Dakota. He arrived as Sitting Bull was being lowered into his grave, but Bear Coat went not to Standing Rock—there was no "unrest" at Standing Rock—but to the south. He made his headquarters at Rapid City, South Dakota, near the Pine Ridge Reservation, where agent Daniel Royer (Young Man Afraid of His Indians) was so fearful of trouble.

With Sitting Bull gone, Red Cloud, the elder statesman of the Oglala, whose agency had become the Pine Ridge Reservation, saw the potential for very big trouble. He recognized that in the increasing tension, and among the growing number of soldiers, there was a disaster waiting to happen. He invited Big Foot and the Minneconjou to come south from Cheyenne River for a peace conference.

Meanwhile, Miles had ordered Lieutenant Colonel Edwin Sumner to detain Big Foot because any large numbers of Lakota on the move were seen as provocative. However, Sumner hesitated because he didn't see Big Foot and his movements as a clear and present danger and his orders from Miles allowed him to use his own discretion. As a result, Big Foot and several hundred Minneconjou followers were able to leave the Cheyenne River Reservation on December 23, heading south, accompanied by some of Sitting Bull's Hunkpapa band who had not gone back to Standing Rock.

The following day, Miles issued specific orders to intercept Big Foot. He put elements of three regiments into the field, including the 6th Cavalry under Colonel Eugene Carr, the 7th Cavalry under Colonel James Forsyth, and the 9th Infantry Regiment under Major Guy Henry.

On December 28, 1890, a four-company detachment of the 7th Cavalry led by Major Samuel Whitside succeeded in intercepting their quarry on Porcupine Creek near Pine Ridge. The two sides parleyed, and Big Foot explained that they were going to the Pine Ridge Agency to have a council with the Oglala. Big Foot, who had just come down with pneumonia, agreed to their being escorted to the agency.

By evening, the Lakota and their cavalry escort had reached Wounded Knee Creek within the Pine Ridge Reservation. Here they made camp and were joined by Colonel Forsyth and the balance of the 7th Cavalry, along with a battery of guns from the 1st Artillery Regiment. The troops were

Members of 1st Artillery, Battery E, and Lakota scouts at the Pine Ridge Reservation
in 1891. This was one of the units who fired upon the Indians at Wounded Knee.
(*Library of Congress*)

posted around the perimeter of the Lakota encampment. The number of
Lakota present was estimated at 120 men and 230 women and children.

The following morning, Forsyth ordered the Minneconjou and
Hunkpapa to be disarmed, and their weapons were stacked. Forsyth then
ordered a search for concealed weapons, and two rifles were found. One
man, Black Coyote, balked at giving up his gun, there was a scuffle, and a
shot was fired.

As had happened with Conquering Bear at Ash Hollow, with Crazy
Horse at Fort Robinson in 1877, and at Sitting Bull's cabin two weeks earlier, a single shot was the catalyst for a hellstorm. Almost instantly, nervous soldiers began firing into the crowd as the Lakota grabbed their
weapons. The 1st Artillery cut loose with a withering barrage from their
Hotchkiss guns, which had been positioned on a hill overlooking the
Wounded Knee campsite.

The ensuing fight, known to history alternatively as the Wounded Knee Massacre or as the Battle of Wounded Knee, cost the lives of 153 Lakota, including an estimated 62 women and children, although some who escaped may have died from their wounds without having been counted. Big Foot was found among the dead. Meanwhile, the 7th Cavalry suffered its greatest number of casualties of any engagement since the Civil War, with the sole exception of the Battle of the Little Bighorn. The regiment lost twenty-five men killed in action, and thirty-five wounded.

The carnage at Wounded Knee, rather than being an end to the bloodshed in South Dakota, was merely another terrible engagement in a new cycle of violence on the Plains. The following day, a large number of Lakota burned a building near the Drexel Mission and attacked a wagon train on White Clay Creek, killing one soldier. When Forsyth rode out from Wounded Knee to intervene, the 7th Cavalry was pinned down under heavy rifle fire for most of the day until they were relived by four companies of the 9th Cavalry. Forsyth lost two men killed in action and seven wounded.

Farther north, Captain John Kerr and units of the 6th Cavalry were involved in a fight with the Lakota on the north bank of the White River, near the mouth of Little Grass Creek on the first day of 1891. That same day, wagons finally came out from the Pine Ridge Agency on New Year's Day to collect the remains of the Lakota who had died at Wounded Knee Creek. Most of them, like Sitting Bull on December 15, had been frozen stiff in the subzero cold.

Wounded Knee was the last major engagement between the U.S. Army and the Lakota, and it is still discussed today as an example of unprovoked cruelty against exhausted members of an exhausted culture. It was indeed a massacre, although the Lakota obliged the Army to pay a heavy price for its "victory." Forsyth had mishandled the situation very badly, and Miles attempted to censure him for incompetence. However, Miles was overruled by General John Schofield, the Commanding General of the U.S. Army.

General Miles and his staff surveying the Indian encampment at the Pine Ridge Reservation on January 16, 1891. (*Library of Congress*)

Miles went into the field himself in January 1891, leading 5,500 men. Without further loss of life, he was able to calm the frayed nerves of the wasichu and gently nudge the remaining Lakota bands back to the reservations. On January 15, Kicking Bear finally handed his Winchester to Miles. The "insurrection" was over.

In his January 12, 1891, letter to Herbert Welsh of the Indian Rights Association, James McLaughlin wrote, "This conflict, which cost so many lives, is much to be regretted, yet the good resulting therefrom can scarcely be overestimated, as it has effectually eradicated all seeds of disaffection sown by the Messiah Craze among the Indians of this Agency, and has also demonstrated to the people of the country the fidelity and loyalty of the Indian police in maintaining law and order on the reservation. . . . Everything is now quiet at this Agency, and good feeling prevails among the Indians, newspaper reports to the contrary notwithstanding."

The mood of the nation had come a long way in a few short weeks since the great sigh of relief that had accompanied Sitting Bull's death. Far from being the end of the "unrest," it had been merely an element of it. The death of Sitting Bull had no apparent effect on the Ghost Dance movement, although many people still continued to imagine him as its leader, just as they imagined him the leader of the victorious hordes at the Little Bighorn.

Many at the top, however, began nervously to regret Sitting Bull's death. Some time later, Benjamin Harrison would cross paths with Buffalo Bill Cody in Indianapolis, and would admit that in retrospect, he wished he had not rescinded the orders of General Miles. "President Harrison informed me that he had allowed himself to be persuaded against my mission in opposition to his own judgment," Cody recalled in his autobiography. "[He] said he was very sorry that he had not allowed me to proceed. It developed afterward that the people who had moved the President to interfere consisted of a party of philanthropists who advanced the argument that my visit would precipitate a war in which Sitting Bull would be killed, and it was to spare the life of this man that I was stopped! I found that General Miles knew exactly why I had been turned back from my trip to Sitting Bull. But he was a soldier, and made no criticism of the order of a superior."

Just as Harrison regretted not letting Buffalo Bill talk to Sitting Bull, many came to regret having ignored the counsel of Dr. Valentine McGillycuddy, who had cautioned, "If the troops remain, trouble is sure to come."

Nor had anyone listened to those who had suggested that the Ghost Dance movement, if ignored, would soon lose momentum. In fact, interest in the Ghost Dance had begun to wane within a month of Wounded Knee, not because of Wounded Knee, but because such things run their course, and because the Ghost Dance offered no real solution to the problems for which it had been promoted as a remedy. The Ghost Dance failed simply because it failed.

Was it an assassination? Speculation that Sitting Bull was deliberately murdered has continued since the day he died. The word "assassination" has long been used to describe the events of that icy morning, even in the mainstream press (*Bismarck Tribune*, December 11, 2006, for example).

Despite the whispers, those who have looked carefully at the details of his death have concluded that it was just a case of nervous men with nervous trigger fingers. Shots were fired and as happened so often in the West—even including that other terrible morning two weeks later at Wounded Knee—things got out of hand.

However, questions that cannot be answered still remain. If Red Tomahawk and Bull Head had gone to Grand River, not to arrest Sitting Bull, but purposely to kill him, his death certainly would have been murder.

Bull Head may have been trying to hit Catch the Bear and missed. Why Red Tomahawk shot Sitting Bull in the head at close range is less explicable. Did he panic it the midst of what he may have seen as an angry mob? Was there some secret understanding between McLaughlin and Bull Head, or between Bull Head and his men, that Sitting Bull was to be killed at the first sign of trouble? We'll never know.

If James McLaughlin had explicitly directed that Sitting Bull was, despite McLaughlin's own directive, to be killed and not arrested, that would have been murder. However, malice aforethought involves deliberate, rational thinking. There is a case to be made that McLaughlin could not have rationally plotted to kill Sitting Bull, because nothing about his perspective on Sitting Bull was rational.

James McLaughlin insisted that Sitting Bull was "in open rebellion against constituted authority, was defying the Government, and encouraging disaffection, made it necessary that he be arrested and removed from the reservation." If he thought that Sitting Bull's death would be celebrated, he was right. If he thought his death would be universally celebrated, he was wrong.

Gradually, the press began to question the actions of McLaughlin's Indian Police, and this doubt got the attention of Congress. Just eight days after Sitting Bull was killed—assassinated if you will—Congressman Newton Crain Blanchard, the future governor of Louisiana, stepped onto the floor of the House of Representatives and called for an investigation. "Whereas," Blanchard began his resolution. "The recent killing of the Indian chief, Sitting Bull, appears to have been accomplished under circumstances recognized neither by the laws of war nor those of peace. . . . Resolved, that a committee consisting of five members of the House, who are members-elect of the House of Representatives of the Fifty-second Congress, to be appointed by the Speaker of the present House, is directed to inquire into and investigate the killing of the said Indian Chief, Sitting Bull, and the immediate causes leading thereto, and whether a state of war existed which justified his summary taking of, and, if not, what justification, if any, there was for his violent death at the hands of Indian Police in the employ of the government."

At the same time, Congressman William McAdoo of New Jersey also "offered for reference a resolution reciting that it is charged in the public press (to the invoking of the national honor) that certain Indian reservation police officers, acting under the civil and military powers of the United States, did unjustifiably kill the Sioux chief Sitting Bull and afterward barbarously mutilate his remains."

In the face of all this, McLaughlin repeatedly stood up for his men. In his letter to Herbert Welsh, he would write, "I cannot too strongly commend the splendid courage and ability which characterized the conduct of the Indian police commanded by Bull Head and Shave Head throughout the encounter. The attempt to arrest Sitting Bull was so managed as to place the responsibility for the fight that ensued upon Sitting Bull's band, which began the firing."

Ultimately, the congressional investigations came to naught, overtaken by other events—the Wounded Knee debacle among them. For his part,

McAdoo was already a lame duck. Having not even been renominated in 1890, he left the House of Representatives in March 1891. If an indictment were to have been sought, a case could have been made for involuntary manslaughter—or criminally negligent homicide. In the case of Crow Foot, it's another story. The killing of an unarmed boy, both contemplated and brutal, cannot be anything other than murder. We leave it to the lawyers to calculate the degree, but it doesn't matter because no charges were brought.

McLaughlin's nervous postscript to his arrest warrant, "You must not let him escape under any circumstances," was ominous. It gave Bull Head a great deal of latitude, but did McLaughlin mean to be giving Bull Head a "dead or alive" order?

The reports from Fort Yates on the day after Sitting Bull died are telling. The idea that there was "a complete understanding from the Commanding Officer to the Indian Police that the slightest attempt to rescue the old medicine man should be a signal to send Sitting Bull to the happy hunting ground," indicate that many people at the scene believed a deliberate assassination was the intended outcome of the mission to Grand River.

The time has long since come and gone for indictment to be made. The issue is merely one for reflection. Two things that can be said with certainty are that after Sitting Bull's death, he was at last, beyond McLaughlin's reach, and that McLaughlin was brought to justice under that most ironic of laws—the law of unintended consequence. By having made Sitting Bull the "high priest" of the Ghost Dance movement, he ensured for him a place of importance at the time of his death. McLaughlin had wished to see Sitting Bull fade quietly into the forgotten pages of obscurity. Instead, through his own obsession, he helped to give his rival immortality.

While McLaughlin had constantly insisted that Sitting Bull was a liar and prevaricator, his old friend, Long Lance James Walsh, set the record straight. Upon hearing of Sitting Bull's death, his words form a fitting epitaph. Said Walsh, "He was not the bloodthirsty man reports from the prairies made him out to be. He asked for nothing but justice . . . . He was not a cruel man, he was kind of heart; he was not dishonest, he was truthful."

As time and the winter snows softened the contours of the killing fields at Grand River and Wounded Knee, the Lakota went back to pondering their future as "civilized" Indians, knowing that Sitting Bull was gone — but not forgotten.

This remarkable photograph of four generations of Sitting Bull's family was taken by an unknown photographer, possibly at Fort Randall. Grouped around Sitting Bull in the center, they are (clockwise from the left) Her Holy Door, his mother; Good Feather, his sister; Walks Looking, his daughter; Many Horses, another daughter; and Tom Fly, his grandson and the son of Many Horses. The picture is undated, but it was probably in about 1883, as Her Holy Door died in 1884 and Tom Fly was born in 1882. In 1883, Walks Looking was 15 and Many Horses was 20. (*State Historical Society of North Dakota*)

7

LIGHT COME SHINING

S ITTING BULL, LIKE ALL GREAT MEN AND GREAT WOMEN, cast a strong light across the history of subsequent generations. He was like a campfire on a dark and moonless Dakota night. The flickering warmth can be seen forever and from all direction of the compass.

Of course, part of the measure of greatness is how, and how long, a person is remembered. To remain a household word after a century is an assurance of a permanent place in the collective memory of one's era. Indeed, Sitting Bull is remembered by more people today than the Grandfathers in Washington who occupied the White House during much of his life.

Sitting Bull is certainly better remembered than Agent James McLaughlin, who had worked so hard in that failed effort to assure that Sitting Bull would be forgotten. McLaughlin remained in his post at Standing Rock for five years after Sitting Bull's death, driven crazy, no doubt, by the flood of interest in Sitting Bull that deluged the agency.

First came an interest in Sitting Bull's worldly possessions. On February 14, 1891, less than two months after his body was cold, Senator Lyman Casey of North Dakota wrote to Indian Commissioner Thomas Morgan proposing that the "Indian Bureau take the necessary steps to come into possession of as large a part of the personal effects of the late Sitting Bull, the Indian chief, as shall prove to be practicable as they cannot fail to be objects of curiosity and interest for many years to come to citizens of the United States." Casey went on to ask Morgan, "if you succeed in obtaining possession of such effects you will permit the use of them to the State of North Dakota for exhibition at the World's Fair."

Five days later, Morgan bounced the memo down the chain of command to McLaughlin, asking him to look into this matter, to "see what there may be of value or interest, and how much it will cost to secure possession of them for the purpose indicated by Senator Casey."

In fact, Sitting Bull's house, the structure in which he was rudely awakened on that terrible morning, was to be displayed as part of the North Dakota exhibit at the World's Columbian Exposition in Chicago in 1893. Tenaciously loyal to his metal breasts, McLaughlin insisted that it be presented as the place where brave Indian Police gave their lives, but instead, it was shown for what it was—Sitting Bull's house. Ironically, it was the type of wasichu gift-house that Sitting Bull had long said he would never be chained to. By 1893, only one narrow aspect of his memory was chained to the house.

At this same time, Buffalo Bill Cody set up shop on a fourteen-acre site adjacent to the Columbian Exposition fairgrounds, where his Wild West had one of its most successful runs ever. The Wild West's opening parade that April was led by a rider carrying the American flag, mounted on the light gray show horse that Buffalo Bill had given to Sitting Bull in 1885.

At least Cody had the decency to buy the horse back from Sitting Bull's widows. Most of Sitting Bull's other personal property was just expropriated. "We lost all our household goods," One Bull complained to Stanley

Vestal a number of years later. "Everything, trunks, boxes, and provisions in Sitting Bull's house were taken, his cattle—all that he had—all disappeared. Some of the horses were also missing. We were overwhelmed with grief."

In 1895, McLaughlin was kicked upstairs, transferred to Washington, D.C., as an inspector for the Bureau of Indian Affairs. In his 1910 book entitled *My Friend, The Indian,* he looked back at his life in the service of civilizing the Indians. His intentions, he insisted, had always been friendly. He died in 1923 at the age of eighty-one in Washington, but he was buried in, of all places, the Standing Rock Reservation, near the town that now bears his name. Under the Dawes Act, which had allocated reservation land to individuals, the land on which the town of McLaughlin was built had been allocated to Bear Soldier. He had ridden with Sitting Bull in the Battle of the Rosebud, and in his later years, he was a source of information about Sitting Bull for wasichu ethnographers.

RED TOMAHAWK, the metal breast who shot Sitting Bull in the head, became a minor celebrity, the beneficiary of McLaughlin's tireless efforts on behalf of his loyal Indian Police. He epitomized what McLaughlin defined as a successfully "civilized Indian."

It's strange to see a man become a celebrity for doing something for which he should have been ashamed. Neither shooting someone in a panic, nor murder, are much to be proud of, but for those who would rather live with stereotypes than facts, then perhaps it was comfortable to have Red Tomahawk become a celebrity.

By the early twentieth century, the former police sergeant had gradually taken on the mantle of North Dakota's greatest living "Indian chief." Red Tomahawk's having killed Sitting Bull, the archvillain of "civilization," was now perceived as something to be celebrated. After leaving the police, he retired to his home near Cannon Ball, where according to the

Sioux County Pioneer of December 29, 1927, he "often meets famous personages who visit the state before whom he is called to represent his people as a prominent type of the old time Sioux."

In 1926, when Queen Marie of Romania— a granddaughter of Queen Victoria—made her extensively publicized visit to the United States, her journey included a stop in North Dakota to call on Red Tomahawk. He made her an honorary Lakota, and presented her with a headdress, formally praising her highness for her heroism during World War I when she she volunteered as a Red Cross nurse to help the sick and wounded.

"We want to honor you. A woman does not wear an eagle's headdress unless she performed some splendid act of heroism," Red Tomahawk said in words reported in the *Ward County Independent* on November 4, 1926. "Your part in that great war has endeared you to us. . . . Therefore, I present you with this honorable badge of bravery and give you the name 'Winyan Kipanpi Win,' (Calling Unto Her Woman) and you are my sister now." As the paper reported, Red Tomahawk then drew blood from her forefinger and mingled it with his own on his forearm.

Among the others who came west to call on Red Tomahawk was General Charles Summerall, the U.S. Army's Chief of Staff. What a different scene from the 1870s and 1880s it must have been to have the head man of the U.S. Army coming to pay tribute, rather than to conduct warfare. It must have seemed strange to Lakota who still remembered, and who had been at Wounded Knee, to watch the biggest bluecoat of them all—now clad in khaki—shaking hands with the man who shot Sitting Bull in the back of the head. The two had never faced one another in battle. Summerall did not graduate from West Point until 1892.

Red Tomahawk later returned the favor with a trip to Washington. As the Associated Press reported on June 20, 1929, "Chief Red Tomahawk of the Sioux tribe of Indians in North Dakota was in the capital today to make big whoopee with Chief General C. P. Summerall of the army general staff in return for the visit the general paid Red Tomahawk last year.

He will also pay his respects to Big Chief President Hoover at the White House and to that other noted Indian chief, Vice President Charles Curtis. . . . Red Tomahawk, who is more than 80 years old, is noted among his tribe for being the man who killed Sitting Bull and speaks only the Indian language. He will be put up as General Summerall's guest at one of the capital's big teepees, the Carlton Hotel."

Vice President Curtis was, in fact, part Indian. The mother of the former U.S. Senator from Kansas was one quarter each Kaw, Osage, and Pottawatomie, and the vice president spent part of his early life on a reservation. As predicted, Red Tomahawk met with Hoover and Curtis the next day.

In 1923, North Dakota officially honored Red Tomahawk as it had no other of its citizens. By this time, even though the United States still did not have a comprehensive coast-to-coast paved highway system, many

The profile of Red Tomahawk, the man who killed Sitting Bull, was adopted for both North Dakota highway signs, top, and the official seal of the North Dakota State Patrol, bottom. (*North Dakota State Patrol*)

states were making great strides in this regard and North Dakota was especially proud of its paved roads. When the Road Marking Division of the State Highway Commission was created, Chief Engineer W. B. Black had the distinction of picking a symbol for the standard state highway sign. The symbol he chose was the profile silhouette of an Indian wearing a feather headdress, over which was superimposed the number of the highway. The Indian whose profile he chose was Red Tomahawk. Within two years, the highways of North Dakota were adorned with 8,590 pressed steel portraits of Sitting Bull's killer. In 1951, the profile of this Indian policeman was added to the doors of North Dakota highway patrol cars. The image of Red Tomahawk is still in use in the twenty-first century.

As we consider Sitting Bull's detractors and enemies, we might also give a thought to what happened to his last wasichu friend, the enigmatic Catherine Weldon. We call her an enigma because that is how she appears in the accounts of his life. Most stories of Sitting Bull's life introduce her suddenly and leave her at the dock in Cannon Ball, waiting for a steamboat with her only son, who is about to die.

Thanks to letters gathered long ago by Stanley Vestal, and to the essential research work done by Eileen Pollack in the 1990s, the story of Weldon in the days following her last parting with Sitting Bull is now complete. After Christie's agonizing death from tetanus on the boat at Pierre on November 19, 1890, Weldon had his body prepared for burial and continued downriver on the Missouri to Kansas City. Here she had relatives, and here she would inter her son and spend the next year of her life. However, her luggage, including at least two of the portraits she had painted of Sitting Bull, had been stranded in Pierre as the Missouri River steamers stopped running for the winter. She may or may not have reclaimed all of this luggage.

From Kansas City, she wrote a couple of letters to Sitting Bull in which she admitted to considering suicide after Christie died, and signed them as "Woman Walking Ahead," the name he had given her. She never received a reply, so she assumed that he had not gotten her missives, but he had. However, within a couple of weeks of her arrival in Kansas City, Sitting Bull was also dead. She later exchanged letters with his family, although she probably never visited them again.

As noted previously, she was born Caroline Schlotter, and in later years she returned to using the name Caroline, rather than Catherine. Indeed, she had already resumed using that name while in Kansas City in 1891.

She spent a couple of years there, living with her sister's son, Frederick Schleicher, a teacher at a Catholic school. She also maintained her contacts with the National Indian Defense Association, contributing some writings to its publications.

Pollack can also be credited with locating a second of Weldon's four portraits of Sitting Bull. The one purchased by Lieutenant Matthew Steele for two dollars had been with the State Historical Society of North Dakota since 1953, but the location of the others was unknown. According to documents at the State Historical Society, a second painting, presumably in Weldon's possession during the 1890s, was deeded by her to Louise Van Solen and Louise's daughter Lucille in February 1912. Weldon stated that it should go to the Historical Society after their deaths, and it was exhibited briefly in Bismarck around 1914. However, after Lucille died in 1929, this painting disappeared without a trace.

Half a century later, a portrait of Sitting Bull signed by "C.S. Weldon" turned up, listed in a 1976 inventory of American art as belonging to private collector who wished to remain anonymous. After extensive detective work, Pollack traced the painting to Mary Delia Prather in Little Rock, Arkansas. She was the great-granddaughter of U.S. Senator James Kimbrough Jones, who had been Chairman of the Senate Indian Affairs Committee early in the twentieth century. Pollack went to Arkansas thinking that this painting, a head and shoulders portrait, was the Van Solen painting, but discovered that it was a *third* portrait. Weldon had given it to Jones in about 1901, eleven years before she gave the other painting to the Van Solens, and it had been in his family ever since.

By 1912, when she gave the painting to Louise Van Solen, Catherine/Caroline Weldon was living in Brooklyn again, and apparently she remained there for the rest of her life. According to her tiny obituary in the *Brooklyn Daily Eagle*, she died an even more violent and painful death than her son. At her home at 384 Baltic Street, on the night of March 14, 1921, her clothes accidentally caught on fire from the flame of a candle. Woman Walking Ahead died later of third degree burns to her face and body. She was eighty-three.

By the time that McLaughlin came "home" to Standing Rock in 1923, the reservation itself was changing, growing, and evolving. The population stood at 4,096, including 1,739 Hunkpapa, in 1890, the year that Sitting Bull died. It declined slowly thereafter, reaching 2,929 in the 1910 United States Census. The death rate among the very old and the very young outpaced the number of children who reached adulthood. By the teens and twenties, however, the population was expanding considerably, up to 10,557 in 1920 and to a twentieth-century peak of 14,222 in 1930. A big part of this increase in population was probably accounted for by wasichu settlers, because portions of Standing Rock were opened to homesteading in 1909. Meanwhile, both North Dakota and South Dakota experienced a great deal of growth statewide through the early twenties as well. North Dakota grew by 81 percent during the first decade of the twentieth century, while South Dakota grew by 45 percent.

During World War I, a number of young Lakota men living at Standing Rock enlisted in the U.S. armed forces, despite the fact that about a third of the Indians living in the United States were still technically not yet citizens. Richard Blue Earth was the first from Standing Rock to enlist, and Albert Grass among the first killed in action. In 1919, the Indian veterans were granted citizenship, but it was not until 1924 that Congress passed legislation granting American citizenship to all Indians born in the United States.

During the Great Depression, the population of the Standing Rock Reservation fell 21.4 percent from the 14,222 peak in 1930 to 9,864 in 1940, as many tribal members left the reservation to seek employment in the wasichu world. Living conditions on reservations had always lagged far behind those elsewhere in the United States, and during the Depression, everyone's standard of living plummeted. During the 1940s, the population fell nearly 12 percent as people continued the economic exodus, this time to answer the demand for workers during the industrial expansion of World War II. There was no major industry at or near Standing Rock and there still isn't.

With this, the place where Sitting Bull had spent the last year of his life watching crops fail and his people go hungry was gradually marginalized even further. In 1948, a year after the Office of Indian Affairs became the Bureau of Indian Affairs, the agency formally undertook its Relocation Program, in which people were lured off reservations all across the country to be retrained for higher paying jobs in major metropolitan areas. Created by Glenn L. Emmons, who served as the head of the Bureau of Indian Affairs from 1953 to 1961, the Relocation Program provided transportation, job placement, subsistence funds, and counseling, as well as vocational training. The program continued through the 1970s and was good for the individual, but less good for the reservations and for the people who remained. It took away perhaps the best and brightest, or at least the most ambitious. Between 1950 and 1990, the population at Standing Rock dropped from 9,864 to 7,956. Indeed, conditions on the South Dakota reservations had still failed to live up to the promises made to Sitting Bull when he was convinced to return from the Grandmother's Country in 1881.

Things boiled over again in 1973. The attention of the wasichu world focused once again on Wounded Knee, as the entrenched American Indian Movement activists held off FBI agents and the National Guard in a bloody ten-week stand-off. As in 1890–1891, the focal point was at Pine Ridge, but as before, the image and words of Sitting Bull were part of the media stereotype. He had lived and died at Standing Rock, but many of his descendants were now living also at Pine Ridge.

Sitting Bull had come to live on the reservation with the promise of a good future there for him, his people, and the future generations. He was ordered to stay there, not to leave, and promised that all would be well. Ironically, a half century later, those future generations were streaming away from Standing Rock and Pine Ridge looking for the economic necessities of the twentieth century, the modern equivalent of the buffalo.

DESPITE James McLaughlin's attempt to discredit Sitting Bull in wasichu eyes, he is an enduring and popular image in popular culture. Just as he had marketed autographed pictures of himself during his 1885 season with Buffalo Bill's Wild West, postcards with his likeness have been marketed in racks all across the West almost continuously since his death.

Sitting Bull was photographed, by the reckoning of Markus Lindner in *North Dakota History* magazine in 2005, at least eighteen times, with multiple photographs taken on several of these occasions. However, Sitting Bull never appeared in a motion picture, although the technology was in its infancy at the time that he died. His old wasichu show business friend, Buffalo Bill Cody, embraced the fledgling medium early on, and he first appeared in a short entitled *Indian War Council* in 1898. Cody was hooked by the potential of film. American Mutoscope & Biograph shot *Buffalo Bill's Wild West Parade* in 1900, and over the next several years, Cody arranged for performances of the Wild West show to be filmed for theatrical release. After spending an immense amount of capital filming his own movie about the Indian Wars, Cody went on to star as himself in the 1914 biopic *The Adventures of Buffalo Bill*.

Though the decades, Sitting Bull would appear often as a character in motion pictures. The film that is believed to be the first such theatrical release was *Custer's Last Raid*—also known as *Custer's Last Fight*—a thirty-minute short feature released in 1912. The first man to portray Sitting Bull was William Eagle Shirt, a fellow Lakota, who appeared in a dozen other films between 1912 and 1917, usually listed in the cast as "Indian Chief." He is said to have been the favorite Indian actor of Thomas Harper

Ince, the former stage actor turned Hollywood producer who directed and/or produced hundreds of motion pictures, many of them Westerns, in the early days of Hollywood. Filmed in Santa Ynez Canyon, north of Los Angeles, *Custer's Last Raid* was directed by Francis Ford, who also portrayed Custer. The older brother of the legendary director John Ford, Francis went on to a minor career as a character actor, occasionally appearing in his brother's films.

The marquee poster for the first theatrical release that featured Sitting Bull, *Custer's Last Fight* (1912). Sitting Bull appears in the upper right corner.

Sitting Bull continued to be featured in films throughout the twentieth century, including Edward Laemmle's *In the Days of Buffalo Bill* (1922), *With Sitting Bull at the Spirit Lake Massacre* (1927), *Battling with Buffalo Bill* (1931), *Heroes of the West* (1932), and *Custer's Last Stand* (1936). *They Died with Their Boots On* (1941), starring Errol Flynn and Olivia de Havilland, is the motion picture that did a better job of polishing the classic myth of the "noble and heroic" George Armstrong Custer than any other in Hollywood history, but Sitting Bull is an incidental character. *Annie Get Your Gun* (1950), based on the highly successful 1940s Broadway musical, portrayed Sitting Bull as a song and dance man, merely a foil for Buffalo Bill and Annie Oakley. *Fort Vengeance* (1953) and the Disney film *Tonka* along with its spinoff television series, *Cheyenne*, which ran from 1955 through 1963, continued the string of film and television portrayals of Sitting Bull and the Old West during the golden age of the Hollywood western. Television programs that featured Sitting Bull in the 1960s included *Branded*, starring Chuck Connors, and John Houseman's *The*

Great Adventure, which dramatized milestones of American history. Two episodes of the latter were devoted to Sitting Bull: "The Death of Sitting Bull" and "The Massacre at Wounded Knee." The latter was the first time that Wounded Knee was dealt with as the focal point of a program on national television.

Early in the twenty-first century, two television projects featuring Sitting Bull as a character portrayed his life and times with a complexity that had not previously been attempted. The first of these was the epic 552-minute, six-part miniseries *Into the West*, which was produced by Steven Spielberg and first aired in June 2005. It dealt somewhat realistically with both the death of Sitting Bull (played by Eric Schweig) and with the Wounded Knee massacre, and should be viewed favorably for using an Indian cast and for having Lakota characters actually speaking Lakota.

Two years later, another television film focused even more closely on Sitting Bull's death, and on the Wounded Knee massacre. This television film shared a title with Dee Brown's milestone 1970 book, *Bury My Heart at Wounded Knee*, but Daniel Giat, who wrote the teleplay, limited the scope of the film treatment considerably. Rather than looking at the broad spectrum of nineteenth-century American Indian history as Brown had done, the film version was limited to the Lakota, and to the years leading up to the massacre. Directed by Yves Simoneau for HBO Films, the film was condemned by many Indian critics for its positive portrayal of Senator Henry Dawes, as well as many inaccuracies.

Despite their shortcomings, however, in the twenty-first century films we can get a sense of Sitting Bull as a person, rather than as a caricature that he was in most twentieth century portrayals. As Maureen Ryan wrote of *Bury My Heart at Wounded Knee* in the *Chicago Tribune* (May 24, 2007), "the filmmakers don't flinch from showing the formidable Sitting Bull as a flawed, real man."

While Hollywood did a poor job of portraying the American Indian until late in the twentieth century—using non-Indian actors and preferring to emphasize fully fictionalized accounts of the nineteenth-century American West—it is thanks to the intense interest by Hollywood that the image of the Indian became such an icon of popular culture. Especially during that golden age of the Hollywood western in the middle of the century, Indians in general, and Sitting Bull in particular, retained a high profile in the consciousness of wasichu the world over.

During the 1950s, Hollywood Westerns also brought forth a tidal wave of tie-in merchandise from books to comics, as well as toys, from headdresses to cap guns to playsets from the Marx Toy Company. Famous for its playsets that allowed children to replay Hollywood's historical films—from Davy Crockett to Fort Apache—Marx was also a pioneer in plastic action figures of famous people. Among the dozens they produced were ones for both Custer and Sitting Bull.

There were baseball cards, but there were also "Indian chief" cards. Roughly between 1933 and 1940, the Goudey Gum Company of Boston marketed a series of Goudey Indian Gum cards in which Sitting Bull was Number 38. Post also featured a Sitting Bull cut-out card on its cereal boxes at about the same time. In the 1950s, Sitting Bull was Number 14 in the series of cards from Quaker Oats.

Even to this day, countless "collectibles" contain Sitting Bull's image. These items, visible from Ebay to roadside gift shops across the West, include expensive "collector" plates, medallions, and dolls, as well as less expensive t-shirts and coffee mugs. Certainly among the most kitsch was the seven-inch, double-faced mug of Sitting Bull and Custer issued in 1984 as part of Royal Doulton's "Antagonists Collection."

The pop culture obsession with Sitting Bull has not been limited to North America. There has always been an enormous fascination with American Indians in Europe. In the late 1940s and 1950s, Sitting Bull was everywhere in Italian and French comics. Franco Donatelli drew him for Agostino Della Casa, while Pierre Duteurtre (also known as "Dut") drew him in cooperation with Marijac (Jacques Dumas). Jean Giraud (also known as Moebius) drew Sitting Bull comics and illustrations for Far-West, and Jean-Claude Pascal included Sitting Bull in the series he did for Collection Mondial Adventures.

In Germany, where interest in American Indians runs high, there are numerous reenactor organizations in which Germans spend their weekends dressed in the stereotypic costume of nineteenth-century Plains Indians, pretending to be in another time and culture. In 1999, the Hessian State Museum in Darmstadt, Germany, held an exhibition entitled "Sitting Bull: Der Letzte Indianer." The show looked at the legend of Sitting Bull as "built up by American press after the Battle of the Little Bighorn and by Buffalo Bill," according to Markus Lindner, and expert on Sitting Bull as a photography subject and a research fellow at the Johann Wolfgang Goethe-Universität Institut für Historische Ethnologie in Frankfurt. The exhibit featured a collection of modern products using Sitting Bull's name—including a power drink from Austria.

And so it is that Sitting Bull's legacy survives in two worlds, with one foot in history, where he remains complex and difficult to understand, and the other foot in popular culture. Here, the man who was photographed with Buffalo Bill and painted by Catherine Weldon is cast as a noble individual in a feathered headdress, easy to see and therefore easy to comprehend.

Long ago, when Jerome Stillson went in search of an understanding of Sitting Bull, he told him, "Your face is dark, my people do not see it." Today, more than a century after his death, one might say that his face is brilliantly illuminated by the pop culture glare, but the wasichu cannot see beyond that glare.

DURING the years that Sitting Bull became a household word throughout the wasichu world, his image as a patriarch has endured at Standing Rock. Today at Standing Rock, his face is everywhere. Red Tomahawk may still be on the highway signs, but Sitting Bull is the patriarch toward whom Standing Rock turns.

The anniversary of his death, December 15, is a holiday at Standing Rock, a day when nearly everyone stays home from work. As for the actual place where his cabin stood on that terrible morning, it is tribally owned and inaccessible to non-tribal members. Tribal members can go, but with restrictions, because it is preserved as a ceremonial site for the annual Sitting Bull Sun Dance held in the month of July. As LaDonna Brave Bull explained, the tribe does not want tourists near the death site, and the road to it is deliberately not well maintained.

On the other hand, there are numerous annual festivals, called wacipi (which literally means "dance" in Lakota) at Standing Rock where outsiders are welcomed. These are held during the summer months at many places around Standing Rock, including Bullhead, Cannon Ball, Fort Yates, Kenel, Little Eagle, McLaughlin, Shields, and Wakpala.

At Fort Yates, Standing Rock has a college. Recognizing the need for an institution of higher education which would provide opportunities for people in the immediate area, the Standing Rock Sioux Tribal Council granted a charter on September 21, 1973, to create the Standing Rock Community College. There had been college courses offered at the reservation, but there was a need for a single institution within the borders of Standing Rock that could grant associate degrees. The college received full accreditation in 1984, and later began offering bachelor of science programs.

Six years past the centennial of Sitting Bull's death, the college got a new name. On March 6, 1996, the Tribal Council voted to officially rename the school Sitting Bull College. The school in turn adopted as its motto a saying ascribed to its namesake: "Let us put our minds together to see what we can build for our children."

The grave of the Sioux Chief Sitting Bull.
Old military burial grounds, Fort Yates, N.D.

Sitting Bull's original grave site at Fort Yates, North Dakota. The fence and marker were added some time after he was hastily buried here in December 1890. (*From an old postcard*)

8

Blood, Spirit, and Bones

After his death, Sitting Bull's family was greatly disrupted. Some remained at Standing Rock, but others moved—or were forcibly moved—to the Pine Ridge Reservation. One Bull assumed a prominent role in tribal affairs at Standing Rock, while others assumed a low profile because of the rift that developed within Hunkpapa society between those who had supported Sitting Bull and those who had fallen into line with McLaughlin and his metal breasts.

The obituary that was published for the record on December 16, 1890 in the *San Francisco Chronicle* and other papers, noted his two wives, Seen by the Nation and Four Robes, and stated that a third wife was dead. In fact, three wives—Light Hair, Snow on Her, and Red Woman—had preceded him in death. Of his children, the obituary said they were "all bright, handsome boys and girls, nine in number; one young man about 18, is in a Catholic school near Chicago." The source of the latter statement remains a mystery.

Crow Foot is described in the obituary as the little boy who handed his father's Winchester to Major Brotherton at Fort Buford and who was "bright as a dollar with eyes that fairly snap like whips." It was known by the time of the obituary that one of Sitting Bull's sons had died with him at Grand River, but the published report does not identify the bright-eyed boy as the same son who had just been killed. In looking at how Sitting Bull's legacy affected future generations, one should not forget, nor fail to mourn, the tragic loss of the unfulfilled future that might have been represented by Crow Foot.

The phrase in the obituary stating that his children were "bright, handsome boys and girls, nine in number," is not exactly true. Bright and handsome they may have been, but some were adults, no longer boys and girls, and nine, while probably close, would not have taken into account his stepsons and adopted sons.

The names of some of Sitting Bull's children are well known, but others not. One Bull, identified almost universally as his adopted son, is well documented and remained with him until the end. Of his natural children, certain names, such as Crow Foot and his daughters Standing Holy and Many Horses, are familiar both in numerous references and in photographs. Other names are more enigmatic. Many of these names are hard to pin down because they often changed. Indeed, Sitting Bull's own name had changed several times, and so did that of his children. Among the Lakota, this is expected and understood. As LaDonna Brave Bull put it so well, "people have different names at different times in their lives."

When I decided to make an effort to sort out what happened to Sitting Bull's children, I realized that even with my best effort it would be difficult, and the results not necessarily complete.

The facts can be somewhat pieced together from a list of his family members at Fort Randall in 1882, and from the United States Indian Census records for Standing Rock for the years through 1891 that are in the National Archives. These annual agency censuses are dated to June 30 of their respective years. I am also indebted to LaDonna Brave Bull at

Standing Rock and Bill Billeck at the Smithsonian Institution's Museum of Natural History, as well as to Ernie LaPointe, Sitting Bull's great-grandson, and his wife Sonja, who provided me with the most detailed family tree for Sitting Bull that I have seen.

LaDonna Brave Bull also furnished me with some information about what happened to Sitting Bull's sister, Twin Woman, who was also known as Brown Shawl Woman, Brown Robe, and Mary Four Woman. She married Herbert Hawk Shield, the son of Hawk Shield, and they had two children who lived into adulthood, Lillian (1899–1980) and Herbert, Jr. (1901–1944). Three others, Abbie, Edith, and Henry, died in 1906 as children.

The Standing Rock censuses are an essential part of tracking Sitting Bull's family. However, they are only as good as the census takers' ability to understand the Lakota language and to accurately record the data. Certain errors are immediately obvious when one examines these old documents. For example, Seen by the Nation and Four Robes advance in age from fifty-four and forty-nine to fifty-five and fifty, respectively, in the 1888 and 1889 censuses. However, they suddenly lose more than a decade in age, and are listed as aging from forty-two and forty to forty-three and forty-one, respectively, in the 1890 and 1891 censuses. The latter ages agree with the data provided to me by the LaPointes.

The 1882 Fort Randall Census lists ten children, including Many Horses and Walks Looking, Sitting Bull's daughters by Snow on Her. Many Horses, his oldest living nonadopted child at the time of his death, was born in 1865, and is noted in the Fort Randall census as being eighteen years old. Walks Looking is mentioned as being fifteen at Fort Randall, which agrees with the LaPointe genealogy, where she is listed as having been born in 1868. Many Horses had married Thomas Fly in 1881, and Walks Looking would marry Andrew Fox in 1885.

Two older boys, Blue Turtle, age fourteen, and Stood by Him, age fifteen, are listed at Fort Randall in 1882, although no mention is made of their mothers. These may be alternate names for the stepsons, Little Soldier, who was fourteen in 1882, and his brother, Refuses Them, who would have been around fifteen or sixteen when Sitting Bull was at Fort Randall.

Also listed in 1882 as Four Robes's three-year-old son is On the Hill (or Not Afraid). Bill Billeck suggests that this may be Left Arrow in Him (also known as Arrows Left in Him), the twin brother of Runs Away From, who is also listed in 1882 as being a three-year-old son of Sitting Bull and Four Robes.

Some sources have also identified Left Arrow in Him as the twin brother of Crow Foot. However, this is obviously implausible given that Crow Foot is listed as being seven at Fort Randall. Even the most inattentive of census takers would probably notice the difference between a three-year-old and a seven-year-old. Still other sources, including the LaPointes, list Crow Foot's birth date as 1873, making him about nine during the Fort Randall period. In subsequent censuses, Runs Away From continues to be listed as three years younger than Crow Foot.

The youngest child in the 1882 Fort Randall list is a daughter who was one day old when the census was taken, and who does not appear in later censuses. According to material shared with me by LaDonna Brave Bull, several of Sitting Bull's children died at birth or at a young age during the 1880s. The LaPointe genealogy also includes three sons of Sitting Bull who died younger than four years of age. Born in 1857, 1870, and 1886, they are listed merely as "Hoksila," or "little boy." A pair of twins born in Canada in 1880, named Sitting Bull and Sitting Eagle, also died young, in 1880 and 1884, respectively. Rounding out the 1882 Fort Randall list, Standing Holy (called Standing Sacred) is listed as being four and Her Lodge in Sight as five years old.

By the time of the 1888–1891 censuses, the two older daughters are no longer listed. Walks Looking died in 1887, and Many Horses was living with Thomas Fly after leaving Fort Randall. By 1888, the oldest child mentioned as living with Sitting Bull is his stepson Little Soldier, age twenty. He, along with Refuses Them, were the boys who became Sitting Bull's stepsons when he married Seen by the Nation and Four Robes.

Crow Foot is identified as being thirteen in 1888, and both Runs Away From and Standing Holy are listed as being ten, data which generally agrees with that in the Fort Randall census and the thesis that Crow Foot was born in about 1876. Also listed as being ten is Arrows Left in Him (also known as Left Arrow in Him), whose birth date is given by the LaPointes as 1878. An unnamed one-year-old girl is mentioned in the 1889 census and not in later censuses, leading one to believe that she is a daughter of Four Robes who died at around this time. A two-year-old called "Sitting Bull Junior" rounds out the list.

In the 1889 Standing Rock Census, names that recur from the previous year include Little Soldier, Crow Foot, Standing Holy, and Runs Away From, each listed as being one year older than they were in the 1888 census. Left Arrow in Him does not appear, but the name of an eleven-year-old named Wounded *does* appear and Bill Billeck notes that the Lakota names of the two boys that are given in the two censuses agree.

Sitting Bull Junior is no longer included in Sitting Bull's household in 1889, indicating that he may have died during the year. Once again, we are reminded that infant and small child mortality was much higher in the 1880s than today, and higher still among people living on the reservations, so the number of deaths of children in Sitting Bull's family is understandable. As previously noted, another son named Sitting Bull was born in 1880 and died as an infant.

In the 1890 Standing Rock Census, Little Soldier, Crow Foot, and Standing Holy are all included as in the previous two years. Her Lodge in Sight was not included in the 1888 or 1889 Standing Rock censuses, but reappears in 1890, this time simply as "Lodge." Her age is listed as fourteen, which is consistent with her having been five years old at Fort Randall in 1882, and with her having been born in 1875 as listed in the LaPointe genealogy.

In 1890, Runs Away From is listed by his Lakota name, but it is translated as the Christian name Theodore. Another twelve-year-old, Red Scout, appears for the first time. Bill Billeck suspects that this may be Left Arrow in Him, although the Lakota names do not match. Other boys in this age group who do not appear in the 1890 census are Next on the Hill (Not Afraid), Runs Away From, and Wounded—boys who would have been about twelve in 1890. Possibly there were further name changes.

Listed in the 1890 Standing Rock Census as Sitting Bull's grandson is a four-year-old named Chase Near, who was also known as Andrew Fox. Walks Looking, the deceased daughter of Sitting Bull and Snow on Her, was married to a man named Andrew Fox and had a child in 1885 who would have been around four in 1890. Many sources agree that Chase Near and the younger Andrew Fox were the same person.

The 1890 census took place in June, half a year before Sitting Bull and Crow Foot were killed, so the Standing Rock census taken one year later, in June 1891, gives us a portrait of a decimated family. Seen by the Nation and Four Robes are both still living in the household, along with Standing Holy, Her Lodge, and Theodore (Runs Away From). In this census, Chase Near is listed as Andrew Fox and is age six. Left Arrow in Him does not appear because, according to the LaPointe genealogy, he also died during 1890.

Refuses Them, listed as age twenty-five, appears in the 1891 list, having not appeared in those taken during the previous three years. Perhaps this suggests that he had rejoined the household of his widowed mother and aunt as its eldest male.

Thereafter, the family fell apart as a unit and it is difficult trace its members through census records, because many of Sitting Bull's relatives went from Standing Rock to Pine Ridge, and because there were so many Lakota people with the same or similar names at both reservations. As we have seen, there were also occasional errors in data, such as the recording of ages. In later years, errors by people transcribing the old handwritten

Sitting Bull's family members in front of a tipi belonging to Sitting Bull, photographed in 1891. From left to right, they are Standing Holy, Seen by the Nation, Theodore, Many Horses, and Four Robes. (*Library of Congress*)

documents crept in. In one instance we found, Sitting Bull himself is transcribed as "Sitteng Duce," and in another, Refuses Them is rendered preposterously as "Pefeuss Theur."

Sitting Bull's oldest daughter, Many Horses, continued to live at Standing Rock until her death in 1897. In the meanwhile, her Blackfoot Lakota husband, Thomas Fly, took a second wife, a part-Lakota woman named Alma Ramsey. Both Thomas and Alma are believed to have been students at the Hampton Normal & Agricultural Institute in Hampton, Virginia. The school was founded in 1870 by Samuel Chapman Armstrong as one of the first colleges specifically for African-American students. It later was widely attended by American Indian students. Many Horses, however, is believed to have never attended such a school.

In about 1881, Many Horses and Thomas Fly had one son, known both as Courting a Woman and Thomas (Tom) Fly Junior. Sonja LaPointe told me that Thomas and Alma had several children, including Felix, Margaret (or Marguerite), Rosa, and Regina. The 1900 U.S. Census lists Thomas and Alma Fly, aged thirty-seven and thirty-three, respectively, at Standing Rock. Their five children are Joseph Fly, age sixteen; Margurite (possibly a misspelling of Marguerite) Fly, age eight; Rosa Fly, age five; Felix Fly, age five; and an infant born in November 1899 named Regina Fly. Joseph Fly may be an alternate name for Thomas Fly Junior, or Thomas Fly Junior may already have left his father's household and Joseph was a younger half-brother.

More is known of Joseph Fly than of many others of Sitting Bull's early descendants. Like his father, he attended the Hampton Institute. School records list Joseph as the grandson of Sitting Bull, indicating that Hampton believed that his mother was Many Horses rather than Alma Ramsey. The transcripts also note that he dropped out of the Hampton Institute in November 1901 because of chronic eye trouble. Hampton's files also say that he worked as both a general laborer and a musician, although it is not noted which instrument he played.

A photograph in the collection of the North Dakota State Archives Historical Research Library (0334-006) pictures the grave of Joseph Fly, with the epitaph: "Grandson of Sitting Bull, died Sept. 18, 1912, Aged 27 years." These dates are consistent with the 1900 census data, but if he is the same person identified as Thomas Fly Junior in the photograph taken at Fort Randall in 1882, he would have been at least thirty in 1912.

Andrew Fox, the husband of Walks Looking, also attended the Hampton Institute between 1878 and 1881 and for several months in 1884. He left due to illness.

Sitting Bull's daughter, Her Lodge in Sight, died in 1898, one year after her sister, Many Horses. In the meantime, she had married Obed Scares, and their daughter, Jenny Scares, was born in 1898. It has been supposed that Her Lodge in Sight died in childbirth, but there is no known documentation. Jenny married Reuben Bear Robe and they had two children before their deaths in 1941. These were Julia Bear Robe (1921–1934) and Raymond Bear Robe (1927–1998).

Sitting Bull himself heads this page, left, from the Indian Bureau's 1890 census of residents at the Standing Rock Agency. He is number 1169, followed by Seen by the Nation and Four Robes. Somehow, changes in calculations, reporting techniques or translation make Sitting Bull three years older than he had been in 1889, while Seen by the Nation is eight years younger and Four Robes is five years younger. The census on the right, completed at Standing Rock on June 30, 1891, shows the remnants of a decimated family. Both Sitting Bull and his son Crow Foot have been dead for half a year. His wives, Seen by the Nation and Four Robes, head the third grouping from the top at numbers 811 and 812 (*National Archives*)

Best known among Sitting Bull's male heirs are those who took on Christian names and used "Sitting Bull" as a surname. Stepson Refuses Them apparently became Louis Sitting Bull, and still later went by the name John Sitting Bull. Sitting Bull's biological son by Four Robes, Runs Away From, also appears to have used two Christian names. Through 1889, he was listed as Runs Away From, but in the 1890 Standing Rock census, he used the name Theodore. Later, he is believed to have become

William Sitting Bull. A William Sitting Bull who is found in the 1898 Pine Ridge Census is probably him, although it gives his age as twenty-three when he was probably closer to twenty. The LaPointe genealogy lists his birth date as 1878. After his father was killed, Runs Away From (William Sitting Bull) had been exiled along with his family to Pine Ridge by McLaughlin, who feared that he would be a troublemaker.

Several years later, William Sitting Bull was the subject of a series of internal memos that crossed desks at the Department of the Interior. These discuss requests for his relocation back to Standing Rock from Pine Ridge. From these, we learn that his mother was still alive and living with her son at Pine Ridge in 1908.

In the document dated May 2, 1908, the Acting Commissioner of Indian Affairs notes that James McLaughlin, the former agent and at that time an inspector with the Indian Bureau in Washington, believed that William should not be transferred. Even eighteen years after Sitting Bull's death, the mere mention of the name disturbed the obsessed McLaughlin, who is quoted in this Bureau of Indian Affairs report as saying, "Sitting Bull, father of this William Sitting Bull, was a disturbing element and a source of much trouble on the Standing Rock Reservation. His attitude throughout his life was detrimental to the advancement of the Indians among whom he lived and should this son of his be transferred to Standing Rock Agency I am fearful that the former adherents of his father would make an effort to install him their leader thereby fostering disaffection among the former followers of Sitting Bull who are now well disposed and steadily advancing in civilization." In conclusion, the bureau was "very unwilling to permit the transfer."

William Sitting Bull was never transferred back to Standing Rock, and he almost certainly died on the Pine Ridge Reservation. Various sources, including the LaPointe genealogy and a document among the Walter Camp Manuscripts at the Indiana University Library, date William's death to the winter of 1909–1910.

Meanwhile, William Sitting Bull married Scout Woman and they had a daughter, born in 1903, whom they named Nancy Sitting Bull. She in turn, married George Stewart, and later Frank Kicking Bear. According to the LaPointes, Nancy's three children were Sifroy Stewart, born in 1929; Lavern Kicking Bear, born in 1934; and Casey Kicking Bear, born in 1936.

In some references, William Sitting Bull is said to have been deaf and dumb, but apparently it was Refuses Them (John Sitting Bull) that actually had this disability. The 1898 Pine Ridge census has William Sitting Bull living with a brother whose name is listed as "Deaf and Dumb." This brother is identified as having been thirty-one years old in 1898, making him the same age as Refuses Them (John Sitting Bull) would have been.

Juti Winchester at the Buffalo Bill Historical Center confirmed for me that William Sitting Bull had toured with Buffalo Bill's Wild West during the 1902 season. She also told me that John Sitting Bull was with the show during the 1903–1906 European tour, and that he was hearing impaired. She said that the Buffalo Bill Center is constantly getting inquiries from people in Europe who insist that Sitting Bull visited the continent with the Wild West. In fact, the man they saw (or heard about) was *John* Sitting Bull. He was in his mid-thirties by that time, making him still young enough to ride in the show, but old enough not to have the facial appearance of a youth.

There are a number of further references to John Sitting Bull. An Associated Press story datelined Rapid City, South Dakota, on September 2, 1924, found him with a group of older Lakota at Custer State Park, noting that "six of the Indians who took part in the Custer massacre held a reunion today. They are old men now. But as to the massacre which they call a battle, their opinions are unchanged. They would do it again. The warriors still are proud of their people's triumph over the white general at the Little Big Horn on June 25, 1876. They are only sorry the Sioux are not strong enough to chase the white man out of their hunting grounds and their Black Hills, which they believe to be inhabited by the Great Spirit."

At the time of the Rapid City reunion, John's age is given as eighty, which is too old for him to have been Sitting Bull's son. However, the age is in line with the other Lakota men who were there that day, and is consistent with someone who could have participated in the Little Bighorn fight. John, being mute, could not have told the reporter his age, so someone else may have guessed eighty. If he was thirty-one in 1898, he would have been fifty-seven in 1924. In the photographs taken that day by William Groethe, a professional photographer from Rapid City, he appears to be more or less the same age that Sitting Bull was when he was last photographed, which was when he was in his late fifties. Groethe later noted that John Sitting Bull had not taken part in the Little Bighorn fight.

David F. Barry, the Bismarck photographer who took some of the best-known portraits of Sitting Bull in the 1880s, also photographed *John Sitting Bull* four decades later, according to a January 17, 1993, article in the *New York Times* by Vivien Raynor. This session took place while Barry was working in New York in 1926. Citing Barry's notes, Raynor describes John Sitting Bull as "a deaf mute who had joined the Sells-Floto Circus." The Sells-Floto Circus was a show similar to Buffalo Bill's Wild West that toured in the years after the Wild West folded its tents. Many of the Indians who had worked for Cody later signed with Sells-Floto, and Cody himself did some work as an announcer with the show for a couple of years.

John Sitting Bull also worked for a time with Colonel Tim McCoy's Wild West, which operated in the 1930s, both independently and as part of the Ringling Brothers & Barnum and Bailey Combined Show. At one point, a group of Indians, including John Sitting Bull (billed as John Sitting Bull, Jr.), posed for a publicity photograph with an Indian brand motorcycle. A headdress and shirt worn by John Sitting Bull are now in the collection of the Gene Autry Museum of the American West in Los Angeles.

Sitting Bull's youngest daughter to survive to adulthood, Standing Holy, was also his last surviving offspring. She married Urban (sometimes called Abraham) Spotted Horse (1873–1919) and passed away in 1927 at the age of fifty-one. Their daughters, Angelique (known within the family as Angeline) and Sarah, were born in 1903 and 1907, respectively.

Sarah married David Little Spotted Horse (1910–1975), and Angeline married twice, to David's older brother, Allison Little Spotted Horse (1900-1990), and to Claude LaPointe (1898–1965). It should be noted that the Spotted Horse and Little Spotted Horse families were unrelated. Angeline's children were Margaret Little Spotted Horse, born in 1930; Lydia Little Spotted Horse-Red Paint, born in 1932; Marlene Little Spotted Horse-Anderson, born in 1935; Ethel Little Spotted Horse-Bates, born in 1937; Eli Little Spotted Horse, born in 1939; and Ernie LaPointe, born in 1948.

Today, many people at Standing Rock and Pine Ridge—and elsewhere—trace their blood line to Sitting Bull. Still others, who are without such a direct lineage, trace a spiritual descendance from him, as he is still seen as a patriarch among the Hunkpapa.

Of the physical objects touched by Sitting Bull during his life, probably the most important and certainly the most intriguing—are the various editions of what Stanley Vestal called his "Hieroglyphic Autobiography," which has been mentioned often in the earlier chapters of this book. By Vestal's reckoning, there were sixty-three events recorded in Sitting Bull's original collection, and Vestal describes thirty-two of these. The first pictograph represented an event that took place in 1846 when Sitting Bull, as a teenager, counted coup on an enemy. The second image records another victory in 1853, and the remainder are of events occurring between 1856 and 1869.

As we have earlier noted, the original portfolio was lost in 1870, and while he subsequently recreated many of the 1846–1869 pictographs, Sitting Bull never executed any drawings describing later events. We have also seen that his uncle Four Horns recreated copies of fifty-five pages from the Hieroglyphic Autobiographies of both Sitting Bull and his adopted Assiniboine brother Jumping Bull. In turn, Sitting Bull re-created at least three sets of selected pictographs himself while he was at Fort Randall in 1881 and 1882.

An obvious question to consider when looking back on Sitting Bull's life is what happened to these intriguing collections?

The original set of drawings is reported to have to have been sold by an unnamed Lakota man to Dr. James Peleg Kimball, a U.S. Army doctor at Fort Buford, in 1870. As the Smithsonian Institution puts it, "An unidentified Sioux brought the copies [implying that they may not have been Sitting Bull's originals] to Fort Buford, where they were acquired by James C. [sic] Kimball, Asst. Surgeon, in August 1870."

Dr. Kimball later transferred this Hieroglyphic Autobiography to his boss, Dr. Joseph K. Barnes, who served as the U.S. Army's Surgeon General in Washington, D.C., from 1864 to 1882. In tracing this transaction, one can easily lose track of the chain of custody because the Surgeon General of the Army is often confused with the Surgeon General of the United States, although the two posts are different and distinct.

This document made its way from the "unidentified Sioux" to Kimball to Barnes to the Library of the Surgeon General's Office. Also known as the Army Medical Library, it was established in 1836 as part of the office of the U.S. Army Surgeon General. Between 1866 and 1887, the library shared quarters with the Army Medical Museum in, of all places, Ford's Theater in Washington, D.C. It is amazing to imagine Sitting Bull's Hieroglyphic Autobiography being stored—and possibly exhibited—in the same building where President Abraham Lincoln was murdered less than a decade before Sitting Bull's property arrived there.

Sitting Bull drawing of him in battle with the Crow. By the time he executed this set of pictograms, he had mastered the art of signing his name in wasichu cursive writing. (*Manuscript 1929B. Sitting Bull pictographic autobiography, 1882. National Anthropological Archives*)

In 1956, the Army Medical Library collection was transferred from the control of the Department of Defense to the Public Health Service and became part of the National Library of Medicine. The Library was then transferred to the National Institutes of Health. In 1962, it moved to its current quarters at the National Naval Medical Center in Bethesda, Maryland. Today, it is the world's largest medical library. Within the library, items created before 1913 are held apart from current materials, and within this collection, in Box 2085, No. 3, is the item listed as "Hieroglyphic Autobiography of Sitting Bull (54 sheets of colored crayon drawings)."

Also as noted earlier, Sitting Bull's 1882 Fort Randall drawings were given to or taken by Lieutenant Wallace Tear, who sent them to General John C. Smith in Chicago in April 1882. The chain of custody of Sitting Bull's Fort Randall Hieroglyphic Autobiography passed from General Smith to his son, Robert E. Smith. In 1923, Robert, then living in South Bellingham, Washington, donated them to the Bureau of American Ethnology.

The Bureau of American Ethnology (Bureau of Ethnology until 1897) was established by Congress in 1879 simply as a means of transferring materials relating to the Indians of North America from the Interior Department to the Smithsonian Institution. However, the bureau's founding director, John Wesley Powell, embraced the larger, more proactive mission of actually conducting anthropologic research in America. Indeed, Powell conducted many such expeditions in the West himself.

These historic projects, which are beyond the scope of this work, formed the true legacy of the bureau, but suffice to say, this was a natural repository into which the Sitting Bull Hieroglyphic Autobiography would have fitted when Smith made his donation in 1923. In 1965, the Bureau of American Ethnology merged with the Smithsonian Institution's Department of Anthropology to form the Smithsonian Office of Anthropology within the United States National Museum, now the National Museum of Natural History. In 1968, the Office of Anthropology holdings became the National Anthropological Archives, whose collections, including Sitting Bull's Fort Randall Hieroglyphic Autobiography are now at the Smithsonian Institution's Museum Support Center in Suitland, Maryland.

The 1870 copy by Four Horns of Sitting Bull's Hieroglyphic Autobiography, which also contains copies of pictographs from Jumping Bull's Hieroglyphic Autobiography, eventually found its way to the Bureau of American Ethnology as well. These drawings, with explanations obtained from other Indians were delivered to the Medical Director's Office of the Department of Dakota, then headquartered at St. Paul, on March 14, 1871. Later in the same year, this Hieroglyphic Autobiography was transferred to the Army Medical Museum at Ford's Theater, where it possibly preceded the portfolio that had been in Kimball's custody. In turn, the Four Horns copy was transferred to the Bureau of American Ethnology on May 15, 1915, by Dr. D. S. Lamb of the Army Medical Museum. This document was accompanied by a letter signed by "John P.

Williamson. Fort Randall, Dakota Territory December 12, 1881." John Poage Williamson had been a Presbyterian missionary at Fort Randall.

It was at the Bureau of American Ethnology that Stanley Vestal was able to refer to the Four Horns and Sitting Bull copies of the original Hieroglyphic Autobiography. He makes no mention of the Hieroglyphic Autobiography then in the collection of the Army Medical Library, now part of the National Library of Medicine. Vestal cautions in his own work that the Smithsonian's "interpretations of some of these exploits do not tally with the information given me by Indians who were present in the fights portrayed." For this reason, we have ignored the Smithsonian interpretations and have relied on Vestal for descriptions given earlier in this book. While eyewitness testimony is often suspect, we are always inclined to take the word of someone who was there, rather than to rely on an interpretation by someone else in a far removed time and place.

As we have noted, the 1882 drawings that were sent to the Bureau of American Ethnology were not the only pictographs that Sitting Bull did at Fort Randall. The drawings that he rendered for the family of regimental quartermaster Captain Horace Quimby remained with his family until the death of his daughter Alice in 1947. They were then given to the Fort St. Joseph Historical Association Museum in Niles, Michigan, where they are now on display.

In 1938, a *third* set of Fort Randall drawings came to light. Mrs. G. H. Pettinger of Oswego, Oregon, wrote to the Smithsonian Institution to make them aware of a collection of thirteen Sitting Bull drawings that she had inherited from her late uncle, Daniel L. Pratt of Seattle, who had been the post trader at Fort Randall in 1882. These drawings, bound together inside an oil cloth cover were done on sheets of letterhead marked "D.L. Pratt, Post Trader, Fort Randall."

In 1938, the Smithsonian Institution published a monograph entitled "Three Pictographic Autobiographie of Sitting Bull," written by M. W. Stirling, then the Chief of the Bureau of American Ethnology. The three

dors of the various offices of the Smithsonian's many campuses, as one person referred me to another and then another, who suggested that I phone yet another. It was at this point that I came in contact with Bill Billeck, whom I have previously mentioned. As I crossed paths with Billeck, who is the Program Manager at the Repatriation Office of the National Museum of Natural History, he was coincidentally preparing to repatriate—of all things—two artifacts that once belonged to Sitting Bull. These were a pair of leggings and a scalplock—a lock of hair not unlike a short pony tail—that had been taken from his body at Fort Yates shortly after he was killed.

Billeck explained that these items had been loaned to the National Museum in 1896 by Dr. Horace M. Deeble, the post surgeon at Fort Yates, who six years earlier had examined Sitting Bull's bloody, partially frozen body. The loan papers did not say exactly how they were obtained from Sitting Bull's body, but one may surmise that they were taken by Deeble himself, or stripped from the corpse in his presence. This was the first confirmation I had that someone other than McLaughlin had clipped some of Sitting Bull's hair post mortem. To the question of taking DNA samples from the hair, I am told that one needs to extract it from the roots, and no roots were present in the sheared-off scalplock.

It should be mentioned here that the Smithsonian created the Repatriation Office in 1991 to implement requirements of the 1989 National Museum of the American Indian Act. This law affirms the right of native peoples to have artifacts collected by the Smithsonian's museums through the years returned to them if they fall into one of four categories. These groupings are human remains, funerary objects, sacred objects, and objects of cultural patrimony.

Billeck pointed out that he approached the two Sitting Bull artifacts with two questions. The first was to ask whether these, of the many artifacts attributed to Sitting Bull, really had been his. Having determined to his satisfaction that these two items really had, he considered whether they fit one of the four repatriation categories under the law. He determined that the scalplock—being human remains—did, while the leggings did not. However, it was determined that because of the way they were acquired, the museum would offer to return them as well.

SETTING aside the question of the locks of Sitting Bull's hair, the question arises as to what happened to the rest of Sitting Bull's human remains after they were buried at Fort Yates on December 17, 1890. Those remains, like the man himself, are surrounded by controversy and mystery. The U.S. Army officially withdrew from Fort Yates in 1903, but most units had gone before that time, leaving it as just another town in North Dakota that happened to have the name of a former military post. The military graves at Fort Yates were dug up and the bodies relocated to Fort McKern—except that of Sitting Bull. Fort Yates also remained—as it does to this day—home to the administrative center of the Standing Rock Reservation. After the mid-1890s, men in blue uniforms could still be seen at town, but they were mainly Indian Police, the metal breasts.

Sitting Bull rested in peace—as peacefully as one can rest if one is buried with quicklime—at Fort Yates for only a few years. One moonlit October night in 1897 or 1898—or possibly as late as 1905—Sitting Bull's peaceful slumber was interrupted by two grave robbers. They were not ghoulish entrepreneurs out for a fast buck, but a pair of bored and inquisitive teenagers, James E. Davies and Frank B. Fiske. The latter was the son of a former Fort Yates soldier and had been a seven-year-old boy living at the post at the time of Sitting Bull's funeral. The elder Fiske continued to work as a wagon master at Standing Rock after he left the service.

The two boys were attending a dance that night when they decided to go see for themselves whether Sitting Bull was actually buried in Sitting Bull's tomb. They told nobody about what Fiske later described as their "sinister purpose," not even their dates at the dance. Fiske surmised that the two girls assumed that they had gone out to procure booze from the cowboys, "who were in the habit of stepping out for something to pep them up, such as might be afforded by certain medicines of high alcoholic content."

As Fiske later told the story to many listeners, including a reporter for the *Fargo Forum*, he and Davies "walked briskly to the home of the chief of police, Thomas J. Reedy, in the west part of the agency, where we procured a pick and shovel. From there we struck due south, in the same brisk manner, to the grave of Sitting Bull."

The Indian Police, who usually "allowed nothing to escape their watchful eye," had their attention focused on the dance hall, so the two young men were undisturbed as they dug. Soon, as Fiske related, they "had a hole large enough and deep enough to allow one of us to push in a portion of the decayed wooden coffin that contained all that was mortal of the great Sioux chief. We pulled out pieces of rotten canvas, which proved that part of the story of the burial was correct. . . . Then we took the bones. I took out a nice large thigh bone. Then Jimmie got down and felt around until he found a rib. These we took for relics."

The two apparently never sold these "relics" to collectors, but rather kept them merely as souvenirs. Reportedly Fiske returned in later years to rebury the bone that he took, but there is a contradictory story that he showed it off to a *Fargo Forum* correspondent as late as 1949. The newspaper reported that an "anthropologist who also saw the bone at about that time, told the writer it was not a thigh bone but rather a humerus, or upper arm bone."

After the violations of the turn of the twentieth century, Sitting Bull's final resting place presumably remained undisturbed for half a century. An iron fence was erected, and eventually began to rust away. Gradually, it was crushed under the weight of sightseers who came to Fort Yates to view the place. In August 1928, amid promises that the grave would be cared for, concrete was poured on the pile of stones that lay at the foot of the grave, and a granite headstone containing an inscription of his death was installed.

Over the coming decades, ideas of caring for the gravesite blossomed and faded. The Great Depression dried up the funds, and World War II distracted attention. The winters came and went, and the site gradually continued to deteriorate. Weeds overgrew the place even as the tourists paid their respects.

In December 1944, President Franklin D. Roosevelt signed the Flood Control Act of 1944, which authorized the construction of thousands of dams and levees across the United States, including a series of projects in the Missouri River Basin built by the Army Corps of Engineers and managed by the Interior Department's Bureau of Reclamation. One of the largest was to be the Oahe Dam, built on the Missouri River in South Dakota, but with a 2.35-million-acre-foot reservoir extending into North Dakota. As work got under way on this enormous project in 1948, it was widely believed that among the places submerged beneath this reservoir would be Fort Yates and the grave of Sitting Bull.

Against this backdrop, there was naturally discussion of relocating his remains from the admittedly dilapidated gravesite to a new memorial on higher ground. As various cities and organizations discussed the issue, the entity that gathered the most steam was an ad hoc group of business leaders from Mobridge, South Dakota. Then boasting a population of 3,800 (3,574 in 2000), Mobridge is about fifty highway miles south of Fort Yates across the state line.

In 1952, these men from Mobridge, including Dan Heupel, Julius Skaug, Walter Tuntland, and George Walters, formed the Dakota Memorial Association, whose expressed purpose was to move Sitting Bull to South Dakota and provide him with a proper burial site. They proposed a site on a bluff overlooking the Missouri River—and well above the water level of the proposed reservoir. It was within the boundaries of the Standing Rock Reservation, and across the Missouri from Mobridge, which is not within the reservation.

Plans were made to raise money for a suitable memorial, and a bust of Sitting Bull was commissioned from Polish-American sculptor Korczak Ziolkowski, who was already working on a massive statue of Crazy Horse in the Black Hills that he had designed to dwarf Mount Rushmore (on which he assisted Gutzon Borglum). The tourism potential for a site near Mobridge might have been apparent, especially because the members of the organization had ties to the Mobridge Chamber of Commerce, but this aspect was underplayed.

The moving of Sitting Bull's remains across the state line from the place where they had remained for sixty-three years was controversial, just as it was obviously going to be ensnarled with jurisdictional squabbles. North Dakota weighed in with an opinion, and its governor, C. Norman Brunsdale, was inclined to refuse permission to open the grave. However, as a former military post that was now located on a reservation, the Fort Yates site was on federal land. Ultimately, the jurisdiction fell to the U.S. government, under the Preservation of American Antiquities Act of 1906 that made "excavation, theft or destruction of historic or prehistoric ruins or objects of antiquity on federal lands" a federal crime. In the case of Sitting Bull's grave, the Department of the Interior determined on April 3, 1953, that it would defer to the wishes of Sitting Bull's family.

By this time, the Dakota Memorial Association was working with Clarence Gray Eagle, the seventy-eight-year-old son of Sitting Bull's brother-in-law. As a teenager, he had been present at the Grand River fight in which Sitting Bull had been killed, and he weighed in heavily in favor of moving the remains to the site near Mobridge. Also supporting their removal from Fort Yates were several of Sitting Bull's descendants, including Jennie Weasel Bear and Helen White Bull Mountain, as well as Angeline Spotted Horse LaPointe, who was the daughter of Sitting Bull's daughter, Standing Holy. According to Ernie LaPointe, the son of Angeline Spotted Horse LaPointe, his mother had agreed that Sitting Bull's remains should be moved, but she wanted them to be moved far away. Half a century later, he would resurrect this idea in a proposal of his own.

A late spring snowstorm was blowing across the Plains on the night of April 7 as several vehicles made their way to the ground that once was the military cemetery at Fort Yates. Among the men digging and observing were Clarence Gray Eagle and a retired Mobridge mortician, Al Miles. Despite the fact that the Interior Department claimed jurisdiction and deferred it to the family, there was still a great deal of opposition to the plan both from the State of North Dakota and from people living at Standing Rock. The gravediggers fully expected to be stopped if they were caught, so they planned and executed the exhumation quietly and secretly in the dead of night. They wanted to get in and get out as fast as possible.

Having opened the grave, they hurried Sitting Bull's bones across the state line to the new site, reburied them, and covered them with a reported twenty tons of concrete to prevent anyone from repeating the disinterment.

In a telephone interview with the *Fargo Forum* published on April 12, Miles explained that the party removed approximately twenty-five pounds of bones, including part of a skull and a few teeth, ribs and vertebra, one humerus, pairs of tibia and fibula, the pelvic bone, both femurs, and a number of smaller bones from the hands and feet. The recovery of just a single humerus tallied with Fiske's account of having removed the other one a half century before. Miles also reported small pieces of leather, probably from a buckskin garment, and a few buttons. As for the reports going back to Waggoner's account, Miles was asked whether there was evidence of the bones having been drenched in quicklime. Miles claimed to have detected no evidence of the bones having come in contact with a corrosive substance.

The fact that the work had been done during a snowstorm, in the dark, and not very carefully, almost certainly meant that parts of Sitting Bull's

Indeed, the Little Bighorn Battlefield is located on Crow land. Ernie LaPointe told me that he had spoken with the Crow people in June 2007. As he explained in our conversation, he told them, "we need peace through unity. We should have healing with each other as tribes. We don't need this thousand years of hating each other. It's time for us to get together and unite to fight the biggest battle that is before us, which is saving the air and the water for future generations. Instead of living in the past we need to look ahead to tomorrow." He told me that the Crow agreed with him.

Visitors to the Mobridge site are often disappointed by what they find. LaPointe relates the story of a family from Germany who drove back to Mobridge, bought a bucket and cleanser, and returned to clean the monument. Although LaPointe has a welcome ally in Darrell Cook, the superintendent of the Little Bighorn Battlefield National Monument, as of now, no decision has been made about reburying his great-grandfather.

This monument, located on a bluff overlooking the mouth of the Grand River, South Dakota, stands atop the second resting place of at least part of Sitting Bull's remains. The bust of Sitting Bull is by Polish sculptor Korczak Ziolkowski, who conceived the massive Crazy Horse memorial megalith in the Black Hills. (*Bill Yenne*)

EPILOGUE: LEGACY

It's cold tonight on the Grand River—and dark. The dirt roads that follow the ruts on which his mortal remains made the first leg of their journey to Fort Yates are as impassable in a blizzard in the twenty-first century as they were back in the waning years of the nineteenth. Tonight there is a pervading sense that time has stood still.

The meadowlark who sings here in August, and who spoke often to him in a language that he understood, is silent tonight, but ghosts walk these hills. Is it Bull Head? The town that bears his name is just down the road. Or Red Tomahawk or McLaughlin? The grave to which the agent had his body shipped from Washington is across the ridge. Ghosts, trapped by the incongruity of history, are condemned to walk these hills in their long black veils.

In these hills above the Grand River, Sitting Bull is everywhere. The site where his cabin stood on that terrible night so long ago is nearby, even though the logs and lumber are long gone. His spirit is here, there, and everywhere.

As they move his bones, it is really just an academic exercise. These decaying artifacts, soaked or not soaked long ago in quicklime, are no longer him. Where are his bones? Were these bones or those bones *ever* really him?

They moved those bones, just as Custer's bones were moved from the Greasy Grass to West Point overlooking Washington Irving's beloved Hudson, and they paid tribute to those bones. But did they get all of Custer's bones? Did they get *any* of Custer's bones? Does it matter?

What hills does Custer's ghost wander? Is it the hill above the Greasy Grass that still bears his name? Or is it the hill above the Gettysburg battlefield where he had his greatest Civil War triumph, the same battlefield that Lincoln immortalized with his address? Does it matter?

We assess the legacy of Sitting Bull, as we assess the legacy of all great persons, by the permanence of their influence and our collective memory of who they were and what they continue to mean to history.

We conclude as we began, recalling that Sitting Bull was, at the time of his death, the most recognized of all American Indians, and he remains as such today. "You can stand in the middle of China and say his name and people know who you are talking about," LaDonna Brave Bull Allard said.

As Mark Holman, the librarian at Sitting Bull College, told me: "People immediately recognize him, and have some idea about him, even if they don't know where Standing Rock is, or who the Lakota people are. His name is transcendent."

This most famous of American Indians has been viewed by many people, at least since 1876, as either the hero or the villain of the greatest clash of cultures that took place in the American West in the late nineteenth century—but the truth is always more complicated than the stereotype.

This popular, if not exactly accurate, image of Sitting Bull as the victor in the Battle of the Little Bighorn—the man who led the Plains Indians to their greatest triumph—has remained the same, even as the popular image of the Little Bighorn has changed. At the time of his death and for many decades after, the Little Bighorn was seen in popular culture as the savage massacre of the great Custer and his brave soldiers—and Sitting Bull was the villain. By the late twentieth century, Little Bighorn came to represent a victory of an oppressed people over blind and savage imperialism—and Sitting Bull was the hero. Both images still have their devotees, though the truth is more complicated than either stereotype.

Many people still regard Sitting Bull as the leading voice of opposition to the seizure of Lakota land by the wasichu in the 1880s, but the reality is more complex. He went to Washington in 1888 prepared to negotiate. He went there, not to blindly oppose the wasichu, but to drive a hard bargain. He understood the nuances of the game the wasichu were playing, and he understood the value of the wasichu dollars and the fact that their culture would inevitably eclipse that of the Lakota.

When General Phil Sheridan once insisted that Sitting Bull was not a real person, but a concept, a composite of many people, he was quite absurdly wrong. Yet when we assess the legacy of Sitting Bull, we come to find that Sheridan was closer to the truth than we might realize. As time goes by, as the winters come and go in the Grand River Country, the truth emerges that Sitting Bull is, in fact, a composite of many realities. His legacy is a composite of the many people he represented. He was a warrior, a leader, a shaman, and an "Indian chief." He was an itancan, a wikasa wakan, a father, and an inspiration to his people.

He was the wikasa wakan who foretold the Battle of the Little Bighorn. He was the wikasa wakan who stood on that battlefield and foretold the fate of his people. The Little Bighorn is cast as the ultimate battle in an epic struggle, and history has cast him as one of its principal protagonists. As Sitting Bull himself foretold, it was a turning point, for it was that moment which clearly accelerated the inevitable demise of a way of life for the Plains people. If we accept the Little Bighorn as the ultimate battle, and that Sitting Bull is an integral part of our memory of it, then perhaps it is within that battle that we should pick up the thread that leads to an understanding of Sitting Bull's true legacy. Where was he on that fateful day? The movies find him riding, shooting troopers, and killing Custer. The reality found him riding, not on Custer Hill, but through the great encampment on the Greasy Grass, concerned with and looking after the welfare of the weakest among his people, especially the young children.

It is in his concern for the children, and for the future of his people, that we find his legacy. Of all the words that I heard and read while working on this book, those that have stayed with me were spoken about his vision of future generations. "The name is recognized by both young and old," Dr. Laurel Vermillion, President of Sitting Bull College, said in our conversation about the decision to name the school for him. "It's a perfect fit, because his dream was to really provide for our youth and our young people, and for the generations to come." When she said that, I could see him riding through that camp, his brow wrinkled with concern for the young ones, and for the future of his people.

His legacy is that this concern paid off. More important than the fact that his name will endure is the fact that his people will endure. This is what he *really* wanted. "Because of him, our people are never going to die," LaDonna Brave Bull Allard once told me. "We are always going to be here."

APPENDICES

Appendix 1

SITTING BULL'S CHILDREN

(Names and ages of children with him as listed in various censuses)

Fort Randall 1882

Blue Turtle (14)
Crow Foot (7)
Her Lodge in Sight (5)
Infant-daughter (one day)
Many Horses (18)
On the Hill/Not Afraid (3)
Runs Away From (3)
Standing Holy (4)
Stood by Him (15)
Walks Looking (15) (Died in 1887)

Standing Rock 1888

Arrows Left in Him (aka Left Arrow in Him) (10)
Crow Foot (13)
Little Soldier (20) (Adopted)
Runs Away From (10)
Sitting Bull Junior (2)
Standing Holy (10)
(Many Horses was with her husband, Thomas Fly)

Standing Rock 1889

Crow Foot (14)
Girl (1)

Appendix 1 (Cont.)

Little Soldier (21) (Adopted)
Runs Away From (11)
Sitting Bull Junior (3)
Standing Holy (14)
Wounded (aka Left Arrow in Him) (11)
(Many Horses was with her husband, Thomas Fly)

Standing Rock 1890

Crow Foot (16)
Henry (24)
Little Soldier (22) (Adopted)
Lodge (14)
Red Scout (12)
Standing Holy (13)
Theodore (Runs Away From) (12)
(Many Horses was with her husband, Thomas Fly)

Appendix 2

VITAL STATISTICS OF THE STANDING ROCK AGENCY/RESERVATION

For selected years while Sitting Bull lived there, plus 1895 for comparison
(Source: Annual Reports of the Commissioner of Indian Affairs)

	1882	1885	1890	1895
Total Population:	3,755	4,450	4,096	3,763
Percent Hunkpapa:	40.5	40.6	42.3	N/A
Percent wholly wearing "citizen's dress":*	10.7	44.9	67.1	97.9
Percent involved in "civilized pursuits":**	20	c.25	30	30
Percent dependent on government rations:	70	70	70	70
Percent routinely speaking English:	0.9	3.3	7.8	14.6
Annual Births:	142	176	208	N/A
School enrollment:	763	N/A	586	542
Number of wood frame dwelling houses:	315	750	1,000	1,000
Corn cultivated (bushels):	N/A	20,190	15,000	20,000

Note: Disease statistics for 1895 were not found in the Annual Report, so data for 1893 is substituted.

*This esoteric statistic was compiled by the Indian Bureau as a means of tracking the progress of the Indians becoming "civilized."

**Including agriculture.

N/A: Not available from the source.

Appendix 2 (Cont.)

	1882	1885	1890	1895
Vegetables cultivated (bushels):	N/A	30,361	18,200	15,970
Horses owned:	N/A	N/A	2,805	5,365
Cattle owned:	N/A	N/A	4,560	14,000
Cases of disease treated:	N/A	2,655	2,546	1,092
Deaths attributed to disease (under age 5):	N/A	19	1	2
Deaths attributed to disease (over age 5):	N/A	50	17	1
Total deaths:	151	N/A	213	N/A
Bronchitis cases:	N/A	417	105	100
Chicken pox cases:	N/A	20	2	0
Cholera morbus cases:	N/A	34	0	12
Conjunctivitis cases:	N/A	287	257	235
Consumption/ tuberculosis cases:	N/A	62	40	120
Influenza cases:	N/A	0	536	147
Rheumatism cases:	N/A	92	73	0
Smallpox cases:	N/A	0	N/A	N/A
Typhoid cases:	N/A	0	2	0

Appendix 3

LAKOTA POPULATION OF THE NORTH AND SOUTH DAKOTA RESERVATIONS
IN 1890*

(Source: Report on Indians Taxed and Not Taxed in the United States at the Eleventh
Census: 1890)

North Dakota:
Devil's Lake:	1,038 (plus 1,458 non-Lakota)
Standing Rock:	4,096 (incl. 1,739 Hunkpapa Lakota)

South Dakota:
Cheyenne River:	2,823
Crow Creek & Lower Brule:	2,084
Pine Ridge:	5,016 (plus 517 Northern Cheyenne)
Rosebud:	5,381
Sisseton:	1,522
Yankton:	1,725

*Total Indian Population of the United States in 1890: 248,253

BIBLIOGRAPHY

Interviews and/or Conversations with the Author

William Billeck, Program Manager, Repatriation Office, National Museum of Natural History

LaDonna Brave Bull Allard, Tribal Tourism Coordinator for the Standing Rock Sioux Tribe

Stephen Greenberg, History of Medicine Division, National Library of Medicine

Mark Holman, Director of Library Services, Sitting Bull College

Ernie and Sonja LaPointe, Sitting Bull's great-grandson and his wife

Robert Leopold, Director, National Anthropological Archives

Markus Lindner, research fellow at the Johann Wolfgang Goethe–Universität Institut für Historische Ethnologie, Frankfurt, Germany

Laurel Vermillion, President, Sitting Bull College

Juti Winchester, Curator of Western American History, Buffalo Bill Historical Center

Bill Yellowtail, Katz Endowed Chair in Native American Studies, Montana State University

Manuscripts

Indian Rights Association. Manuscript Collections (1884–1967). Historical Society of Pennsylvania.

Manuscript 1929A. Four Horns copy of Sitting Bull and Jumping Bull pictographic autobiographies, 1870. National Anthropological Archives.

Manuscript 1929B. Sitting Bull pictographic autobiography, 1882. National Anthropological Archives.

PRINTED SOURCES

American Council of Learned Societies. *American National Biography*. New York: Oxford University Press, 2000.

Armstrong, William John. "Sitting Bull and a Michigan Family—Legacy of an Unlikely Friendship." *Michigan History* (January-February 1995).

Bourke, John Gregory. *On the Border with Crook*. New York: Charles Scribner & Sons, 1950.

Branch, E. Douglas. *The Hunting of the Buffalo*. New York: D. Appleton & Company, 1929.

Brown, Dee. *Bury My Heart at Wounded Knee: An Indian History of the American West*. New York: Holt, Rinehart & Winston, 1970.

Buechel, Eugene (Editor), and Paul Manhart. *Lakota Dictionary: Lakota–English/English–Lakota: Comprehensive Edition*. Lincoln: University of Nebraska Press, (2002.

Byrne, P. E. *Soldiers of the Plains*. New York: Minton, Balch & Company, 1926.

Cody, Colonel W. F. *An Autobiography of Buffalo Bill*. New York: Cosmopolitan Book Corporation, Farrar & Rinehart, 1920.

Commissioner of Indian Affairs. *Annual Reports*. Washington, D.C.: Department of the Interior, 1888, 1889, 1890, 1891.

Congressional Record, 48th Congress, 1st Session; Senate Ex. Doc. No. 70; Senate Reports 148 through 348.

Custer, George Armstrong. *My Life on the Plains*. New York: Sheldon & Company, 1874.

De Barthe, Joe. *The Life and Adventures of Frank Grouard, Chief of Scouts, U.S.A.* St. Joseph: Combe Printing Company, 1894.

Fechét, Major Edmond G. "The True Story of the Death of Sitting Bull." *The Cosmopolitan* (March 1896).

Hamilton, Andy. "LaPointe Tells Story of Sitting Bull." *Niles* (Michigan) *Daily Star* (October 3, 2006).

Hornaday, William T.: *The Extermination of the American Bison.* Smithsonian Institution. Washington, D.C.: U.S. Government Printing Office, 1889.

Huntley, Stanley. "Interviewed, A Tribune Emissary Practicing His Art Under Difficulties." *Chicago Tribune* (July 5, 1879).

Hyde, George E. *Red Cloud's Folk: A History of the Oglala Sioux Indians.* Norman: University of Oklahoma Press, 1937.

Isenberg, Andrew C. *The Destruction of the Bison: An Environmental History, 1750–1920.* New York: Cambridge University Press, 2000.

Johnson, W. Fletcher. *The Life of Sitting Bull and History of the Indian War of 1890–'91.* Edgewood Publishing Co., 1891.

Kappler, Charles J. *Indian Affairs: Laws and Treaties, Vol. IV, Laws (Compiled to March 4, 1927).* Washington, D.C.: U.S. Government Printing Office, 1929.

Lear, Jonathan. *Radical Hope: Ethics in the Face of Cultural Devastation.* Cambridge, Mass.: Harvard University Press, 2006.

Linderman, F. B. *Plenty–Coups, Chief of the Crows.* Lincoln: University of Nebraska Press, 1962.

Lindner, Markus. "Family, Politics, and Show Business: The Photographs of Sitting Bull." *North Dakota History* 75, nos. 3–4 (2005).

McClam, Erin. "Battle over Memorializing Sitting Bull." Associated Press (June 16, 2007).

McMurtry, Larry. *The Colonel and Little Missie*. New York: Simon & Schuster, 2005.

Michno, Gregory F.: *Encyclopedia of Indian Wars: Western Battles and Skirmishes 1850–1890*. Missoula, Mt.: Mountain Press Publishing, 2003.

Moses, L. C. *Wild West Shows and the Images of American Indians*. Albuquerque: University of New Mexico Press, 1996.

Phillips, Charles. "Wounded Knee Massacre: United States versus the Plains Indians." *American History Magazine* (December 2005).

Pollack, Eileen. *Woman Walking Ahead: In Search of Catherine Weldon and Sitting Bull*. Albuquerque: University of New Mexico Press, 2002.

Raynor, Vivien. "Where the Faces, Not Artifacts, Are the Center of Attention." *New York Times* (January 17, 1993).

Sherwell, Philip. "Last Stand to Save Grave of Sitting Bull." *London Sunday Telegraph* (August 8, 2007).

Stillson, Jerome. "Sitting Bull: The United States Commission Arrive at Fort Walsh." *New York Herald* (October 22, 1877).

———. "Sitting Bull Talks." *New York Herald* (November 16, 1877).

Stirling, M. W. "Three Pictographic Autobiographies of Sitting Bull," *Smithsonian Miscellaneous Collections* (Volume 97, number 5) Washington, D.C., 1938.

Thackery, Lorna. "Marker Will Stand as a Memorial to History and Why it Happened." *Billings Gazette* (June 24, 2003).

———. "Sitting Bull's Kin Seek Home for Chief's Bones." *Billings Gazette* (February 22, 2007).

Utley, Robert M. *Frontier Regulars: The United States Army and the Indian, 1866–1891*. New York: Macmillan, 1974.

———. *Frontiersman in Blue: The United States and the Indian, 1848–1865*. New York: Macmillan, 1967.

_____. *The Lance and the Shield: The Life and Times of Sitting Bull.* New York: Henry Holt, 1993.

Vestal, Stanley. *New Sources of Indian History 1850–1891.* Norman: University of Oklahoma Press, 1934.

_____. *Sitting Bull: Champion of the Sioux.* New York: Houghton Mifflin, 1932.

Viola, Herman J. *Diplomats in Buckskins: A History of Indian Delegations in Washington City.* Washington, D.C.: Smithsonian Institution Press, 1981.

Walsh, Richard. *The Making of Buffalo Bill.* New York: A. L. Burt Company, 1928.

Yenne, Bill. *Indian Wars: The Campaign for the American West.* Yardley, Pa.: Westholme, 2005.

NEWSPAPERS AND PERIODICALS

Bismarck Tribune

Chicago Tribune

Fargo Forum

Indian Country Today

Minneapolis Tribune

Nation

New York Daily News

New York Herald

New York Sun

New York Times

San Francisco Chronicle

San Francisco Examiner

Sioux City Journal

Sioux County Arrow

Sioux County Pioneer

Sioux County Pioneer Arrow

Time

Ward County Independent

Washington Post

West Magazine

INDEX

ACKNOWLEDGMENTS

THANKS to the following people who were helpful to me while I was working on this book: William Billeck, Program Manager Repatriation Office, National Museum of Natural History; LaDonna Brave Bull Allard, Tribal Tourism Coordinator for the Standing Rock Sioux Tribe; Stephen Greenberg in the History of Medicine Division of the National Library of Medicine; Mark Holman, Director of Library Services at Sitting Bull College; Ernie LaPointe, Sitting Bull's great-grandson and his wife, Sonja; Barbara Larsen of the National Archives Central Plains Region in Kansas City, Missouri; Robert Leopold, Director of the National Anthropological Archives; Dr. Laurel Vermillion, President of Sitting Bull College; Dr. Juti Winchester, the Curator of Western American History at the Buffalo Bill Historical Center; and Bill Yellowtail at Montana State University.

Thanks, too, to Bruce H. Franklin of Westholme Publishing who was the original champion of this project, copy editor Noreen O'Connor-Abel, and Tracy Dungan, for his maps.

Everyone who writes about Sitting Bull, and related subjects, stands on the shoulders of Stanley Vestal, aka Walter Stanley Campbell (1877–1957), the Kansas-born Rhodes Scholar and author of many books on the American West. Beginning in the mid-1920s, he interviewed many old men who had known Sitting Bull when they were young men. These included his nephews White Bull and One Bull, the latter of whom Sitting Bull adopted as a son.

About the Author

Bill Yenne is the San Francisco-based author of more than two dozen books on historical topics, including many on Western history. Mr. Yenne grew up in Western Montana where his father was a backcountry trail guide and trails supervisor at Glacier National Park. He graduated from the University of Montana and has traveled extensively in all of the western states. Among his books on Western history are *Indian Wars: The Campaign for the American West*, *On The Trail of Lewis and Clark, Yesterday and Today*, *Images of America: Glacier National Park*, *The Opening of the American West*, and *The Encyclopedia of North American Indian Tribes*.

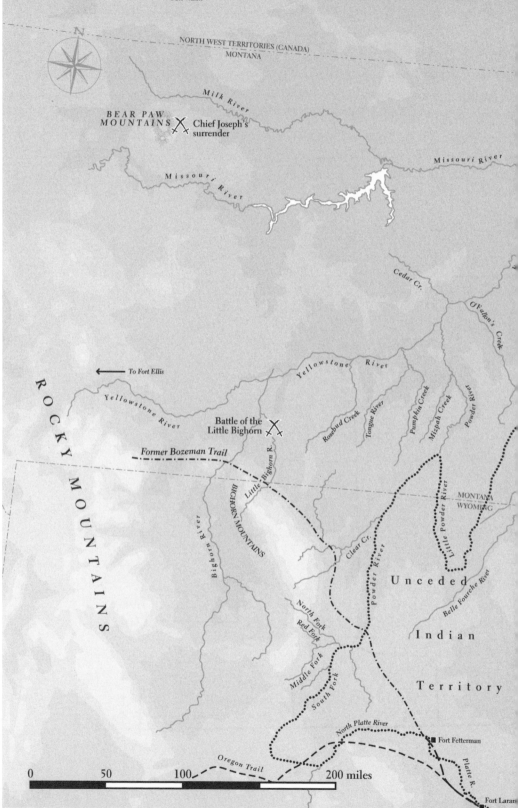

■ Fort Walsh

N

NORTH WEST TERRITORIES (CANADA)
MONTANA

Milk River

BEAR PAW
MOUNTAINS ✕ Chief Joseph's
surrender

Missouri River

Missouri River

Cedar Cr.

O'Fallon's Creek

← To Fort Ellis

Yellowstone River

Yellowstone River

Battle of the
Little Bighorn ✕

Rosebud Creek

Tongue River

Pumpkin Creek

Mispah Creek

Powder River

Former Bozeman Trail

Little Bighorn R.

R O C K Y   M O U N T A I N S

BIGHORN
MOUNTAINS

MONTANA
WYOMING

Bighorn River

Clear Cr.

Powder River

Little Powder River

U n c e d e d

Belle Fourche River

North Fork

Red Fork

I n d i a n

Middle Fork

South Fork

T e r r i t o r y

North Platte River

■ Fort Fetterman

Oregon Trail

Platte R.

0   50   100   200 miles

■ Fort Lara[m]